1-9-18
KEEP IT CLEAN!
THANKS

FROM THE BOTTOM UP

CHAD PREGRACKE WITH JEFF BARROW

INTRODUCTION BY TIM WALL

ONE MAN'S CRUSADE TO CLEAN AMERICA'S RIVERS

NATIONAL GEOGRAPHIC

WASHINGTON, D.C.

Published by the National Geographic Society

Library of Congress Cataloging-in-Publication Data:
Pregracke, Chad, 1974–
  From the bottom up : one man's crusade to clean America's rivers / Chad Pregracke With Jeff Barrow.
    p. cm.
  Includes index.
  1. Water—Pollution—United States. 2. Water quality management—United States. 3. Nonprofit organizations—United States. I. Barrow, Jeff, 1956– II. Title.
TD223.P73 2007
363.73'94—dc22
                          2006035078
ISBN: 978-1-4262-0100-4

Illustration Credits: Front, spine, and back cover photographs by Greg Boll. Half-title page and last page artwork from a photograph by Greg Boll. All interior photographs courtesy Living Lands & Waters unless otherwise noted: 182, Ali Selim; 229, Mark Christmass; 267, Bob Wiatrolik/Illinois EPA.

Founded in 1888, the National Geographic Society is one of the largest nonprofit scientific and educational organizations in the world. It reaches more than 285 million people worldwide each month through its official journal, NATIONAL GEOGRAPHIC, and its four other magazines; the National Geographic Channel; television documentaries; radio programs; films; books; videos and DVDs; maps; and interactive media. National Geographic has funded more than 8,000 scientific research projects and supports an education program combating geographic illiteracy.

For more information, please call 1-800-NGS LINE (647-5463) or write to the following address:

NATIONAL GEOGRAPHIC SOCIETY
1145 17th Street N.W.
Washington, DC 20036-4688 U.S.A.

Visit the Society's Web site at www.nationalgeographic.com/books

For information about special discounts for bulk purchases, please contact National Geographic Books Special Sales: ngspecsales@ngs.org.

Printed in U.S.A.

Interior Design: Cameron Zotter

CONTENTS

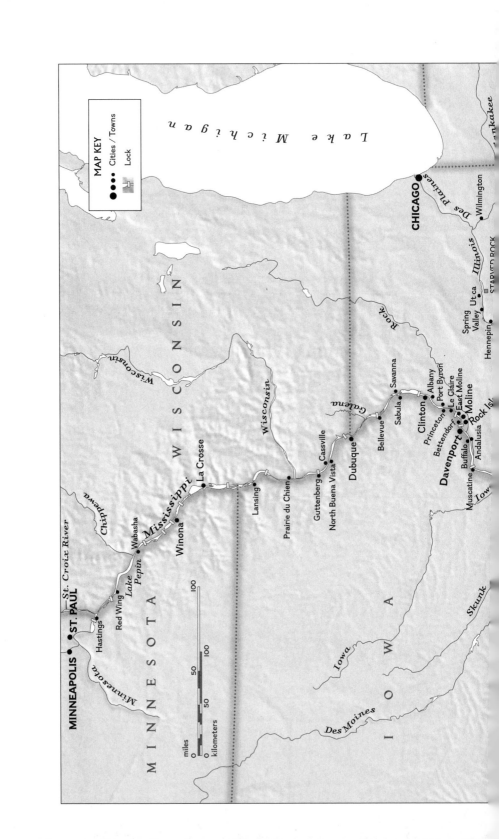

MAP KEY

Cities / Towns

Lock

Lake Michigan

MINNESOTA

WISCONSIN

IOWA

Minnesota

St. Croix River

Chippewa

Wisconsin

Wisconsin

Mississippi

Rock

Galena

Iowa

Des Moines

Skunk

Illinois

Des Plaines

Kankakee

MINNEAPOLIS

ST. PAUL

Hastings

Red Wing

Lake Pepin

Wabasha

Winona

La Crosse

Lansing

Prairie du Chien

Guttenberg

Cassville

North Buena Vista

Dubuque

Bellevue

Savanna

Sabula

Clinton

Albany

Port Byron

Princeton

Le Claire

East Moline

Bettendorf

Moline

Davenport

Buffalo

Rock Isl.

Andalusia

Muscatine

CHICAGO

Spring Valley

Utica

Hennepin

Wilmington

STARVED ROCK

miles
0   50   100

kilometers
0   50   100

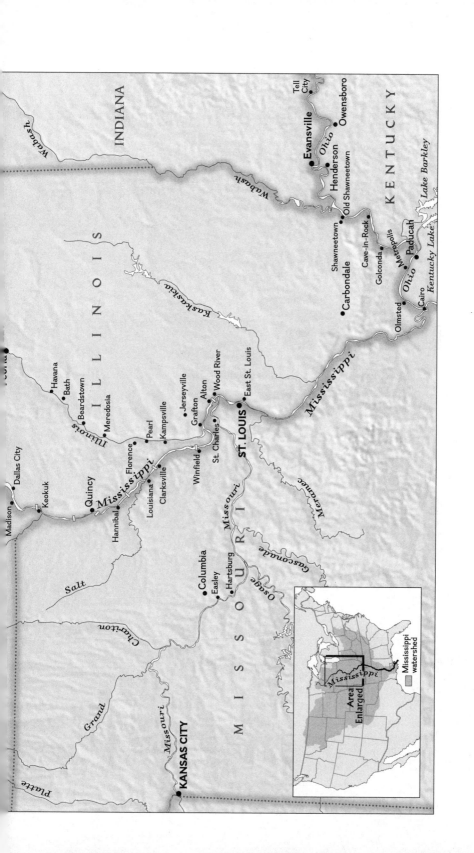

INTRODUCTION

The summer of 1997 was steaming along at CNN's headquarters in Atlanta, and the 10 o'clock news show was in need of compelling stories. The show's producer, Steve Redisch, was trawling the wires, looking for something unique and noteworthy. An AP story out of the Quad Cities caught his eye: "One man sets out to clean up the Mississippi River this summer." Stories about ordinary people doing extraordinary things had become my favorite kind to do. Redisch could sense this tale of indomitable American spirit might be right up my alley, and he passed the article on to me.

The first time I heard Chad's voice on the phone I had to hold the receiver away from my ear a bit. On the other end was an exuberant, non-stop, groove-talkin' dude who tried to simultaneously tell me his life story, his love for the Mississippi, his mission statement, and his amazement and appreciation for my call.

In September, I headed to Illinois to meet this young idealist. To help envelop myself in the region's feel, I decided I would camp out somewhere along the banks of the river rather than retreat to the homogenized confines of a roadside motel. Getting off the interstate at the last exit before Iowa, I found a small family-run campground on the Illinois side of the Big River just above Moline.

The historical relevance of the Mississippi is unavoidable. Long before Lewis and Clark showed up, the native peoples spoke of the Mississippi in godlike terms, the pulsing heart and lifeblood of the continent. I could sense that I was bedding down alongside a significant ancient highway. Each mile could tell a story. I stretched out at my riverside campsite and imagined river life as it was. The next day, I hoped I would get a good taste of river life as it *is*.

Chad had been pushing a wheelbarrow up and down the banks of the Mississippi River 12 hours a day all summer long, picking up whatever he could along the way. Aluminum cans, plastic bottles, soggy boxes, old tires, rusted appliances, the list is endless…and it was all making its way from Chad's grasp to recycling centers or landfills. I imagined an action-packed day with Chad along the river could be rich with motion and sound, and his story would be all laid out before the romantically majestic backdrop of the Mighty Mississippi.

It rained off and on all night. I was concerned that the trip might have been in vain if we got too much rain. By first light, things weren't looking much better. The rain had left a thick fog that would let through only the distant horns of barges approaching the local locks on the Iowa side. I packed up and moved out. I met Chad just a few miles away, at his folks' house along the Great River Road. By the time I arrived, the fog was beginning to lift. I had two days to capture this story. Hopefully Mother Nature would cut me and Chad some slack.

The weather had no effect on Chad's energy. After introducing me to his parents, KeeKee and Gary, Chad was anxious to show me everything he had accomplished that summer. He showed me local and regional articles that had already given him some print. He showed me photos of junk before and after it had been picked up. He showed me piles of tires and other refuse he hoped to recycle. When the weather cleared a bit, he showed me his backyard, a Tom Sawyer utopia, that had shaped this indefatigable idealist that stood before me. It was clear that the Mississippi didn't just flow *near* him; it flowed *in* him.

With his older brother, Brent, Chad had become intimate with everything the river had to offer, from work to play. They were "river rats," an affectionate term for locals whose lives were completely entwined with the river culture, the history, the fishing, the barges, and so on. They had even spent the last few years earning their keep under the surface, harvesting commercial mussels. It was this intimate daily relationship with the river's health that eventually would shape Chad's mission.

I wanted to capture as much of that passion as I could in my weather-hampered two days, so I put a wireless microphone on Chad and off we went. Climbing in and out of his aluminum workboat, and his beat-up red Ford pickup, we dodged intermittent showers, but I did get a tour of the immediate area, the shorelines and urban centers that form the Quad Cities: Moline and Rock Island, Illinois, and Bettendorf and Davenport, Iowa. These environs had been the starting point for his efforts, but now, Chad told me, with the help of friends an estimated 100 miles of shoreline had been cleared.

Because of the weather, by the end of the day's light I had put very little on tape. Chad now needed help moving a powerless houseboat he had acquired out of a marina on the Iowa side of the river to a beach on an island on the Illinois side. That's where we planned to spend the night.

Using his aluminum work boat to push and maneuver the houseboat, we eventually got the behemoth across the river while making passage in the total moonless darkness. We were navigating the old-fashioned way. Dead reckoning, I think it is called. I was beginning to have a strong understanding that once Chad set his mind to do something, very little could deter him. We were going to get that boat onto that island and we were going to sleep there. Period.

I relished the opportunity to experience the river firsthand, from sunrise to sunset. It's what Chad did every day, and if I was going to have him tell his own story, that was where we needed to be. It was humid in the dank houseboat—a condition the orchestra of mosquitoes seemed quite comfortable with. Chad nestled into his familiar space on board for the night, and I chose a wide padded bench near a screened window. It was a warm and muggy evening. In the foggy distance, I could hear the horns of barges making their way up and down the waterway. I was drenched in mist and sweat. Chad seemed unaffected.

I awoke first, eased myself outside to the 2x10 driftwood gangplank, and descended to the island's beach. I grabbed my video camera on the way out. The river was glassy, foggy, and gorgeous. However, there was trash everywhere—in the water, on the beach, and back in the island's woods.

I began to get some shots of the river's beauty at sunrise, juxtaposed with empty cans of beer and yellow antifreeze bottles. The peaceful yet poignant scene was soon over though. My taskmaster was arising. "Good mornin' dude! Did you get enough sleep?" he asked. Obviously young Mr. Positive did. He had his overalls on, along with his soggy sneakers, as he pulled on work gloves, Chad began grabbing gear and then bounded down the 2x10. Game on! I put the wireless microphone back on him as soon as possible.

Weeks later, in edit, I would open the short piece with this initial scene, accompanied by some appropriate but simple harmonica music. The vibrant young Mr. Pregracke would do the rest, introducing himself, describing his waterborne background, expressing his passion for his mission, and mostly, through his sweat and deeds, cleaning up the shores of the nation's greatest river, one piece at a time. Chad owned the screen anytime he was on it. His tireless efforts were surmounted only by his earnest descriptions of the task at hand and the future it promised.

Chad's looks have been compared to Tom Cruise's, with similar height, athletic build, and a winning smile. However, balancing the silver-screen good looks were heartland hybrid traits—lots of freckles, some reddish hair, and bib overalls—that ended up giving him a modern-day Huck Finn look. In an aw-shucks mode on camera, Chad denied any conscious similarities to Cruise or Finn. His focus was on the river only. He explained for the camera that "all the beaches were totally trashed and nobody was coming out to pick them up...so I thought, well...if I don't do it, who's going to?"

As Chad combed the island's shores, he quickly filled a series of industrial-strength garbage bags. "What I find here is basically a lot barrels, tires, bottles, cans, mattresses, refrigerators, TV sets," he told me. "Everything you could find in a city dump, you could find out here."

We motored a little way back upriver toward Rock Island and suddenly I heard a loud exclamation. "Yeah!" As we passed some fisherman casting off a small boat, Chad spotted a pile of barrels on the shore just beyond them. It was as if he had found a pot of gold. "There's a barrel pile that's probably 50 or 60 years old! And there's probably 30 barrels here." This cathartic moment seemed to make his mission crystal clear.

The task now was to get these newly found barrels off the river, and hopefully recycled. With a tireless series of grunts, crunches, rips, tosses, and heave-hos, Chad began to make a dent in the pile. Before long, the aluminum workboat was full of scrap metal and Chad was shoving the laden craft off its sandy perch and back into the river's currents. This scene in particular later caught the eye of CNN's audience. When the piece aired, CNN's viewer response phone-line began to ring off the hook.

Chad started the reluctant motor again and headed back to a nearby boat ramp. Standing at the helm with the tiller in his hand, Chad explained that Alcoa had given a him a grant to get started, and a waste management company had given him Dumpsters for recycling. "And I've picked up 30,000 pounds of trash, 92 barrels, 156 tires..." All acquired in just the first summer of his efforts, all just tokens of what lay ahead.

The piece ran on CNN many times as an *American Voices* segment that fall of 1997. Our audience was quite receptive. Chad's enthusiasm and noble cause clearly translated well on camera. He was learning that a key ingredient to making ends meet would be making the most of public appearances and sharing the limelight with the helping hands that were going to help his cause endure.

Having the tale of his project airing on worldwide satellite television brought a great deal of attention to Chad and his campaign. Other broadcast networks sent crews, national newspaper and magazine outlets sent photographers and scribes. Chad Pregracke had become a national spokesman for what he considered a national treasure, the Mississippi River. His good looks and charm were coupled with his sweat and tenacious spirit, creating a noble goal that corporate movers and shakers elsewhere were thinking they just might want to become a part of. Chad now seemed to be ready to raise the bar on his dreams.

Bit by bit, Chad met with more and more potential sponsors. With videotapes and other nationally published articles in hand, Chad was relentless in knocking on doors for support. It made it easy for some donors to get on board when they saw the good press that was associated with their allegiance. I kept in touch with Chad to take the project's pulse from time to time. After three years I was able to convince my superiors at CNN that it was time for a follow-up. In the early fall of 2000, I headed west from Atlanta.

Chad picked me up at the St. Louis airport in his old red pickup and drove me upstream to Grafton, Illinois, where his crew and their crafts were based on an island for a few days. Chad was finally about to fulfill his promise to clean the shores of the Mississippi from Dubuque, Iowa, to St. Louis. That's hundreds of miles of shoreline, littered with everything you can imagine—tires, barrels, appliances, tractors, prosthetic limbs, condoms, a horse's head, EVERYTHING! They had most of it loaded up on their barge and they were headed to a big community cleanup down in St. Louis, sponsored by Anheuser-Busch. I would ride with them downstream, spending several nights on board documenting the legion's march into their Rome.

St. Louis had dominated the Upper Mississippi since before Lewis and Clark in the early 1800s, and certainly during Mark Twain's times later. It seemed oddly poetic that the first major milestone achieved by the Living Lands & Waters team would be marked by their arrival under the Gateway Arch. It also seemed appropriate that Anheuser-Busch was participating, along with Alcoa and other sponsors, since so many of their containers ended up in or on the banks of the river.

As we cruised downstream, I tried to imagine what the riverbanks and bluffs probably looked like before Manifest Destiny, the Industrial Revolution, Pampers, and pop-tops. The expanse of water, the passage of the sun, the sights and sounds of Mother Nature unfolded before me as I sat on one of the barge bows and watched the gleaming Alton Bridge glide above us. The shores seemed relatively clean as we rode by, but a slight turn over my shoulder revealed the harsh reality of months of toil.

Tons and tons of garbage from months of Living Lands & Waters cleanups and community efforts lay piled in organized recyclable heaps. Rubber, steel, plastic, glass, you name it, was stacked 15 feet high in places on the barges. The ugly but proud array of refuse would stand the next day at the base of the arch as a testament to what was possible, what could be done. And coming up was the grand finale for the season— getting down and dirty with the corporate ranks of a major American corporation. Tomorrow this motley crew of idealists would be sharing their vision with the boardroom bosses and their entourage. How far had this one-man project come? From tiny acorn to mighty oak.

The next day, one well-coiffed Budweiser assistant struggled along with her coworkers to unearth a heavy barge cable that had been discarded in the sandy banks opposite downtown St. Louis. When they dislodged it, she turned to my camera and said, "It's one thing…to say your company is taking an environmental stance, but it's another thing to come see your senior directors and managers picking up trash on the Mississippi River!" Jennifer, one of Chad's sidekicks, added, "They've put a piece of garbage on this barge and they feel good about it."

By the next day, we had tugged back upriver to a major recycling and salvage depot in Alton, Illinois. *Crunch*, the barge's heavy load rams the facility's bulkhead, although from the looks of it, worse contact has been made in the past. It would take two to three days to unload what the river had yielded to Chad and his stalwart crew.

Chad commandeered a skid-steer to move tires and other items. I videotaped him in silhouette against a setting sun and strangely smooth Mississippi waters. I had begun this second installment with a synopsis of my first piece, but quickly showed the transformation from a one-man operation to a legitimate nonprofit success story. In a voice-over at the end of the piece, Chad told our audience that next year they would tackle the Illinois River, the Missouri, then the Ohio, the Hudson, and eventually even the Potomac in the nation's capital. "Coming to a river near you" had become his slogan. That was in 2000.

As I write this, it is fall 2006. After six years, a lot of water has passed under the bridge, or barge. Chad was approached by Robert F. Kennedy Jr. to participate in Kennedy's Riverkeeper organization, but while Chad was honored by the offer, he kept true to his roots and remained the captain of his own armada. In 2002 Chad received the Jefferson Award in Washington, D.C., sharing kudos with Bill and Melinda Gates and Rudolph Giuliani. Not bad company for a mussel diver from the Quad Cities.

But despite all the accolades, the awards, the positive press, and the donations, Chad thanks profusely those who have helped Living Lands & Waters along the way. Jeff Barrow, the coauthor of this book, myself, CNN, other media, the Living Lands & Waters staff, Chad's parents, the financial donors, the legal and financial advisors—everyone has been an individual ingredient of a greater cause that Chad Pregracke has kept together with the glue of his contagious, positive, can-do attitude. And Chad's tenacious vision continues to push its horizons. This past year Chad staged his second Potomac River cleanup and more notably provided enormous logistical and laborious help to those who suffered in Hurricane Katrina's wake.

If I wasn't married with children, I would truly consider joining up with Chad and Co. Chad's job is one of the most challenging yet rewarding occupations available. I have traveled all over the world in my 25 years at CNN. I have met presidents, covered world sports championships, dodged revolutionaries' gunfire, run the rapids of the mighty

Colorado River, and gotten drunk with Hunter S. Thompson, but my proudest achievement has been lending a hand in some small way to the growth of this noble cause.

This past summer my 22-year-old son Patrick signed on with Chad and Living Lands & Waters for two and a half months. I knew what he was getting into and I was skeptical of his survival in that role. When he returned home in August, after all those weeks of cleaning up on and in various rivers I asked him, "Well, whaddya think?" "It was the best job I ever had," he answered. "I want to do it again."

Tim Wall
Senior videographer, CNN Atlanta

When people hear the name of the Mississippi River, they think "mighty" and "historic" and "legendary." When I hear "Mississippi," I think "backyard."

I grew up on the shores of the Mississippi River in a rural section of East Moline, Illinois, The river's edge was 67 feet from my back door. As a kid, I didn't know the Mississippi River was of great importance. I saw it every morning from my family's breakfast table and judged the upcoming day by its moods—a blue reflection in the water meant clear skies and fair weather, while a silver-gray reflection meant clouds and possibly rain. The Mississippi was my playground when I came home from school. My parents made sure I knew how to swim at an early age, trusted my judgment, and didn't worry about me playing on the water. However, as I grew older, they worried about me working on the river.

My brother Brent was five years older than me, and I naturally followed his lead. Along with him, I learned to fish and ski and drive a boat before I was eight years old. When I was nine, I made five dollars a day trapping muskrats right off our dock. When I was 15, Brent took me on the river to help him as he dove commercially for mussels.

My parents wanted us to have good, decent, regular jobs and worried about the hardscrabble livelihood that went with working on the river. My mother, KeeKee, was director of the early childhood laboratory school at Black Hawk College, and my father, Gary, taught drafting at a vocational high school. At home, he taught Brent and me the value of hard work—that you can improve the world by persistent endeavor. My parents resisted our efforts to work on the river, but my brother probably said it best: "You raised us on the river, so don't try to fight us about working on the river."

I loved the adventure—every day on the water was different and brought something new. I liked working outside and the freedom and responsibility of being my own boss. I liked the variety of jobs I did and the character of the people I knew on the river. They treated you with the respect you deserved (high or low), because the river revealed what kind of person you were.

By the time Brent was 20, he was learning the techniques of shell-diving from his friend Randy David. Our families lived in the country within a mile of each other and we grew up playing together. We especially liked climbing up under the Interstate 80 bridge near our home, crawling out on the girders 50 feet above the water, and jumping into the river.

Randy himself had learned about shell-diving from an older guy known as "Hose Head." He'd earned that nickname because he sometimes breathed directly out of the air hose when he went "clamming" instead of using a diver's regulator. Hose Head was a typical mussel diver—self-reliant, fearless, and tough.

It is dangerous, miserable work, and shell divers typically spend six hours on the bottom of the river in pitch-black water with heavy currents. The only way to join the shell-diving industry is to apprentice with experienced "shellers," and when I was 15, Randy and Brent inducted me into this fringe element on the river.

There are more than 350 species of mussels in North America, and the vast majority live in rivers or streams. Most freshwater mussel species, which are called "clams" by commercial divers, require flowing water to bring food and take away waste, and they thrived in the Mississippi River because of its dependable current. On a good day, skilled shell divers could make $100 or more an hour collecting mussels from the mud, sand, or gravel at the bottom of the river. On a bad day, they earned nothing.

The mussels weren't valued for their meat but for their shells. These were cleaned and sorted for export to Japan, where the shells were cut up and rounded into little spheres. These mother-of-pearl beads were then implanted inside oysters, and the saltwater mollusks would coat each nucleus with layers of nacre—the calcium carbonate material that gives a pearl its iridescent luster. A tiny piece of American mussel shell nestles at the center of nearly every cultured pearl in the world. In the 1990s, the value of U.S.'s mussel-shell exports to Japan averaged $50 million per year.

The chance to make big bucks exhilarated Brent and Randy, but they prized their freedom over the cash. On the river and underwater, they didn't have to put up with a boss ordering them around or a time clock to measure their worth. They typically worked 10-hour days. They would make three two-hour dives with a break in between to sort shells and bail the boat. The rest of the workday consisted of equipment chores, boat handling, and selling the shells to a local buyer.

At first, Brent, Randy, and I used an aluminum boat our family had salvaged 10 years earlier in the high water of a spring flood. My parents paid an insurance company the $75 scrap value to obtain legal title. The boat had seen better days. The hull had cracks and holes, but with a beat-up Evinrude outboard motor on the stern transom, we had a serviceable vessel to use as a work platform.

While some shellers just waded in the shallows to find mussels, more and more were divers who transformed hospital-grade air compressors into portable underwater breathing machines. Powered by small gasoline engines, these were called "hookah" rigs. The compressor pumped air through rubber hoses snaking over the sides of the boat and down to

One of my chores as a 10-year-old was to clear "seaweed" from the bay behind my parents' house on the Mississippi River.

the divers' regulators. Like many other shell divers, Brent and Randy had fabricated air hoses by duct-taping ski ropes to garden hoses. They used the air hoses like gym ropes to descend from the boat and ascend from the bottom. A typical air hose was about 50 feet long.

Once the hookah rig was checked out for leaks, each diver would grab a mesh bag used for hauling the mussels. A dive bag looks something like a horse's feed sack—it hangs hands-free in front of the diver at chest level where a diver can shove shells inside it easily. A metal ring about a foot wide holds the dive bag open, and a short section of rope serves as a collar around the diver's neck. A full bag can hold up to 100 pounds of mussels.

When they were ready to clam, the divers would climb over the gunwales, slide into the water, and disappear into the coffee-with-cream-colored river. A five-horsepower Briggs & Stratton engine roared the whole time the divers were submerged. The pulley on the engine rotated a rubber belt that transferred power to the air compressor. It was a marginal operation, for the air compressor's engine sometimes broke down and the belt often jumped the pulley. An air hose could uncouple from an attachment or a compressor seal could leak air. If a seal failed, the person tending it might not know the air had stopped unless he was watching the divers' bubbles and saw that they had quit rising to the surface.

When the equipment malfunctioned, the air pressure went to zero and the divers would lose their air supply. Shell divers practiced escape maneuvers for just such emergencies. They would jettison their dive bags, drop their weight belts, push off the bottom, and rocket to the surface—being careful to hold their hands above their heads to keep from hitting the dive boat or the propeller as they surfaced. This was a simple and quick routine in slack water. When the river was running hard, however, the scramble for air could become more desperate.

Normally, a diver dropped straight down, holding on to the air hose to control his rate of descent. There is no visibility at the bottom of the river, and shell divers know what it means to be blind. They spend hours at a time groping in darkness where their eyesight has become useless. They discern the layout of this alien world by touching everything with their hands, feet, and bodies. They learn to translate what they touch into mental maps of the river bottom. Their memory of this unseen underwater terrain is astounding. They can often return to the same spot by remembering how a specific rock feels, relating its location to other invisible items in the underwater maze. On large, mud-flat bottoms without identifying features, they tend to walk in circles like lost hikers—favoring either their right side or left.

Divers say they develop a sixth sense because zero visibility forces them to use their brains in a different way. They often sense obstacles just before reaching them—perhaps because they can feel the subtle shift in the current as it passes an obstruction.

Working underwater in the pitch-black depths also requires divers to develop a fearless attitude. They learn to concentrate on doing their risky job without getting distracted by the danger.

On my very first day working on the river, I learned firsthand how dangerous clamming can be. It had rained overnight, and the Mississippi came up hard and fast. The current was ripping when my brother and Randy dove together side by side using the same hookah rig. They brought me along as a tender, and my job was to sort the clams and keep watch on the equipment. But mainly they needed me to bail the leaky boat.

After less than an hour underwater, Randy popped to the surface and shouted that the air supply had been cut off. Brent was still underwater, and his air hose stretched taut behind us in the raging, brown river. Randy quickly scrambled aboard, and we hauled Brent's limp body into the boat. Brent's face was purple, his skin was clammy, and his bloodshot eyes stared blankly into space. He wasn't breathing, and I thought he was dead. I can't express the relief I felt when he started breathing again, although the first thing he did was curse me roundly for not paying attention to his air bubbles. We found out later that a rubber seal had failed in the air compressor and shut off the air supply.

Despite this frightening mishap, I felt like I had found my life's calling that day. Working in a boat outdoors on the water was a perfect job, and I wanted more of it. It was sketchy but satisfying, not to mention fun—you never knew what was going to happen. The only downside was having Brent as my boss, because, as my older brother, he could yell and scream in my face at any time.

I remember vividly my first chance to dive. It occurred 12 months after Brent's near-drowning experience, in the summer between my sophomore and junior years—in fact, it was one day after high school let out for the summer. Brent was shelling at Peoria Lake and asked me to help him. I drove through the rolling, open farmland of central Illinois and descended into the heavily wooded Illinois River valley. I arrived in the late morning at Hamm's Holiday Harbor, a private marina in Chillicothe, Illinois. The Hamm family had lived on the Illinois River for generations, and relatives could be found in every town along the waterway. They were famous for being connected with that river through hunting and fishing, and some of them were notorious along the river for their game fines and as outlaws. Dale Hamm, the family patriarch, even published a book about making his livelihood poaching in the 1940s and '50s, entitled *Last of the Market Hunters*.

Dale's son, Dick, settled in Chillicothe on the shores of Peoria Lake—a reservoir pooling for 20 miles behind a dam built by the Army Corps of Engineers. Dick Hamm owned and operated a protected harbor on the river and opened a private marina.

When I left home that morning, my parents had repeated their mantra, "No diving! No diving!" They knew I was going to the river to help Brent, but they didn't want me to be exposed to the dangers of working under-water. But when Brent picked me up, he informed me that his ears were getting infected. He had swimmer's ear—a clammer's worst enemy—and I would have to dive. I couldn't believe my luck.

Brent steered the boat out on the water while I suited up. The depth in Peoria Lake usually measured 3 to 4 feet, but spring rains had brought the level up to 12 feet. The bottom consisted of mud flats interspersed with stumps and sunken logs that were far apart. The slack current and shallow depth made for easy diving conditions. Brent assured me that I would run into nothing but clams.

I slipped over the side and sank into the silty water while Brent tended the boat. I couldn't see a thing and dropped straight down. I was scared and breathing hard, almost hyperventilating. It was an eerie feeling to dangle from the clear surface through layers of progressively murkier water to the complete and utter blackness at the bottom. My mind was racing, wondering what I would feel down there—sunken trees, wrecked vehicles, jumbles of barbed wire, concrete chunks with steel rebar sticking out? I was relieved to land safely in the soft mud.

When I reached the bottom, I leaned forward blindly and spread my arms to feel for the clams. I found my first mussel, put it in the dive bag around my neck, and moved forward to find a second one. The shells were far apart but plentiful. I ran along while feeling for the mussels. The reservoir was big—20 miles long and up to 3 miles wide—and the bottom was smooth. Brent was right—there were few obstacles. The air-hose line went from the boat to my weight belt and I dragged the vessel behind me. For the next seven hours with only a few breaks up top, I proceeded to run along the bottom, pulling the boat four or five miles. Because I had trained to run long-distance in track, my ability to keep moving on the bottom was exceptionally good.

When I reboarded the boat at 6 p.m., I had collected 300 pounds of legal mussels, a haul that would yield $336 at Hamm's. I counted about 80 boats with mussel divers in the waters near Chillicothe that day—I saw more clamming boats and more money than I'd ever seen in my life. At that time, clamming was like a gold rush, except you couldn't stake a claim and you couldn't completely protect your spots.

We spent many days that summer working on Peoria Lake. In addition to the experience I gained on the water, something else stands out in my mind that would have a big impact on the work I do now. At that time Dick Hamm was just starting to get into the barge business. Every morning when Brent and I went out to dive, I would see Dick and a couple other guys working on the towboats and the barges—moving them, tying them up, fixing them, welding them, pulling engines. Dick was maybe 50 years old, and I was amazed to watch him scrambling around the towboats like he was 20. I remember thinking, "Someday, I want to work with barges."

Another event that summer also made a strong impression on me. Brent and I teamed up with Rick Hamm, Dick's son, and went 60 miles downriver to look for clams at Bath Chute, a narrow offshoot of the main channel about 14 miles long. This chute was the largest of its kind on the Illinois River, and clammers had been picking it over for years. To be successful there, any new clammers would have to search overlooked spots or dangerous places where other divers didn't venture, such as log jams. We decided to dive directly off the boat launch and beneath a floating tavern, because we didn't think anyone would dive there.

There were tons of garbage down there—metal barrels, tires, bottles, cans, and random junk. Brent came up and reported that he had found a toilet and a car. The river bottom was like a small landfill, as though people had been disposing of garbage in the river for years. The pebble bottom kept the junk from getting buried by mud. The biggest mussel that day was actually found in the toilet bowl. Brent crawled into a car that was lying on the bottom of the river and sat behind the wheel pretending to drive—just to say he did it. I laughed, but the reality of all that trash really disturbed me.

That experience was soon repeated closer to home. Brent and I traveled to Andalusia Slough to dive for mussel shells. A slough is a backwater channel, and Andalusia is one of the largest slough areas on the Upper Mississippi River, a 670-mile section of the river that flows from Minneapolis down a 420-foot slope to St. Louis. While the main river channel is maintained for barge navigation, the side channels are cut off in numerous bays and sloughs. The Andalusia Slough braids itself around numerous wooded islands.

The islands and peninsulas are incredibly beautiful. On the islands, towering forests of cottonwood, sycamore, and silver maple interlace their branches into dense canopies that don't allow much light to reach the ground. Intermittent shafts of sunlight pierce the humid air, and at certain times the woods look like a natural cathedral. The groves of oak trees and hickories are full of wildlife.

Although the whole area was lush and green in the summer, hardly any weeds or other low-growing vegetation could survive in this shady jungle. Every year, the river flooded these low-lying islands and turned them into swampy wetlands. Fortunately for us, the ground was dry this late in the season. Yet the high water also brought in rafts of trash and debris. Metal barrels, appliances, and tires were mixed in with the fallen logs and branches. The ground was sprinkled with bottles and cans as far as you could see.

I didn't have plans to go to a four-year college immediately after graduation, so I started attending Black Hawk College in Moline,

Illinois, where my mother worked. Like many first-year students, I didn't know what I wanted to do after getting a degree, but I knew one thing for sure: I wanted to work on the river.

As educators, my parents strongly advocated higher education. They struggled hard against every effort by Brent and me to work on the river—and for good reason, actually. They saw that direction as leading to an uncertain future and a hard life.

I wanted to have the college experience, but felt that higher education was distracting me from my true calling. So I would go to school for a semester and then "stop out" for a semester. At one point, I finally made up my mind to be a commercial fisherman, and I dropped out of school to work with Rick Hamm, my friend and mentor on the Illinois River. He was an excellent commercial fisherman, and I knew I could learn the ropes of what to do and how to do it. I intended to apprentice with him until I had saved enough money to buy my own nets, so I could fish independently on the Mississippi River. After working with him two months, I actually did buy my own nets and went out on my own to make my mark as a commercial fisherman. I lasted four days and sold $70 worth of fish.

It was back to college for me. I did everything I could *not* to work at what my parents called a steady and decent job. They were very happy when I was hired at a Godfather's Pizza restaurant. It was steady and decent, but I hated it. I didn't like having to adhere to a rigid schedule or be supervised by a boss. I worked there for three weeks before I quit.

I still needed to pay the bills, so I partnered with one of my best friends to form a business while we were still in college. We started building willow furniture and called our enterprise Scott and Chad's Willow Shop. In 1996, I transferred to Heartland Community College in Normal, Illinois, and moved the small business into the basement of the house I rented with friends. I had met a farmer whose property abutted the Illinois River, and we worked a deal: I could cut the willows on his land, and all I had to do was leave him a case of Budweiser in his tractor cab every time I went there. As far as he was concerned, the willow trees were taking up land he could till, but to me he owned the biggest willow patch I had ever seen, with the best willow in it for making furniture. I could have cut his patch for years and years.

As I stopped-and-started through college, my higher education included lots of river time—both on shore cutting willows in the winter and on the water shell-diving in the summer. More and more, I noticed the accumulation of garbage out there—even when I was cutting in the willow patch. When I say accumulation, I mean thousands of tires, barrels, propane tanks, cars, tractors—you name it. There were appliances such as refrigerators, stoves, washers, dryers, and air conditioners, and smaller items like cans, plastic bottles, toys, discarded clothes, and building materials. Anything you can find in a landfill, you'll find on the shores of the river. Of course, in the summer months the weeds would get so thick that the garbage was pretty well hidden, but in the winter when the weeds were down, you could literally see islands full of garbage.

Discarded household appliances and 55-gallon drums were probably the most common kinds of garbage—refrigerators were most likely dumped on purpose because you have to pay a fee to get rid of them. The metal drums you might expect to be full of hazardous waste, but they were actually used to float docks on the river in earlier days, so most of them were empty, half-rusted, or full of holes. Some people see the barrels as a sign of illegal dumping, but the vast majority got loose in the river by getting swept away in high water or by developing a pinhole leak.

For many decades, people treated the river as a sewer and garbage disposal. Illegal dumping was common—almost a way of life before cities and counties established landfills and good recycling programs. People dumped in the river because their parents did it and their neighbors did it. Or they dumped in nearby ravines, valleys, or ditches that would be cleaned by heavy rains—so-called gully-washers. Eventually the trash would drain into the nearest river and get hung up on islands and shores. Virtually all rivers in the 32 Midwestern states ultimately flow into the Mississippi River—which translates as "Big River" in the Algonquin language.

On top of all this intentional dumping, river floods played a huge role as well. The high water would pick things up from the floodplain and float them downriver, where they would drop out of the current onto the land as the water level receded. In some places, especially on river islands, the garbage was so profuse that it looked like something you'd see in a magazine article about a Third World country. You certainly wouldn't expect to see such a sight in the United States of America, not on the great Mississippi River—a symbol of our country and one of the great rivers of the world.

The Mississippi watershed comprises 1.2 million square miles, the second largest drainage basin in the world. Only the Amazon River drains a larger area. The river has more than 250 tributaries, and its basin stretches from the high plains in Saskatchewan and the Rocky Mountains in Montana to the Alleghenies in New York and the Appalachians in North Carolina. The Mississippi River supplies 90 percent of the freshwater recharge to the Gulf of Mexico, yet the river has become a huge repository of America's waste.

The Mississippi is mighty, for sure, but I knew it from a very close and personal perspective. After years of camping on the islands with my brother during our shell-diving days, I became disgusted with the extent of the garbage. It got to the point that everywhere I went was littered with trash—no matter how remote the island or side-channel slough.

I frequently camped on the islands near Andalusia and woke up in the morning with the river shining like a mirror. When I looked into the woods, the ground was carpeted with bright plastic bottles—the yellow of oil containers, the red of antifreeze jugs, and a rainbow of brightly colored laundry bottles. In one particular spot, I found dozens of light-bulbs scattered all over the ground. I was amazed that they floated to this place without shattering. How could such fragile glass survive the force of the floods?

I woke up like that many times—loving the natural world and hating the despicable mess. I saw the garbage on the river, and it didn't look right. It may have been commonplace, but I didn't like it and I didn't

accept it. And the more garbage sites I noticed, the more it made me want
to do something about it.

The contrast between the beauty of the river and its ugly burden of
trash became crystal clear for me one Friday evening when I was heading
back after a long day diving for shells just south of what we call the "Quad
Cities," four municipalities that more or less face each other across the
Mississippi (Rock Island and Moline on the Illinois side, Davenport and
Bettendorf on the Iowa side). I was approaching the boat ramp at Sunset
Marina, the biggest marina in the area, and the entrance to Sunset was
busy with ski boats, houseboats, and even million-dollar yachts slowly
cruising out to the river for the weekend.

As I motored upstream with a heavy load of clams, a huge pile of more
than 50 steel barrels that stood exposed in the mud on shore caught my
eye. This ragged mess had probably been rusting there for 30 years
or more, and I had seen the site many times. But this time a 60-foot
yacht was anchored just offshore from the ugly tangle of barrels. The
boat's white hull gleamed in the low-angled sunlight shining off the
water. People were enjoying their cocktail hour on the back deck. As I
looked at this picturesque setting, I thought to myself, "I wish that was
my boat." But seriously and more important, I was thinking, "Is this how
these people have to enjoy the river? Next to a pile of rusty barrels?"

That was the moment I knew what I had to do. If nobody else was going
to do anything about the trashing of the Mississippi River, then I would
do something.

I wasn't sure how I was going to go about cleaning the river. I was barely
making ends meet with shell-diving, so I figured I had to call somebody with
the state of Illinois to see if they had funding to pick up the garbage. With
phone in hand, I started to wade through the government's alphabet soup—I
called every acronym in the directory: the DNR, the DOT, the EPA, and even
the governor's office. I was still a teenager and didn't know whom to call.
I didn't know what to say or how to say it. All the state agencies responded
in the same way: "What garbage are you talking about?" and "Who are you,

kid?" They uniformly said, "No, we don't have any money to support such a project."

But I was doing everything wrong. I didn't present my idea properly and I didn't talk to the right people in the agencies. Clammers usually are not high on the social scale. They crawl all day on the bottom of a river, and it's a tough, dangerous job. I doubt my status as a teenage clammer helped me any in promoting my cause.

I did have some things going for me though. I had saved up enough money to buy a 20-foot flat-bottom boat and had obtained a loan from a local credit union to purchase a 40-horsepower motor. It was an open boat with deep sides and a tiller-arm. It could be used for fishing and clamming—or trash-hauling—and I was willing to use it as a floating Dumpster. I also had experience working on a hundred-mile reach of river and knew it well from the bottom up. And I was dead set on attacking the problem—first, the garbage on the river, and second, the intransigence of the state agencies.

I started to focus on why the agencies were saying no. I didn't believe it was a lack of interest but rather a lack of knowledge about the extent of the problem. These people had no idea about how much garbage had accumulated on the Mississippi's banks and islands. They worked in offices several hours away at the state capital in Springfield, and they couldn't know how bad it was on the river.

So I began taking pictures of some sites similar to the barrel pile that had finally motivated me to take action. I intended to put together a photo album of random shots to show the agency folks the depth of the problem. I was convinced they would support a cleanup project once they knew how bad the situation was.

Meanwhile, I was thinking about how to do a cleanup and had talked to my dad about it. We discussed the tools that would be needed and the potential problems—stuff like how to move the garbage and what to do with it once it was out of the river.

Coincidentally, I needed to make a presentation for an environmental science class during spring semester at Heartland Community College,

*I'm 16 here and helping my older brother, Brent, clean out the Carolina skiff
for the upcoming clamming season from June through August.*

so I actually used the cleanup project to get credit in the class. I made a
big poster with a map of the river and photos I had taken of the garbage.
During my presentation I talked about cleaning the river, but I think the
entire class, including the teacher, thought that I was full of crap.

Then the solution for the funding problem hit me in a stunning
revelation.

I had been out all day cutting willows for my furniture-making
business when I came home and found my roommates on the couch
watching a NASCAR race on TV. I stood behind the couch and saw the
winning driver get out of his car. He walked over to be interviewed
and thanked his sponsors for helping him win the race. Corporate
logos covered his race car and patches were sewn on his jumpsuit. I
scratched my head and narrowed my eyes while looking at the logos
and the patches. I knew it took a lot of money to sponsor a car in a
NASCAR race. In a flash, I connected the dots between sponsors and

race cars. If companies would support NASCAR races, then surely they'd sponsor a river cleanup, too.

My smile lit up the room as I said, "I can wear patches!"

I bolted straight to my room and looked at a map. I traced out a 435-mile stretch of the river from Guttenberg, Iowa, to St. Louis because I wanted to set a goal that I could present to companies for their support. This 435-mile reach was far too ambitious considering my resources, and everybody I told about my idea pointed this out. But, at the time, it didn't seem like too much to me. I thought two workboats and a crew of six people could make a sizable difference. Although I'd never been to three-quarters of the places on that part of the river, I just assumed there would be garbage and plenty of it. I figured I would set my sights high and work as hard as I could every day—that's all one person can do, and that's what I was going to do.

I made a list of local companies that might be interested in sponsoring a river cleanup. Moline is the world headquarters for John Deere, one of the biggest farm equipment manufacturers in the world. Other large companies in the Quad Cities included Case, International Harvester, and Alcoa. These companies were the top employers in the area, and since Alcoa started with an "A," I figured I'd go there first.

When I looked in the telephone directory, there were about 30 different departments at Alcoa. I picked one at random. I got a lady on the phone and said, "My name is Chad Pregracke and I want to clean up a 435-mile stretch of the Mississippi River." I told her I wanted to know who the top person was at Alcoa.

I could sense that she was pretty reluctant to put me through to the person in charge. But I begged her for five minutes and wouldn't let up. Eventually she put me in touch with a vice president at the plant—a man by the name of Tim Wilkinson. I called him and requested a meeting.

At first, I think he was reticent, but I just kept talking and didn't give him a chance to say no. I told him who I was and what I wanted to do. I said I'd been planning to clean up the Mississippi River for the past four years, and I offered to come in and show him all the photos I had taken of the garbage. I begged him to give me just ten minutes of his time. Trying to make it sound easy for him, I said I'd meet him on the way to his car if he couldn't meet me in his office.

He finally agreed to a meeting, but only after asking me if I was a 501(c)3, not-for-profit organization. I told him I had no idea what a 501(c)3 was but that I could be if it would help me out any.

Tim asked this question because he wanted to know if I was an established organization, which I wasn't. Nor did I have any intention at the time of starting an organization. He also stressed that I must have a budget for the project before coming to see him. On that score, I said, "No problem."

My mother's job at the college made her very familiar with budgets, and my job on the river gave me a good idea of what the project would cost. I also realized that one person couldn't clean up a 435-mile reach of the river, so I wanted to buy a second workboat and hire six people to help me do the job. The budget didn't include money to pay me because that was never my intention. I just wanted my expenses to be paid.

I went to see Mr. Wilkinson with photos of the garbage and a budget in hand. My hair was long at the time so I tucked it up in my baseball cap. I was extremely enthusiastic. There was no doubt in my mind that I was going to get a sponsorship.

I had to check my enthusiasm while watching a boring safety video in his office. I was expecting a ten-minute meeting and was worried that this video was taking up seven minutes of my time. When I finally got a chance to make my presentation, speaking in rapid-fire fashion, I jumbled all together who I was, what my goals were, and how I planned to achieve them. I flipped through the photos that I had brought and tripped over my tongue as I narrated their contents to him. Trying to impress on him how important this project was. I explained my attempts to work with state agencies and told him about my idea to get private sponsorships.

By that time I had slowed down. He seemed thoroughly interested in the project, and he complimented me on how much thought and time I had already put into it. He seemed convinced of the need for cleaning the river. Our meeting was already longer than ten minutes and he wasn't ending it. When he asked me how much it would cost, I slipped him the budget my mom and I had put together with a bottom line of $77,000. His eyes widened as he inspected the document on his desk.

"Wow, that's a lot of money," he said.

I told him I knew it was a lot, but that's what the budget worked out to be.

He sat back in his chair and laughed. I couldn't tell if he was laughing at the project, at the budget, or at me. I thought I detected a friendly tone, though. Then he said, "All right, how about ten?"

I said, "Ten?"

"Yeah, ten thousand dollars."

I was so excited that I almost jumped out of my seat. I looked down at my watch and calculated how long I'd been in his office. "Ten minutes, ten thousand dollars," I told him. "You've got a deal!"

He tried to calm me down by saying that the Alcoa sponsorship was conditional.

"You go out there and raise the rest of the money you need," he said. "Then I'll help you out."

I was so naïve at this point that I thought I'd be back in a few days with the rest of the money. As it turned out, I spent the next six weeks trying to get meetings so I could talk about the project. No luck. Some people just blatantly said no without even giving me a chance to explain who I was or what I wanted to do. Others strung me along for the entire month and a half before saying no. But who could blame them for shunning me? I wasn't a nonprofit organization and had never done anything like this. As far as they were concerned, I was just a clammer kid begging for money.

I was near emotional bottom after hearing no from almost everybody that I contacted. I was supremely discouraged. Yet in spite of my despair,

I was determined to make this happen. So I went back to Mr. Wilkinson and told him what I had been doing for the past six weeks.

"To be honest," I said, "I don't know why you're interested in this project—no one else will even give me the chance to say who I am and explain what I want to do." I asked him if he would still consider sponsoring the project.

He suggested that I go to work by myself with what I already owned—a boat, a truck, and some tools—and just concentrate in the Quad Cities area.

"Come back with a budget for what that'll cost," he said.

I went back home and recalculated the budget for a one-man operation—money to pay my expenses for gas, oil, landfill fees, and so on. I went back to him with a budget of $8,400, and the next day he handed me a check for that amount. It took a lot of confidence for him to trust me enough to take that chance.

I was so happy that I didn't have to call any more people who ultimately would tell me no. I still wasn't a 501(c)3 organization, but I opened a bank account with the title "River Cleanup" at the local credit union.

The next day, I started cleaning up the Mississippi River.

arly on a sunny June morning in 1997, I launched my boat at my parents' concrete ramp and drove directly across the river to a bay on the Mississippi known as LeClaire Canal. The sky was clear blue, and a light wind rippled the surface of the river. It was a Thursday and no boaters were out on the water with me.

The site I'd chosen for starting my cleanup used to be a canal for steamboats before Lock-and-Dam 14 flooded the river in 1939. When the pool filled above the dam, the canal became a protected cove out of the main navigation channel. Recreational boaters and fishermen used the bay heavily.

As a child, I had spent countless mornings there fishing with my dad and brother. I used to walk along the shore and look for usable lumber that Dad could salvage for building projects. It was also one of the trash sites I had photographed when trying to get support for cleaning the river. Now here I was cleaning it up.

I found my first piece of garbage immediately. It was an eight-foot section of culvert pipe half-buried at the edge of the river and half-full of mud. I emptied the pipe and tossed it into the boat. There were some

I'm pretty pleased after my first day cleaning the Mississippi River.
I've filled my truck and trailered my boat to haul the garbage.

diesel barrels stuck in the mud nearby, so I rolled them over to the boat and pushed the barrels over its side onto the culvert pipe. The aluminum hull rang when each of these heavy items banged into the bottom.

Blaine's Farm-and-Fleet Store had given me a roll of heavy-duty garbage bags, and I started filling one of them with small items—bottles, cans, plastic jugs, old tarps, and so on. I found pockets of concentrated trash where people fished from shore. This "fisherman's trash" consisted mostly of foam bait boxes, tangles of fishing line, smashed lawn chairs, and beer bottles and cans.

I filled my boat with garbage bags and debris and drove it back to my parents' house. It was no problem since I was used to driving with a heavy load from my clamming days, when the boat would be full of mussel shells. I took a photo of my first boatload of garbage and then unloaded it onto the back of my dad's flatbed trailer. I had spotted a big diesel tank in the mud at LeClaire Canal, so I fetched a pickax from the toolshed and went back to get it.

By then, boaters were coming out and saw me loading my boat. When I tossed in a heavy item, they would hear the racket I was making, too. I was digging out the diesel tank when an older man drove up in his boat and idled offshore about 20 feet. I put my shovel down, and he asked what I was doing. I told him I was cleaning the garbage. I went on to say that Alcoa was sponsoring me to clean up the river, and this was my first day on the job.

"I can't believe you're actually doing something about this," he said. "It's disgusted me for years." He was the first of many people who began to pay attention to what I was doing.

I filled two boatloads that first day and dumped everything on the flatbed trailer. Then I drove it to the landfill and to a scrap-metal yard to dispose of the trash.

I had begun a new work routine. Every day, I motored out in my 20-foot, flat-bottom boat with its small 40-horsepower engine. I wore my standard garb of bib overalls with no shirt and hair down to my shoulders. No matter who was on the river, whether they were boating or fishing or birding—they were curious about what I was doing and why. And when I told them, they thought it was absolutely phenomenal that someone would actually want to clean up the river garbage. In many cases, people would offer me sodas and sandwiches, and some people even got out of their boats and helped me pick up the trash.

I loved cleaning the river. For one thing, I could take a breath of air anytime I wanted to, compared with clamming where you never knew when the airflow would stop. Plus, people were thanking me for cleaning the garbage. Clammers were sometimes considered to be scummy characters, and I wasn't used to being praised. I didn't realize picking up garbage would be so positive. I was learning firsthand that I was by no means the only person who didn't like seeing all this junk in the river.

After a few days, I quit off-loading each boatload onto the trailer. I needed a bigger space, and my first unloading and sorting area was the obvious one—where else but my parents' yard? I piled the barrels in one area and stacked the tires in another. I heaped the bags of garbage into a small hill. The river had washed the trash and the sun had bleached it, so the garbage didn't smell. Luckily, my parents were away on vacation for a couple of weeks. That's when the garbage really started to pile up. We're talking about fair-sized mountains of material.

I especially liked the challenge of digging out refrigerators and metal barrels—they were big and heavy, and usually buried in sand or mud. These were ugly things, dangerous and obviously out of place on the river. It felt supremely satisfying to start removing these barrels, and the fact that they were gone left a big impression. In a couple of weeks, I collected a pile of barrels that towered nearly as high as the second-story deck at my parents' house.

I proceeded to sort the garbage to make disposal easier and cheaper. I didn't want it all to go to a landfill, so I tried to recycle as much as I could. The process involved benefits and costs. I could get money for scrap metal, but I had to pay a disposal charge for appliances and tires.

I was collecting dozens of tires, too—huge tractor tires, semi-truck tires, motorcycle tires, and bicycle tires in addition to automobile tires. Most of them were still on the rim, which made them more expensive to get rid of, but they were typically lighter than rimless tires because they hadn't filled with mud.

I covered the entire yard with garbage. There was a 15-foot-tall hill composed of plastic trash bags filled with all the little stuff I picked up—glass bottles, aluminum cans, antifreeze jugs, bleach bottles, oil containers, paint cans, foam cups, plastic bottles, lightbulbs, batteries, shoes, balls, toys, and an endless parade of small plastic items of every description. I collected another mountain of tires and yet another of appliances. My parents' yard was becoming a Mad Max version of the Alps. I made sure to clear out all the garbage before they got home, though and just in the knick of time! They would have gone crazy to see how I had landscaped their yard with the garbage.

I was extremely proud of the garbage piles I had accumulated in a short amount of time, but I also was disgusted that all of these items were retrieved from less than a mile of riverfront. And that was just on the Iowa side; I hadn't even started in Illinois. When neighbors saw the garbage piling up, they asked me if all that junk came from the river. I answered, "Yes, and that's nothing compared to what's still out there."

I'm not sure who made the initial call, but a river enthusiast told the local TV stations and newspapers about what I was doing. I wasn't answering my parents' phone while they were gone, so they came back to a ton of messages on their answering machine. They said I should return the calls, but I wasn't really interested in talking to reporters—I just wanted to go out on the river and pick up garbage. My parents persisted, however, and eventually convinced me that media coverage would become good publicity for the project. It would show everyone how neglected the river had been in the past and what I was trying to do about it now. I was still hoping to clean up the planned 435-mile section of river, and I thought this attention could help raise money to launch that expedition. So I sucked in a big breath of air and picked up the phone.

I called Lee Nelson at the *Quad City Times*, and she came over with photographer Greg Boll in June 1997. I took them out on the river and explained the project. I thought I was making everything clear, but I was worried that the article would come out cheesy.

The layout appeared on the front page of the Sunday edition with a huge headline, "Love Affair with the River," and a big photo of me, shirtless in my overalls, driving the boat. I didn't particularly care for the article, because I was embarrassed by the attention. It made me feel uneasy to be on the front page. But everyone else seemed to love it.

The next day, the phone at my parents' house started ringing off the hook. All the local television stations called and wanted to cover the story. The *Quad City Times* had advanced the story to the Associated Press, and it seemed like everyone in the country loved it. FOX National News out of Chicago came down right away. Tim Wall of CNN called, followed by Anderson Cooper of ABC's Peter Jennings team from New York and Denver.

When the original article ran, I figured it might be newsworthy for the local area, but I was absolutely awestruck when national news media expressed such strong interest. In the fall, I spent three days with the ABC team, which included Cooper and John Banner. This sparked a follow-up article on the front page of the *Quad City Times* about the notoriety I was gaining—usually the Quad Cities area achieves national attention only when something big blows up or there's a devastating flood.

Later that summer, Tim Wall from CNN came out to do a story. He was the senior producer of a show called *American Voices*, and the clip he produced didn't just run once, it ran numerous times. I got to meet and hang out with a lot of journalists that year and was amazed by their experiences and the many cool stories they told. I was surprised and humbled to be a focal point in their camera sights.

Although the attention made me uneasy, I realized it would help the cause of cleaner rivers. More people would become aware of how badly the rivers had been treated in the past.

After a few weeks of working, I had cleaned the entire bay at LeClaire Canal. It felt great to see the results: the shoreline free of trash. I did notice that bottles and cans started to reappear almost immediately, but the big stuff was gone.

I decided to move south about 20 miles, near Andalusia. Having spent so much time shell-diving there, I knew I'd find a bunch of garbage on the side-channel islands. I started at the point of an island where Turkey Hollow Creek meets the Mississippi River. People called this side-channel Dead Man's Slough because corpses had been known to wash up there from the Quad Cities upriver. In fact, a dead body had been found there just days before I arrived. The man was wearing high-tops and a Chicago Bears jacket, and police believed he jumped from the Interstate 280 bridge about two miles upstream.

Dead Man's Slough is officially named "Swift Slough" on river charts, and it's perfectly situated to capture things floating downstream from the Quad Cities. The river creates stream dynamics that tend to catch and hold floating objects in certain areas. In general, I noticed that trash typically accumulates downriver from a town or city on the outside bends of the curving watercourse.

I planned to stay for a few months while I cleaned up the garbage in this area. My brother let me use his houseboat as a base, and I tied it up to a silver maple tree that hung over the water from the head of the island. The main channel of the Mississippi rolled by on the north, and the slow-moving backwaters stretched south into the densely wooded islands and swamps. It was spooky at night because occasionally people would drive their boats down there with no running lights.

I took the trash to the public ramp at Sunset Marina about four miles up from Dead Man's Slough. The city of Rock Island let me set up there, and I arranged with a waste company to bring Dumpsters down to the

My brother, Brent, let me use his houseboat as a floating base of operations during my first two cleanup seasons in 1997–98.

ramp at no charge. They even hauled some of the scrap metal for me, but I still had to pay to remove tires, appliances, and the leftover garbage after they retrieved the Dumpsters.

I worked a lot by myself but also had help from friends. It was always fun to work in a group and a lot easier to move big, awkward items. Two local environmental groups, the Izaac Walton League and the Quad City Conservation Alliance, called me with offers to help with a cleanup. They made a financial contribution, and about 15 of their members joined me on the river to pick up trash. This was my first experience leading a large group, and it provided the template for future volunteer cleanup events.

First, I thanked them for coming and told them what we were going to do. I had decided to attack the big pile of barrels at Sunset Marina—the same barrels that disgusted me originally. Several volunteers rode out in my boat, others went in a pontoon boat, and the rest were in a private launch. I provided some shovels, and they had brought shovels as well. We worked for about four hours and removed a sizable proportion of the pile of barrels. They returned home to hot showers, and I stayed out to haul the barrels a short distance to the boat ramp next to the marina.

Another "first" was an honor I still treasure: an award from the Illinois Chapter of the National Fish and Wildlife Federation. A local man named Bill Courter nominated me, and soon I was accepting the award in a ceremony at the State Capitol in Springfield. I drove there with my parents and Heidi Hartman, who helped a lot on the cleanup.

I continued to work full-time on the project through the summer, but had to scale back to four days a week once I returned to college. My fall semester schedule required me to attend classes three days a week. College seemed to be a distraction from my mission, but I was close to obtaining a two-year degree.

It was at this time that I found my first message in a bottle. A Rock Island teacher had asked each student in her fourth grade class to write a brief note, and she put them all in a plastic bottle with a little flag attached. She probably launched it with high hopes that it would be recovered in the Gulf of Mexico. Unfortunately, the bottle floated high in the water and drifted into a logjam about 10 feet downstream. When I called the teacher, she asked me where I had found it. I knew the students would be disappointed if they were told the truth, so I fibbed and said I found it "above Muscatine." This was literally true—Rock Island is 30 miles upstream from Muscatine—but I stretched the truth by 99.9 percent.

Later that fall, the CNN piece aired and brought an unbelievable response, spawning hundreds of letters and cards from all around the country and the world. We received enough mail to fill several laundry baskets—and my mom replied to each one of them with a thank-you note. The letters expressed a variety of ideas, but almost all of the writers hit the same three points: first, what a great thing it was to clean up the trash; second, how important the rivers are to them; and third, the need to keep going with the cleanup.

The day after the CNN segment aired, I got a call from the rock star Lenny Kravitz. My friends and I were fans of his music, so his call flattered me and made me very excited—but not so much that I acted like a freaked-out groupie or anything. Lenny told me that his band was in Miami cutting a new album and they'd taken a break in the middle of the day. They were sitting in a hotel room watching the news, and it was so negative they couldn't stand it anymore. They kept switching, but every channel carried bad news. Then they switched to CNN just as the river cleanup story came on the screen—and finally there was some good news to watch on television. We talked for about 45 minutes.

Later, I learned Lenny was inspired to write a song about the cleanup called "Can We Find a Reason?" It is the last song on his 5 album. He sent me a stack of CDs, an autographed 8-by-10 photograph, and a news release with my name in it. Two years later, I actually got to meet him and his supermodel girlfriend in Bloomington, Illinois, where they were playing a show.

I was reassured by knowing how many people cared about cleaner rivers. I could sense a big social movement undergirding my river-restoration efforts. This helped me keep going at times when I was working all alone in the middle of nowhere digging a rusty barrel out of the sticky mud.

Appearing on national television gave me a level of credibility that I definitely needed as a shell-diver with long hair. That fall and winter, I entered the fund-raising battleground armed with the CNN tape and the results I had documented throughout the year—92 barrels and an estimated 45,000 pounds of garbage. I remained focused on cleaning the 435 miles from St. Louis to Guttenberg, Iowa, with two boats and six people, and wanted to launch that expedition the following spring.

I began to look at fund-raising as a game. Rejection was the worst thing that could happen, and that wasn't so bad. I just kept calling and calling unless they said, "Never call again." When that happened, I would find another company to call and begin the process all over again.

Near the end of the year, I got a bunch of my college buddies together to do a cleanup at Starved Rock State Park on the Illinois River. The park is located about an hour west of Chicago, and 1.3 million people visit there every year. When I called the park superintendent to make arrangements, he told me that I couldn't do a cleanup there and threatened to have me arrested.

"Well, you can have me arrested but I'm going to be there on Thursday," I said. "I just want to know if you can help haul the stuff or am I going to have to take it away in my boat?"

As we continued talking, it dawned on me that he was afraid the cleanup would give the park a bad image—implying that it was neglected and dirty. I said, "Look, I don't want to make you look bad, I just want to clean up some of the garbage that floats in from the river."

I explained in detail what we would be doing, and by the end of the conversation he said okay. It snowed during the cleanup, and we never saw anyone at Starved Rock. At the end of the day, we had collected a small mountain of trash, and the Park Service hauled it away.

I returned to the Mississippi River and kept working until the garbage froze into the mud. Yet the ice of the winter season didn't slow my momentum. My first year cleaning the river rolled seamlessly into the next cleanup season. The crusade to make America's rivers pristine had only begun.

In the winter of 1997, I dropped out of college because I knew I couldn't lead a cleanup expedition and go to school at the same time. I completed my last semester of college just three classes shy of earning a degree.

I turned my full attention to the upcoming season. The plan still called for another workboat and six people to do the job, and my original budget showed it would take about $77,000 to pay for everything. I kept pushing forward on fund-raising. Alcoa had already committed to about a quarter of our budget for that year, and I also pursued Honda Marine relentlessly. With my media coverage and a record of accomplishment, Honda gave me both a 75- and a 90-horsepower engine, two of the toughest and most reliable outboard motors in the industry—a handsome donation worth $15,000.

I mounted the 75-horsepower motor on my clamming boat, but I intended to build a new boat for the bigger one. I worked with Rick Hamm in his garage to fabricate a 24-foot aluminum plate boat and a trailer to haul it. I planned on using heavy-duty plate boats in my operations. They are flat-bottomed, constructed out of aluminum plates 3/16-inch thick, and typically are used for commercial fishing. The front ends have upswept "spoonbill" bows that allow the hulls to plane on top of the water even with heavy loads of a ton or more. They are easy to clean and easy to maintain, but require advanced boat-handling skills due to their length and weight.

Back in the Quad Cities, I obtained permission to tear down a flood-damaged building that used to be a strip club called Tuxedo's, but I would need some help. I went to Peoria to see a band called Burnt Melba Toast. It was a very intimate show since my date and I were the only people in the audience. Rodney Shaw, playing bass guitar, knew of me as Brent's little brother. Although I barely knew Rodney, I had heard that he was a jack-of-all-trades, six feet tall, lanky, and with long, dark hair to the middle of his back. He wore denim overalls and had a big tattoo on his arm. He was a very easygoing, steady guy, and I asked if he would help me take down Tuxedo's. I had saved my money from willow-furniture orders and he was the first person I hired, and he would prove to be one of my all-time solid crew members.

We started in January 1998, and for two months Rodney and I ripped down the strip club. Tuxedo's was located in an area completely flooded in 1993 and had been vacant for five years. It was called the "building with nine lives" because all demolition schemes since the flood had been stymied for various reasons. I had passed by the building for years on my way to Rampage, the skateboard park next door. I had a good relationship with the mayor of Davenport from my river cleanups in 1997, and he helped me get in touch with the building's owner. The derelict structure was an eyesore, and everyone wanted it torn down. I offered to do the demolition in exchange for salvaging the steel and wood. I needed materials to build a boat shed and liked the idea of reusing stuff rather than throwing it away. It would also be cheaper than buying new materials.

In addition to Rodney, I hired some of the upcoming summer-crew people on a very limited personal budget. They worked part-time for me that winter knowing that they would be working full-time for the cleanup project in the summer. My dad and brother helped, too. The most spectacular part came at the start of the demolition because we had to remove two giant air-conditioning units on the roof. Brent and I tied 300 feet of barge line to them, hooked it to our trucks, and stepped on the gas in four-wheel low. It took three hard yanks, but the AC units came crashing down.

In January, I got a call from a writer at *Life* magazine who had seen a reprise of the CNN piece on New Year's Day while recovering from a New Year's Eve party. He wanted to do a story, so we set it up for the spring when I planned to be working near St. Louis.

I stayed busy with fund-raising meetings and planning for the 1998 season. When Tim Wilkinson at Alcoa had first asked me about being a nonprofit organization, I really didn't know what he was talking about. But he arranged with attorney Joe Judge to help me with the paperwork. Although I could have borrowed a library book and applied to the Internal Revenue Service myself, having a lawyer was very helpful. Joe understood the legal requirements and knew the people to contact. He fast-tracked the application so I would get the 501(c)3 status as quickly as possible. Even at that, it takes a long time for the IRS to process paperwork, and I lucked out when the Quad City Conservation Alliance took me under its wing. Its members were extremely generous in many ways—establishing a separate account for tax-deductible donations, managing my payroll, allowing me to store equipment and materials, and even donating money to the project.

My mom helped me come up with the first name for the cleanup project: the Mississippi River Beautification and Restoration Project. That name accurately described what we were doing, but Tim pointed out that it was too long. "You can't even fit this on a check. You've got to change the name."

In looking for a new name, I didn't want to get tied down to one geographic area or one river so I didn't want to name it after the Mississippi. And I also wanted to make the name as general as possible so I could branch out into different endeavors. What if in ten years I wanted to do something unrelated to river cleanups, like growing trees? I needed a name that captured a broad, general purpose.

I cast around among my friends and family to find one. When I was a student, I had befriended Curtis Bliss, a professor of English literature, creative writing, and poetry at Heartland Community College, and his wife, Nannie, who was a part-time instructor there. They were both very intelligent, and I told them I was looking for a good name for the organization. I wanted to work on the water and I also wanted to work on the land. Nannie came up with 30 names just out of her head. When she came to number 27—living lands and waters—I said, "Yep, there it is. Okay, it's Living Lands & Waters."

I was highly motivated and very driven to organize everything for the summer. I wrote huge lists and bought equipment for the cleanups and for camping on the shore. I studied maps and planned schedules. I had to expand the project from a one-person operation on a local portion of the river to a six-person crew cleaning two-thirds of the Upper Mississippi.

I set up an "office" at my parents' house—a three-foot by six-foot space behind a little bar area next to the back entryway. My cousin Tiffany Rossman had taken time out from college to work on the project, and she moved from Duluth, Minnesota, to help in the office with correspondence, planning, and answering the phone. My uncle donated a fax machine, and I felt fairly high–tech. I spent hours and hours on the phone being upbeat and talking to potential sponsors.

By March, I had raised about half of the money we had budgeted, and the project had $33,000 in the bank. I had already bought the new boat and equipment we needed and recruited a crew I thought could live together on the river. Rodney was the "old man" at 31, and two of the women were about my age, 23. Heidi Hartman had helped me on cleanups the year before. She was short and strong with a swimmer's build and shoulder-length hair. My cousin Tiffany, besides being athletic and pretty, was smart and had good common sense.

I hired three people who were around 20 years old—Tony Polito, Rachael Carlin, and Jim Jaggers. We called Tony "Young Burt Reynolds" because of his thick mustache. He didn't talk a lot, but when he said something, it was usually worth hearing, and funny, too. Rachael, who had finished high school early, had a wise way about her—an old head on young shoulders. Tony and Rachael had been a couple since high school. Jim, a tall guy with curly, dark hair and glasses, was upbeat and ready for anything.

In early March, we drove down to the Gateway Arch in St. Louis to begin the 435-mile trip upriver to Guttenberg, Iowa. We were really excited but nervous at the same time. We were just getting to know each other as a group, leaving our regular lives behind and starting our river adventure. We also were getting a real jump on spring by driving 200 miles south. The air was warmer, the grass was greening up, and we all felt the surge of spring energy.

I had been working toward this day ever since the moment I first conceived of the river cleanup and drew it on a map. All winter I had been busy building a boat and trailer, buying equipment, calling sponsors, raising money, studying maps, and planning, planning, planning. Now I was apprehensive. I had never been to two-thirds of the places we planned to clean and had never worked with a crew before.

I also had never been on the Mississippi River at St. Louis. I had crossed it a few times on bridges and thought, "Oh, it's wide down there." Originally I had simply drawn a line on a map to establish a goal, and now we were discovering the ground truth underlying the maps. I wanted the start of the project to be big! I felt it would be photogenic and meaningful to start below the graceful, stainless-steel Arch that rises 630 feet above the banks of the river—the Gateway to the West and a symbol of the Mississippi.

We pulled up on the cobblestone steamboat landing right under the Arch. Since it was springtime, the river was high and raging. Huge trees whisked by at a good clip—popping up and getting swallowed by the ferocious current—and the river was so wide that the giant trees looked like

little branches in the turbulent brown water. The March wind was blowing upstream against the flow, and the surface was covered with steep,
cresting waves.

I was scared to death. The crew looked at me and asked, "Are you kidding us? We're not going out there, are we?"

"We can't go out there," I said. "We'll die out there."

This was not a good way to start. I felt like a moron. I checked the
map and saw that the Arch was about 15 miles below the confluence with
the Missouri River—a huge river in its own right—and the mouth of the
Illinois River was another 15 miles above that. I figured that one flood
ing river was better than the combination of three flooding rivers and
decided we should move upstream.

The map showed that Grafton, Illinois, was near the confluence with
the Illinois River. I had never been there and didn't know where the boat
ramps were, but that's where we were bound.

On our trip 35 miles upriver, we drove beneath some of the most
spectacular bluffs I had ever seen. Known as the Piasa Bluffs, they were
named for a Native American pictograph of a mythic bird called the Piasa
painted on a rock wall. The white limestone towered 150 feet above the
Great River Road for 10 miles on the Illinois side. That felt like a more
auspicious sign for the start of our expedition.

We found a boat ramp in Grafton and were able to launch our boats
even though the river was in flood stage. We set up a camp with tents
and makeshift tarps at a place called Bolters Island on the west side of
the Mississippi River, about four miles upstream from the mouth of the
Illinois River. The island was built up with dredge spoils, and the sandy
beach was coarse and steep. It was flat on top, and a small sandy berm
offered us some protection.

We camped under trees that were leafless and gray. It was cold and the
winds just ripped through the camp. Our Bolters Island settlement soon
resembled a homeless camp or something built by messy gypsies. We set
up tents and blue tarps around a fire pit with half-burnt logs. Hammocks

and pans were hung in the trees, and a clothesline stretched out into the woods. After a windstorm, the camp looked even more disheveled with blown-out tarps and pans lying in the sand. We had three dogs running around to add to the chaos: Chuggabob was Tony's black Chow, a fluff-ball with short, stumpy legs; Indie was my young black Lab; and Sierra was a mixed husky-shepherd puppy that Jim had brought along.

Tiffany took care of us with her excellent camp cooking, and we ate hearty meals. When nature called, we had to dig a hole—there was no toilet. There were no showers, either, and we swam in the river to wash off—even when it was really cold. The crew members were all like-minded and could live in the woods. I never heard a complaint from anyone.

As for our mission, we found tons of garbage and created massive piles of it. We started stockpiling garbage next to our camp because it was too far to drive loaded boats every day to the ramp in Grafton. The island began to look like a junkyard set from *Sanford and Son*. The local boaters found out what we were doing and soon everybody in town knew about the project. Grafton is a commercial fishing village with a strong river connection. Almost every house has a flat-bottom boat on a trailer. The buildings are mostly older, with gingerbread molding and lots of stone-work. The Great River Road scenic highway runs through town, and people from St. Louis come out for weekend drives. On good days, there were lots of Harley riders, and cyclists rode the bicycle trail along the river.

The weather was still cold in March, so we didn't see very many people on the river. Still, someone noticed our pile of garbage and called the game warden. He came out and, once he found out why we were there, he gave us his card. He praised what we were doing and told us to call him if we needed anything. He would occasionally stop by to see how things were going, and he was always friendly and helpful.

The river was a lot bigger down here than in the Quad Cities. The current was raging, too, especially when the river level was up. The floodwaters were six feet high in some places, and this allowed us to drive into the woods like an airboat in the Everglades. We could simply pick the garbage out of the water. Hundreds of barrels floated among the tree trunks; Styrofoam blocks from marine docks were scattered everywhere; and propane tanks littered the backwater areas from the 1993 flood. There was so much big stuff that we rarely picked up the smaller items like bottles and cans. There was an overwhelming amount of garbage, more than I had ever seen or imagined.

We found some unusual things, among them a bowling ball and some bowling pins in one area. We also found some messages-in-bottles, which were always fun. Although most were mundane with a name, address, and a request to be contacted, others were more risqué. We also discovered how buoyant refrigerators were. Since they were packed with insulating foam, they floated really high in the water. Fortunately, I had rigged the new plate boat with a boom crane and an electric winch that could lift 500-plus pounds. We dubbed ourselves the Boom Crane Crew. When we passed each other in boats we yelled "Boom Crane!" and saluted with a raised arm and a bent wrist that looked like the boom crane.

Grafton could be a little rough around the edges, but most of the residents were very appreciative of what we were doing. Townspeople talked about us as "those kids living on Bolters Island and picking up the garbage." The police chief sent a water patrol out to make sure we were okay. There were some really nice people who ran the Ruebel Hotel, where we got rooms on occasion during nasty weather. They only charged us half price. Sometimes we would stay on the island during bad storms, and they'd get really nervous and try to call us on our primitive cell phones. A lot of people were keeping an eye on us.

Life magazine called while we were working out of Bolters Island to confirm the appointment with the writer and photographer. Three days before they were supposed to arrive, I was driving my new plate boat in a backwater slough when Tony asked me if I could see the log up ahead. I said, "Yeah, I see it," but we were looking at two different logs. I hit the sunken one in the middle of the slough and it ripped the whole lower unit off the motor. I called Honda Marine and told them what had happened and said, "This is bad; *Life* magazine is coming in three days." Again, Honda responded generously. They sent me a new motor immediately, and the magazine article ultimately included a huge photo of the Honda motor on a boat full of garbage. Honda was pleased with the publicity, so I was able to pay them back to some degree.

So much garbage had collected near the confluence with the Illinois River that we had barely put a dent in it after a month of hard work. That put me in a quandary since I still had my sights set on working the entire reach up to Guttenberg. Originally, I thought we would start at the Arch and move upriver every five days, pitching tents and cleaning an area before moving on. At this rate, we could have stayed for four years at Bolters Island. It was extremely discouraging to leave that much garbage behind, but we had to press on.

In April, we made a jump 20 miles upriver to Winfield, Missouri. My brother brought his houseboat to meet us, and we started living in it. We called it the *Shanty* because it reminded us of a floating shack. It worked well for a couple of weeks before the cost of running it began to sink in. Then we started calling it the "Five-Hundred-Dollar Boat" because it seemed to cost that much money every time we fired up the engine. So instead of using the houseboat engine, we started towing it with our work-boats. All the same, we made monstrous piles in the Winfield area and rented Dumpsters to take the garbage to a landfill.

In May, we moved upriver another 20 miles to Clarksville, Missouri. Clarksville is a small river town with a 200-foot-tall bluff capped by Indian mounds. We set up camp on the lower tip of a giant island where a treeless sandy area provided the perfect spot for us.

Some of the people we met there thought what we were doing was great. They would stop by our camp and offer us beer. Yet the town officials were less accommodating. They had a boat ramp where we wanted to sort the trash before disposing of it, and I spent a lot of time trying to get permission to use it. The officials were afraid that we would just take off and leave the garbage there. They had never heard of anyone cleaning up the river before, and I had long hair, as did most of the crew. None of us were neat or clean after weeks of sleeping on the ground, bathing in the river, and cooking on driftwood fires. We were strangers who had blown in from the river, so the town officials were wary of us at first.

I spent many hours making phone calls and setting up meetings. I had to talk to the mayor and the director of public works. If they weren't in their offices, I had to come back. Ultimately, I worked with a private boat club, and they let us stack barrels, tires, appliances, and tons of garbage on the basketball court next to their ramp.

The difficulties didn't stop there. It took me days to arrange for Dumpsters to haul the garbage to a landfill. I suffered through the same hassles with the local waste haulers as I did with city officials: Who are you? What are you doing? How are you going to pay? BFI, a national waste company, was supporting the project, but they didn't have affiliates in a lot of our remote locations. This haggling occurred in almost every stop along the way.

We also spent an inordinate amount of time handling the garbage. Not only did we move it from the shore to the boat to the ramp, but we also hauled it from town to town. If we couldn't get rid of the tires in one place, we had to take them to the next stop. One scrap yard took everything except a propane bottle full of mud, and we had to haul that around. That's not to mention the physical strain. We continually loaded the garbage and unloaded it, all of it by hand, and everything was heavy. We had only one truck, which I bought at a junkyard and fixed up. We did lots of driving back and forth to shuttle everything whenever we moved. It was frustrating to waste time getting permits and moving trash over and over again when all I really set out to do was pick up garbage out of the river.

Between getting rid of the garbage and setting up in new places, we had no breaks. I probably took off only four days of work the entire summer. The outdoors lifestyle was relentless, too. We were living in tight quarters, day in and day out, whether it was cold or hot, fair weather or foul. We worked together all day, then ate and slept on the houseboat at night.

As a former shell-diver, I was used to living alone and working with an equal partner. I wasn't accustomed at all to being in charge. But I discovered the crew members were looking at me to make the big decisions about schedules, logistics, and spending money. I was also the go-to person for dealing with difficult situations. If one person was messy and another was trying to keep the houseboat clean, then a conflict could erupt. A few times, I had to take brawling people aside to work things out.

Some parts weren't so bad. Tiffany would buy the groceries, and we ate simple, easy-to-prepare food like frozen pizzas, quesadillas, tacos, and rice and beans—meals that were fast and easy to clean up. We didn't have much space on the houseboat, and we had to keep it clean so the flies wouldn't swarm all over the kitchen. That's because window screens in the houseboat never worked and the insects were really awful at certain times. Each species had its particular season to torment us. Once, Rachael slept on top of the houseboat and the biting flies attacked her all night. She woke up with 150 bites on her face. To top it off, we had to do a TV news interview the next day.

One night around midnight, we woke up to a loud noise on the river. A 40-horsepower jet boat was screaming as the driver circled near the houseboat. I got up in my underwear, expecting to see some jacked-up hillbilly with a sawed-off shotgun. Everybody in the houseboat was scared, wondering what was going on, and I stepped out on deck with a racing heart, wondering if I was about to be shot.

The jet-boat driver shined a spotlight in my eyes, blinding me, and I yelled, "Get that light off me. What do you want?"

He put the light down and asked if I'd seen a body floating by. He said he was a game warden looking for a man who had been missing since 7 p.m. They'd found his boat, but the man was gone.

You can imagine how stressful that episode was. But everything was stressful—scheduling, planning, raising money, obtaining permits, repairing equipment, communicating with sponsors, dealing with crew dynamics and logistics. It all fell on me to keep it going.

Tiffany stayed with us until June in Clarksville when she returned to her anthropology studies at college. After that, we started eating a lot of frozen pizzas and gas-station burritos.

When we left Clarksville, I was close to running out of money. I had underestimated the quantity of garbage, the amount of time the collection would take, and the effort involved. I had promised my sponsors and many other people that I would clean up 435 miles of the Mississippi River, and the crew had moved out of their houses and quit their jobs. Now I was almost broke after just getting started.

As we worked our way up the river, I began trying to locate businesses that could help us out. When we came to a new place, I'd go into town and ask questions about the industries there. I would ask people who the biggest employers were and who the managers there were.

I thought I'd be able to raise money on the go, but the plan didn't work. It was extremely difficult to meet people in person, and I had only a cell phone with bad to no reception. Despite the unpredictable phone, I asked friends to send me phone books from different cities along the river, and I'd just call anybody I could. I used a bag phone—an early portable phone that was cumbersome, and I often ran it off a car battery. I'd scramble up on the levee to get better reception, or I'd sit in a lawn chair on an island beach and raise a pole 20 feet in the air with an old car antenna duct-taped to it. The reception was invariably bad, so I'd go to a pay phone when I could—but then the long-haul trucks would roar by. When prospective sponsors realized I was calling from a pay phone, they'd get spooked. I imagined them thinking that I was going to ask them for unmarked bills in a brown paper bag.

I learned, too, that it was the wrong time of the year to be asking for money. Nearly everyone had committed their sponsorship funds the previous fall, so by the time I called, they were already looking to the next year.

Also, nobody in this part of the river knew who I was or had heard about the project. I hadn't received the media coverage here that I had in the Quad Cities, so I couldn't just say, "Have you heard of the river cleanup?"

In early June, my mother informed me that the River Cleanup bank account was down to about $2,000—enough for six or seven days at our normal spending rates. One big repair bill, though, could bring the whole project to a screeching halt. She advised: "Pull the boats. You're done. Close it down." I told her that we weren't done until *all* the money was gone. I knew if we shut down, the crew would disperse and wouldn't come back.

I worked the phones with redoubled energy. The cement plant near Clarksville gave $2,500 to the project, replenishing the bank account. I kept plugging away, and we got a little bit here and a little bit there. Then we got a big one—the Delta Queen Steamboat Company gave $15,000 right when we really needed it.

In June, we cleaned the river in the town of Louisiana, Missouri, and then moved 20 miles upriver to Hannibal, Missouri. We made large jumps as we went upriver because it was such a big headache and so time-consuming to get set up at a new spot. We had to pack all our gear in the houseboat, shuttle the boats and trailers, locate a new base camp, and hassle with getting permits and Dumpsters.

My first taste of Hannibal was terribly disappointing. I was expecting it to be such an icon of the Mississippi River—full of the legends of Huck Finn and Tom Sawyer, since it was the hometown of Mark Twain. Yet, the shoreline was very dirty, complete with a scrap yard whose junk was falling into the river. The levee blocked most of the town's access to the river. As for the people's attitude there, the town was like a number of tourist-based areas—the residents were not as friendly as people who lived in places off the beaten path. On two separate occasions, we got our tools stolen.

That first night, as a morale-booster for the crew, I wanted to get a motel room so everybody could take a shower and sleep in a bed. We must have looked and smelled like homeless vagrants, however, because the clerk would not let us check in.

Nonetheless, we went to work picking up garbage and stacking it near the boat ramp. The mayor of Hannibal turned out to be very supportive, and he found a place for us to park our boats and to stockpile the garbage. Plus, the Hannibal newspaper did a big story.

The reporter came out when we were piling barrels. These were our favorite garbage because they're bulky and big, and it meant something to most people when you told them you'd pulled hundreds out of the river. When they saw the piles, they realized we were really helping to beautify their town.

The reporter became super-excited when he saw us working and exclaimed, "This is it! This is how it starts! Do you realize this is how social movements begin?" It was cool to hear him say that, but we didn't feel like much of a social movement—hell, I wasn't even sure exactly what a social movement was. We hadn't seen anybody back in the sloughs where we lived, and you don't feel like much of a movement when it's just you digging a rusty barrel out of the mud.

A bigger news event took place when the *Today Show* sent a camera crew with David Gregory to capture our efforts. They created a really nice piece about us that produced a groundswell of good responses. When they filmed Rachael, you could see Delta Queen decals on our big plate boat. I was surprised, however, that the story came out so well because the *Today Show* crew seemed so disconnected from our endeavor. Unlike other reporters who had covered our story, they didn't want to camp with us and didn't offer to go out to dinner with us. Once the shoot was over, they packed up their gear and left.

In July, we went 15 miles upriver to Quincy, Illinois. Along the way, we were chased off the water by what we thought was going to be a tornado— the most bizarre sky descended on us with green and yellow clouds, and a huge rainbow. We escaped by truck to some big catacombs—man-made caves where we huddled to wait out the storm. We didn't think we'd find our houseboat still tied up when we got back.

Around the Fourth of July, I had an unpleasant taste of the responsibilities of running a crew. I had to fire Heidi. We were arguing all the time by that point, and nobody could stand the tension anymore. When you're squeezed on top of each other in a cramped living space and people are arguing incessantly, then someone has to go. Since I couldn't leave the project, I told her she had to go.

From the beginning of our stay in Quincy, the locals who knew us asked, "Are you going to get the van out of the bay?" Apparently, a duck hunter had converted a 1970s Ford Econoline into a storage shed for decoys. The flood of 1993 had then washed it out of his backyard and onto an island where it settled in full view of the city's riverfront park. The van floated because it was filled with the buoyant duck decoys.

This eyesore of a van was the final thing on our to-do list in Quincy. Unfortunately, the river had risen three feet and it was still raining when we set out to remove it. The van was completely submerged and we needed a tow truck to haul it out. I called all the tow companies before one finally agreed to do the job. I estimated the job would take an hour, tops.

We had to borrow spare cables and tie them together to reach across to the van on the other side of the bay. Since I didn't have my diving gear and air compressor, I free-dove to hook the cable onto the van's bumper. This worked until the van got dragged into a log jam. I dove again to unhook the bumper and attach the cable around the front. But when the electric winch pulled on the cable, the pressure collapsed the front end. Finally, the operator shouted to me, "You tie it to the steering column and it's coming out." That did the trick, and the crowd laughed to see bubbles rising from the submerged van as the tow truck pulled it across the bay.

Then another obstacle reared its head. The tow-truck driver could only pull the van about 100 feet before he reached the end of the spool on his truck. We had to unhook the cable and run the spool back out to start pulling again. This stop-and-go procedure turned the hour-long job into a six-hour ordeal. The tow company's owner came out to the park, yelling, "Get this damn thing done, damn it!"

As though all these efforts weren't enough, when the van finally reached the shore, our crew helped it over the edge of the bank while trying to stay upright on the slippery, steep slope covered with poison ivy. The tow truck did a wheelie pulling the van up and over the bank, and the van's tireless rims carved ruts into the muddy ground. At least the van-removal job turned out to be excellent news coverage for the tow-truck company, despite the trashing of the park. The entire cleanup crew got a terrible case of poison ivy, but, more important, we got the satisfaction of removing a huge piece of highly visible junk that had been there for five years.

At the end of July, Tony Polito and Jim Jaggers left the project in Keokuk, Iowa, during the same few days that *Time* magazine covered the project and the Australian Broadcast Company (ABC) came to film us. The ABC camera crew spent five days on the river, and they turned out a terrific video. We were continuing to attract a lot of media attention— even people in Australia were interested in what we were doing.

I was expanding the project's reach on an individual basis as well and started to meet with community groups like Rotary clubs. I was receiving a lot of requests for speaking engagements and taking every chance to get in front of a crowd. I showed pictures of the garbage we had collected and displayed a map of where we had been and where we were going. This community outreach helped the river cleanup cause, but it was a burden made more difficult because I lived on the houseboat out in the boondocks most of the time, so I was driving all over.

From Keokuk, we moved 20 miles to Fort Madison, Iowa. This time the cleanup included work-release prisoners from the nearby penitentiary. For the first several days, it was just our crew loading garbage into boats, but at the end of the week, we had arranged for the prisoners to help us unload it into roll-off bins. We filled the plate boat with such a massive pile of scrap metal that it rode low in the water with only about an inch of freeboard. At this point Brent was helping us and, as an experienced boat operator, he offered to drive it to the ramp. I went first and backed my boat off the beach, spun around, and drove downriver. We waited at the boat ramp for a long time.

I was starting to wonder what the heck had happened to my brother when we saw him coming downstream around the bend. The only problem was that Brent wasn't in the boat. He was standing on top of its upside-down hull in the middle of the river. A flotilla of garbage drifted all around him. His overloaded boat had teetered as he backed off the beach, and my boat's three-inch wake was enough to flip it over. Brent had climbed up the side of the boat as it capsized and scrambled out on the bottom of the hull. He didn't even get wet in the mishap, but we lost all the scrap metal we had worked so hard to collect. I didn't hear much older-brother yelling from him that day.

A similar incident occurred in late July. We left Fort Madison and cleaned as we cruised 20 miles upriver toward Burlington, Iowa. The garbage was strewn all over in this area. Of particular interest, Rodney found a rubble pile near Dallas City, Illinois. He attacked it with Rachael and Julie Montgomery, a girl from the Quad Cities who often came out to help us. Within the pile, they discovered a 1950s Chevrolet car, and they chopped it into pieces to fit into their boat. They completely filled the boat for the ten-mile trip upstream to our base camp near Burlington.

The boat was riding low in the water and Rachael warned Rodney that it was going to sink. But Rodney wanted to take the entire load with one trip and said they'd be fine if he drove slowly. They cruised up a cut between two islands and were just heading out into the river when a big cabin cruiser yacht appeared in the channel. It was barreling downstream fast, cranking up huge waves in its wake.

Rodney told everyone to put on their life jackets and slowed down to a crawl. He managed to quarter the boat over the first wave and drop down the backside. When the hull dove into the second wave, however, water poured over the bow and the boat sank immediately. They found them-selves suddenly swimming in the river with the floating trash. Rodney put his feet down and stood up—the water was only four feet deep. He waded to the boat and tied an extra life jacket to it as a marker.

The yacht kept cruising downriver, oblivious, but some other recre-ational boaters rescued the crew and drove them to Dallas City. Rodney called me from a pay phone, and I told him to contact Charlie Gilpin, a local fisherman, clammer, and shell-buyer whom I knew from my mus-sel-diving days. Charlie picked them up, and they rode out to the sunken boat in Charlie's 30-foot plate boat. Rodney, Rachael, and Julie patiently unloaded the pieces of the car and reloaded them into the plate boat. Charlie then tied a line to the bow of the sunken boat and pulled it off the bottom with the power of his 250-hp motor. When our boat planed out on the surface, Charlie accelerated, and the water sloshed over the transom. The boat was still swamped but it was floating. Rodney jumped aboard and pulled the drain plug as Charlie towed the boat at a speed fast enough to drain the rest of the water out of it.

Once in dry dock, Rodney changed the motor oil twice, removed the spark plugs, and turned the starter to force the water out of the cylinders. The motor worked again within a couple of hours. Still, I decided then and there to get another plate boat as a replacement as soon as I could. Plate boats were built with false floors for flotation, so they were harder to sink.

We spent about a month cleaning up in the Burlington area. The peo-ple were really river oriented. Duck hunters, fishermen, and recreational boaters used the river constantly, and the town had restored its water-front with two boat ramps. There was plenty of garbage, and the towns-folk thanked us for cleaning it up.

I simultaneously helped organize a big cleanup based in Davenport, Iowa, and worked closely with the mayor and the Quad City Conservation Alliance (QCCA), the Izaak Walton League, and the Sierra Club. We did most of the planning over the phone. The *Quad City Times* helped with publicity, and we expected a big turnout but couldn't predict the exact number of volunteers who would show up.

I had high hopes, since so many people in the Quad Cities had been calling me. Local churches and school groups, hunting and fishing clubs, and conservation organizations—they all wanted to help. At first, I was reluctant to make plans with them because our progress moving upriver had been so hard to schedule with all the logistical hassles and equipment breakdowns. But then I thought, why not have one cleanup where all these people can come and we'll see how it goes?

We finished in Burlington in late August. Just before we left, I had one of the few negative experiences of the summer. I had seen a game warden driving around, and he always seemed to be hanging out at the boat ramp. Yet, I never saw him go out on the river the entire month we were working there.

On the last day in Burlington, my father was coming to meet me at the boat ramp so we could trailer both boats to the Quad Cities for the big cleanup scheduled the next day. Inside my truck I found a handwritten note from the game warden taped to the steering wheel. It said, "Chad, call me immediately. You've got some explaining to do about these feathers."

Feathers? I was thoroughly confused. I called the game warden and listened to him for five minutes without comprehending what he was talking about. Finally, he said, "The feathers on your necklace."

I was even more mystified. I certainly had feathers from pheasants and turkeys in my truck, but now I wondered if I had accidentally picked up an eagle or a hawk feather. Those birds of prey are both protected species.

At last, I looked at the rearview mirror where I kept a handmade necklace. The game warden had taken it. The necklace was a gift from a good friend from fifth grade who had given it to me while we were in high school. I thought it was awesome and always kept it with me. The necklace was decorated with little feathers about an inch long and pure white. I remembered that they looked like chicken feathers.

I explained this to the game warden and said, "Sir, my friend gave me the necklace and I can have him call you to explain its origin. I mean, I didn't go hunt this bird. They're just little pure-white feathers on a necklace."

The warden replied in a hostile tone, "If they're something, I'm going to find out."

"Wait a second," I said. "You mean you don't know what they are? You just looked in my truck and basically you're trying to pin something on me? If you're a game warden and have no idea what they are, then how would I know what they are?"

He didn't back down from his absurd position, "Well, I don't know but I'm going drive them up to Iowa City to get them tested."

I didn't have any more time to argue with him so I said, "If you want to send me a ticket, then here's my address."

What was his problem? I couldn't figure him out at all. Then it dawned on me that he wanted to be the guy who busted the long-haired "river boy." He was grasping at straws to find some kind of violation. I was shocked because all the other game wardens I had seen on the river were so nice. They worked on the river and didn't like seeing the garbage either. We had met game wardens from three states, and they all were very supportive and helpful to the project.

I told the game warden, "I've been working hard every day in your town for a month. Instead of coming by and saying, 'That's a good thing you're doing, good job,' you leave this note in my truck as a parting gift. Whatever."

The morning of the big cleanup in Davenport was humid, and you could just tell it was going to be a hot day. A few people from the QCCA had set up the tents and tables for registration, and the QCCA provided T-shirts for the volunteers. We had work gloves, trash bags, and bottled water for everyone. The *Quad Cities Times* brought the doughnuts, coffee, and juice. The Izaac Walton League provided some boats and life jackets to supplement ours. Rick Sharp from the League had charts of the river to show the boat drivers and volunteers where we would be working.

The boat ramp and parking lot areas at Marquette Street Landing were new, and hardly any private boats were present. The volunteers parked their cars and walked toward the registration area in small groups. There were also a few individuals who had heard about the cleanup and came out alone to help. The crowd gradually swelled to 150 people. It was a massive turnout.

I gathered the volunteers around me and thanked them all for coming. We really appreciated their help. I explained what our crew had done so far on the Mississippi, and what all of us were going to do that day. I emphasized that the cleanup would be fun and safe. Then we got into the boats and took the volunteers to trash sites we had scouted the day before. The different groups started picking up the garbage and making big piles on shore.

I was overwhelmed with running around and shuttling people up and down the river. There were kids and adults of all ages. The volunteers were stoked and digging like they'd never dug before. I worked most of the time on one island with Rick. We took down several old cabins and dragged out everything, including bedsprings and kitchen sinks. You couldn't even find a pop can when we were done.

I noticed that the people seemed to be releasing their aggressions, beating barrels and just tearing it up. They really wanted a piece of it. It was like they were unleashed animals out there.

We took back the river that day. When the volunteers returned to the boat ramp, they were dirty and tired but really energized at the same time. They told trash stories to each other. They had worked together to accomplish a big project and felt good about doing it. I was amazed to see how much garbage all these people had gotten in one day—it would have taken me years to accomplish what they had done in a few hours. Everybody could see the results, and they were proud of our combined accomplishment. The crew and I spent the next two days hauling all the accumulated garbage to the Dumpsters at Marquette Street Landing.

What we had done with our boats was to create an opportunity for people to go out and do something positive. All we did was plan the cleanup, advertise it in the paper, and take the volunteers out to the sites. The other groups and businesses provided the infrastructure and support for the volunteers.

People were really jumping on board the river cleanup bandwagon. I realized that the animating force wasn't necessarily me or the project— we were just sparking ambitions that were already simmering before we started. People all over were beginning to eye the water quality of the Mississippi River with a new perspective. They wanted to change the neglected and abused situation that had festered for years. They really liked our project because it was so results oriented.

Many organizations had been tackling river issues for a long time, but this project had a David-and-Goliath appeal. I was a young person facing the giant problem of garbage on the Mississippi River. That image seemed to strike a chord with a great many people who cared strongly about the river.

After the big cleanup in the Quad Cities, we returned to our more isolated routine. We went back to Burlington and started pushing the houseboat upriver. As we drove the truck through a small town called Wapello, Iowa, about 15 miles upstream from the mouth of the Iowa River, I noticed a guy with a bandanna and braids standing out in the grass by some Indian mounds with his hands outspread over his head. I drove on for about a mile before my curiosity got the better of me. I said, "Let's go see what that guy was doing."

That's how we met Peter, a man in his forties who had been traveling off and on for seven years throughout the United States. He was making a perfect spiral around the country with his home in Santa Fe, New Mexico, at the center. He would work a little bit and then travel along his spiral path for a while. Peter was very calm and mellow, just a neat dude. I told him what we were doing and, after knowing him a day and a night, asked him to watch our houseboat while I went to New Orleans for the Delta Queen sponsorship.

*A volunteer poses with Rodney Shaw as they prepare to load a refrigerator
on a 24-foot plate boat outfitted with a boom crane.*

I flew to New Orleans to meet with the Delta Queen Steamboat
Company and promote their sponsorship. They operated three steamboats—the *Delta Queen, Mississippi Queen,* and *American Queen.* I was on
the local news and talk shows in Louisiana, where I explained what we
were doing and listed the stuff we had pulled out of the river. That led
to a few humorous moments. One TV moderator asked me if any of the
televisions I had pulled from the river still worked. All I could think to
say was, "You know, I've been so busy that I haven't had a chance to plug
them in."

I returned to Illinois to the nitty-gritty, and there were two issues
awaiting my arrival. First, the game warden had sent me a ticket for the
feathers, and a court date was set for November. Second, Peter informed
me that the houseboat was leaking. We inspected it and found water coming in through a ripped boot on the inboard motor's outdrive. We pulled
the *Shanty* out of the water and trailered it to the Quad Cities, where we

parked it for the rest of the season. Peter resumed his travels, and we cor-
responded for the next few years.

It was September, and we knew that ice would soon be forming on the
river. We decided to jump north 100 miles to Guttenberg, Iowa, and start
working southward to stay ahead of the cold weather. To solve the hous-
ing problem, I called Mark Thompson of Thompson & Sons Trailer Sales,
a company I just randomly picked from the phone book. The old saying
"Ask and you shall receive" is really true. He helped us out by donating a
20-foot camper. Still, it was only half the size of the houseboat and much
more cramped. Rachael, Rodney, and I were the mainstays during these
final months of the season, but friends would come to help, too.

The fall nights we spent in that camper are not among my favorite
memories. Bunk beds lined each side of the camper, and if we had an
extra helper, someone would have to sleep on the floor and get stepped
over. Sometimes people would sleep in a tent, but they still had to store
all their stuff in the camper, lock it during the day, and then pull it all out
again at night. We cooked in the camper, too, and it was always damp and
often wet. The camper soon smelled bad with all of our gear crammed in
such tight quarters. The fall rains were starting and it was getting colder.
It was just miserable.

The work had to go on. When we finished cleaning up in the Guttenberg
area, we journeyed to the village of Buena Vista, Iowa, and lived at an old
gas dock that had been pulled out for the season. We then jumped down to
Dubuque, Iowa, and happened to meet the summer caretakers for the city
park just as they were leaving for Florida. The mayor of Dubuque loaned
us a gate key, and we stayed in the closed park right by the bridge. While
we were there, we met a punk-rock kid from Wisconsin who had canoed
from Milwaukee and was now planning to ride his bike to New Orleans.
We met all sorts of people like that during the year.

Our vagabond crew roamed southward to Bellevue and Sabula, Iowa.
Along the way, we drove beneath high bluffs that rise up from the river
and fan out westward into the rolling plains of Iowa. The river was wide

through here, and the forests in the steep ravines flashed with colorful fall foliage.

We didn't see hardly anyone on the river for the last month and a half. The summer campers were long gone. It was desolate and lonely most of the time. We loved it when friends came to visit.

Although I was in the midst of wrapping up the season and trying to push as far as I could with a bare-bones crew, I still had legal affairs to attend to because of the Iowa game warden and the "case of the feather necklace." When I asked my old friend about the feathers, his dad got so upset that he sent the game warden a letter to explain what happened and even tried to call him on the phone. About 20 years prior to this, it seems, a bird had flown into a church window in Moline, Illinois, and a mail carrier found it dead when he was delivering letters to the church. He picked the bird up and gave it to my friend's dad. My friend was in kindergarten and was attending a YMCA Indian Scouts camp with his dad where they were making Indian jewelry as a crafts project. My friend had taken the feathers and hooked them to the necklace. Much later, he gave the necklace to me. When I bought a truck, I hung the necklace on my rearview mirror, where the feathers got sun-bleached pure white,

I was angry about the ticket, so I decided to hire a lawyer and plead not guilty. In the end, I was acquitted because the state ornithologist didn't testify.

Then the game warden brought federal charges against me. I ended up in federal court, handcuffed, fingerprinted, and locked in a cell for 15 minutes. I was escorted into a big closed meeting with the district attorney. The game warden never showed up. I worked out a plea agreement with the prosecutor and got six months' probation. When I was leaving the government building, I noticed a stuffed bald eagle mounted on the wall. I thought that was pretty ironic.

The state prosecutor was a nice guy and really wanted to uphold environmental laws and bust polluters. I fulfilled my probation by making a map of all the outlet pipes along a 30-mile reach of the river. That's how I paid my debt to society. I paid the $1,000 debt to my attorney with a personal check.

With that legal issue resolved, I had to keep pressing on with planning for the next year. In the winter months, I would have to ask for the money we needed. I compiled a report with lists of where we had been and what we had done. I had good pictures of our boatloads of garbage and a host of news articles and video clips that mentioned our sponsors.

Just before Thanksgiving, I received good news from the Internal Revenue Service in a letter dated November 15, 1998. Living Lands & Waters had achieved official status as a not-for-profit corporation, and now we needed people to serve as officers and directors. Attorney Joe Judge told me just to name anyone, because I would build a board over time. I named myself, my mother, my cousin, and some friends as Living Lands & Waters' initial officers and directors.

We reached Clinton, Iowa, around the first of December, and the weather finally got so damned cold that we just ended the cleanup season there. Rodney, Rachael, and I were the last crew members at the finish. I divided up the remaining money between us and paid everyone as much as I could. Rachael received $5,000 for nine months. That was all I had. Rodney calculated his earnings and joked that he made 32 cents per hour on the project.

What weighed on me was the fact that we hadn't cleaned everything out of the 435-mile reach on the Mississippi. Tons of garbage still remained out there. Maybe I was naïve to think we would actually clean up the entire stretch, but I still felt bummed about it. I had to be satisfied with the knowledge that we did what we could with what we had, and we worked every day as hard as we could. That's pretty much all you can do.

On the plus side, we had become more adept at cleaning the river and had met a lot of supporters along the way. Even more people had seen us and learned about the project. We never sent out news releases and didn't seek media attention. Somebody would see us and tell the media, or else a reporter would notice the piles of garbage and find us. They loved it because it was a scoop. We weren't self-promoting; we were just cleaning up the river.

At the year's end, I could see that I had to stay one step ahead if I was going to make the project a success. For one thing, I had learned that most companies earmarked their money in the fall for the upcoming year.

Rachael moved to Oregon and was done with the project. Rodney stayed with me through the winter and slept on my parents' couch. It was just the two of us, and there was no decompression time. It was simply, "Okay, what's next? Let's do it." We were set to conquer new worlds, or at least a new river. I had already set my sights on the Illinois River. I knew that river well and it needed a good cleaning.

Rodney and I sprinted into the new year with a big event—Bald Eagle Days in the Quad Cities. This is an annual celebration held the first weekend in January and hosted by the Quad City Conservation Alliance (QCCA).

Bald eagles are a major attraction in the Quad Cities. These birds have wintered near the Rock Island rapids since the glaciers receded 12,000 years ago. Because the moving water in the rapids does not ice up, the birds can fish when the Upper Mississippi freezes solid. To help them even more, the Elton Fawks Eagle Preserve was established in 1989 on a 50-acre tract in the Mississippi River hills behind the house where I grew up.

Almost all the conservation organizations and agencies in the region set up displays in the old Weyerhaeuser Lumber Company warehouse that the QCCA has converted into a convention center. Just as a point of his-toric interest, timber magnate Frederick Weyerhaeuser opened his first sawmill in Moline in 1860, where he sawed timber that was floated down in big log rafts from Wisconsin and Minnesota.

Our biggest sponsor, Alcoa, rented booth space in 1999, and we loaded our biggest boat with river trash and parked it inside the building right by the entrance. We hung photos and maps along with a display of interesting things we'd found in the river. Our booth became a star attraction.

I wanted to take full advantage of Bald Eagle Days, because it attracted a crowd of 10,000-plus to a single place. I jumped in front of people and shook every hand I could reach, "Hey, how're you doing? We're cleaning up the river. Check out the booth."

I worked for three days right by the entrance despite the subzero temperatures outside. I started to catch a cold at the end but stayed with the booth. I didn't know who would walk in and didn't want to miss any opportunities to find friends for the project. My dream for the next year was to work on the entire 273-mile stretch of the Illinois River from its confluence with the Mississippi all the way to the Chicago area. Yet I quickly realized that most people couldn't locate the Illinois River on a map, and my sponsors weren't very interested in it. I thought Alcoa would be a big supporter but they said they didn't have any ties to the Illinois. Instead of money, Alcoa gave us some aluminum plate so we could have another plate boat built.

Since I wasn't finding too much interest in the Quad Cities for cleaning up the Illinois River, I figured we could find people in Chicago and St. Louis who had a closer connection to it. I decided to go to some big boat shows because that seemed like a good place to find sponsors. I called John Lally at Honda Marine and asked if he could help us get into the shows. Although I had never met John in person, he had helped me a lot from his office in Georgia. Honda was a great sponsor, and John helped open doors to the boat show at McCormick Place in Chicago.

This show was scheduled for three weeks after the Bald Eagle Days festival, and I was still recovering from pneumonia when it opened. My throat was so sore I had to drink hot water all day to be able to talk to people. Rodney and I worked the show for all ten days until 11 p.m. every night.

We definitely felt unwanted there. Boat-show organizers want to sell new yachts and had filled the brightly lit hall with glossy displays and shiny boats. We loaded our commercial fishing boat with river trash and displayed maps and pictures. We even put out a glass bowl for on-the-spot donations, and Rodney said that we looked like bartenders with a tip cup. They stuck us in the darkest corner, way back in the cavernous building. The people who did come near our display hated our garbage and complained that it smelled—even though it didn't. I tried working the crowd, but the people in attendance were there to look at fabulous boats. They didn't want to talk about cleaning up rivers.

We experienced similar results two weeks later at the Rosemont Horizon boat show in Chicago. They put us in the back of the hall right next to a little swimming pool with a water-skiing squirrel. We hustled hard to get people excited about the project, but they showed no interest. We weren't selling boats.

We learned one good lesson: Don't go to boat shows. Something positive did come from it though. We met people from Harborside Marina in Wilmington, Illinois, located about 45 miles southwest of Chicago. They told us about a sunken 42-foot houseboat in their harbor near where the Des Plaines and Kankakee rivers come together to form the Illinois River. We knew our project needed its own houseboat after the trials we had endured the previous year with the *Shanty*.

The marina owners suspected that the houseboat had been sunk on purpose, and it sat in the river for weeks or months. They were going to pay to have it crushed and thrown into a landfill, but we offered to take it at no charge. The sunken vessel was so big that it took two cranes to pull it off the bottom. When it broke the surface, black muck and brown water poured out of it. It spun in the air as the cranes lifted it onto a cradle. When we got there in February, we saw what was written on the transom: *The Miracle*. Our faces brightened and we laughed hard. I punched Rodney in the arm and said, "That's it! *The Miracle!*"

We spent the rest of the winter and on into the spring fixing it up. The marina let us stay in a guest cabin while we worked. It was a little dome called a Pod and looked like what Tinky Winky lived in. The Pod was insulated with three inches of foam, and it had a spinning vent on top that looked like a funny hat. A small heater kept it warm. The marina rented the Pod to boat owners for $50 a night, but they let us live there for free in the off-season.

The houseboat was a trashed 1975 Delta Clipper, and we gutted it entirely. The hardest part was patching the holes in the fiberglass hull. This repair proved tricky at that time of year because the resin wouldn't set up properly in subfreezing temperatures. The water-filled engines froze and their blocks cracked, so we needed new engines, too. Honda Marine came through again—two 130-horsepower units for the houseboat and one 90-horsepower motor for our plate boat. Rodney and my dad engineered a heavy-duty transom to hold the outboards. Alcoa donated the aluminum and The Schebler Company in Bettendorf, Iowa, contributed the labor to fabricate the motor mounts. The renovation project was featured in the March 2000 edition of *Houseboat* magazine in an article written by Gary Kramer, a family friend.

We worked on the houseboat for two months up in Chicago during the blustery, gray season—or more accurately, Rodney worked up there. I was a part-time boat worker because I spent a lot of time scrambling around for sponsorships. I thought nothing of driving six hours to go to meetings and give speeches. On my minuscule budget, I saved money by sleeping in the truck. I took a towel and an electric iron so I could look halfway decent when I met potential sponsors. I'd find a plug-in on the side of some building or parking lot and iron my clothes right before the meetings.

I traveled a circuit encompassing Chicago, St. Louis, and the Quad Cities—and everywhere in between—to meet with whoever would talk to me. Often these people would tell me about someone else, so I'd call that person to set up a meeting. I pursued a never-ending chain of contacts. I didn't know much about fund-raising but I had Alcoa, Waste Management (formerly BFI), and Honda Marine onboard, so that gave me some legitimacy with other sponsors. In addition, I had a good record of accomplishment.

Still, I had to be relentless. I had called Anheuser-Busch seeking a sponsorship so many times in 1998 that I practically became friends with Kay, the secretary who answered the phone and always told me that people were too busy to take my call. After a while I asked her, "What are the chances on a scale of one to ten of me getting a call back?"

Kay said, "About a two."

I said, "Great! That's better than a zero." I knew that nearly every nonprofit in the country asks Anheuser-Busch for sponsorships. They review thousands of proposals every year.

In February, I decided to call them again. Expecting to hear Kay's voice, I was surprised when a recording of a man's voice came on the phone. I left a message about who I was and what I planned to do. I thought I'd reached a dead end, but 20 minutes later I got a call. "Hello, this is Charles Poole at Anheuser-Busch."

Floored that he had called back, I started to tell him about the river cleanup. He interrupted to say that he had seen me on CNN and Channel 4 in St. Louis. He had just taken the environmental-outreach job at Anheuser-Busch and had been planning to call me. He asked when I could meet him.

"Dude, I can be there in four hours," I said. "I'm leaving right now."

He answered, "Whoa, how about tomorrow morning at nine? Bring your tapes."

I packed up and drove down that night, sleeping in my truck in a park near East St. Louis. The next morning, I walked into his office expecting to see only him, but the room was filled with people. He had invited his whole team of professionals and consultants. We sat around a big table, and I introduced myself and the cleanup project.

Partway through, Charles asked for my videotapes. He explained, "I want everyone to watch this right here."

Once he had played both news segments, he announced to the others, "This is exactly what I want the entire Anheuser-Busch program to be modeled after—exactly what Chad's doing: real action, real people, and results."

Charles set me up with two graphic artists from Rio Creative and told them to create an attractive brochure for the project. Two months later, Anheuser-Busch sent a $25,000 sponsorship check to us.

By late March, the houseboat was nearly fixed up and I really wanted to start cleaning the river, but I had less money in the bank than at the beginning of the previous year. Despite my new relationship with Anheuser-Busch, new sponsors were scarce, and I didn't know who else to contact. Yet despite the financial situation, I wanted to clean up the Illinois River and was going to make it happen. I planned to do "on-the-fly" fund-raising similar to what I did on the Mississippi River the year before. We would go upstream cleaning the river and, right before we pulled into a town, I would see if anyone there would sponsor us. That technique hadn't worked so well in 1998, but I was willing to try it again. I really had no other choice.

Before starting our cleanup season on the Illinois, I first wanted to complete the 35-mile stretch of the Mississippi River we had missed last year—from the Arch in St. Louis up to Grafton, Illinois. On April Fool's Day, I left Rodney to finish working on *The Miracle* and took a plate boat and my Labrador retriever, Indie, to the Mississippi River to start the cleanup season. I lived in my truck next to a Dumpster under the Alton Bridge. Indie was really territorial, and I made him sleep in the cab so he wouldn't bite anybody. He didn't like to be cooped up all night, and the first thing he did each morning was to find something dead—like a fish or bird—and roll in it. Then he wanted to get back in the truck. I would take him to a car wash, tie him to the bumper, and hose him off with a light, misty spray. He hated taking the bath and, just to be spiteful, would find something new to roll in. At least the cold weather kept things from rotting in the Dumpster and prevented flies from swarming. As for me, I took a bath by swimming in the river.

I lived on the Illinois side of the river and piled garbage on the Missouri side, where the Army Corps of Engineers gave me permission to use their boat ramp. Other people noticed what I was doing and asked if all that junk came out of the river. They were astounded when I said, "Yes—and that's nothing compared to what's still out there."

The river naturally accumulated trash along this stretch. The watercourse snaked in an S-curve similar to the plumbing under a sink, and the shores formed a landing beach for garbage. There also was a lot of development in the lowlands, and the high water during floods carried debris downstream. In a very short time I had gathered a massive amount of trash—and big stuff, too, like 1,000-gallon diesel drums, 55-gallon barrels, and wrecked boats.

All the same, I was lonely and plagued with self-doubt. I thought, "I'm 24 years old and living in my truck under a bridge next to the river. I don't exactly feel like I'm really kicking ass."

Fortunately, I received some positive feedback at that time when the Putnam Museum in Davenport gave me its Environmental Award. I also had friends counting on me for a job that summer. I just had to carry on.

In mid-April, Rodney drove the houseboat all the way down the Illinois River. The trip probably should have taken a week, but I asked Rodney to get there in time for a television crew that wanted to cover the project. He did the trip in three and a half days, and on the final stretch, he drove all day and all night to get to Alton in time for the *Missouri Outdoors* camera crew.

Rodney called me on the cell phone at dawn when he reached the Mississippi. I went out in the plate boat to meet him and felt a thrill when I caught sight of *The Miracle* cruising downstream. The houseboat looked spectacular beneath the Piasa Bluffs. It was early spring and the forests were turning faintly green with bursts of purple-pink redbud trees. *The Miracle* cut a big white wave in the water, and Rodney waved from inside the cabin. I was overjoyed.

We moored *The Miracle* in a bay on the Missouri side of the river where the old lock-and-dam had been demolished. We tied off all four corners to keep the houseboat from shifting in the winds and getting smashed on rocks or holed by sunken stumps. With the plate boats tied alongside, we created our own little marina. Rodney installed my car stereo in *The*

Miracle, and we listened to music at night while watching the white-and-gold lights of Alton reflecting in water. It's amazing how much your mood can change when you have company.

In May, the rest of the crew caught up with us in Alton. Tony Polito came back after spending the winter in Oregon, and he had recruited his friend Cliff Anthony, who originally hailed from Lawrence, Kansas. We called him Cliff Dawg. I hired Heidi Buracker, a friend of my brother's, who was getting her master's degree in teaching at the University of Oregon. Her curiosity had been piqued when her mother sent newspaper clips about the project.

Her introduction to the river cleanup was certainly memorable. I picked her up in the Quad Cities and drove back through a violent lightning storm. After the storm had passed, Rodney drove a plate boat to pick us up at the boat ramp and, on the way, he "prop-chopped" an Asian carp. It was the first time we had ever seen this invasive, non-native species, but their populations were mushrooming quickly in the Mississippi and its tributaries. As Heidi carried her bags to the boat, she could see the fish flopping on shore with its bloody head hanging by a thread. I turned to her and said, "Welcome to river cleanup!"

When Heidi boarded *The Miracle,* I had a premonition and told Rodney, "Man, it's her. You guys are going to hook up."

I felt we had a good solid crew with some of our "repeat offenders" on board. I also didn't feel like the project all depended on me. Rodney and Tony were my right-hand men and they knew everything.

That didn't mean I didn't have many lessons to learn. One of the more instructive ones began while we were working in the Alton area. I got a call from a lady in Meredosia, Illinois, a small town about 70 miles upriver from the mouth of the Illinois River, and she was with a group called Friends of the Illinois River, a newly forming organization. She had heard of Living Lands & Waters and congratulated me on what we were doing. She wanted to know what our plans were for the year.

I told her we would be getting off the Mississippi in a couple of weeks and would be moving from town to town as we went up the

I'm running in shallow water while carrying two handfuls of trash to the boat.
Another day on the river, another boatload of garbage.

Illinois. I said we wanted to recruit volunteers to help us clean up and would try to raise money in the towns as we moved upstream. I was glad to learn about another river-oriented organization and wanted to help support them.

The abundance of garbage on the Mississippi made for slow progress, and we crept up toward the mouth of the Illinois River. While tied up in a slough, we saw a cooler floating downstream and then a seat cushion. It looked like flotsam from a sunken boat, so we zipped upstream to investigate. We found a man clinging to a log on a slippery mud-bank. His boat had sunk, and he couldn't get out of the river. We rescued him and recovered his tiny craft. It was so small that we just picked it up and nested it inside our plate boat.

In May, we filled our gas tanks and headed up the Illinois. We had one truck, three workboats, and the houseboat. *The Miracle* was a wonderful addition to the project because it didn't leak, had reliable engines, and was bigger than the "five-hundred-dollar" *Shanty* houseboat we used last year.

The Miracle had a separate room in back with a built-in bunk bed, and I made some willow furniture for it, too. We put a chest freezer against the back wall, and I built a willow bed over the top of it with just a sliver of headroom. I suffered through many hot nights trying to sleep in that claustrophobic space. My difficulties were compounded by another aspect of the houseboat: *The Miracle*'s gas-powered generator—which ran the electric appliances and charged the 12-volt batteries—produced a lot of heat and noise, and it sat on the roof about two feet above my pillow. The freezer cranked out heat, too, and my bed was sandwiched between the two hot-running machines. I was destined to bake all summer.

My truck had a small radiator and overheated when I pulled a trailer, so I had to keep the heater on to cool the engine. All the while, I was continuously trying to raise money, which required that I keep the windows up so I could talk on my cell phone. When the outside temperature rose into the high 80s, it felt like a sauna inside the cab. I spent many hours like this on the phone and always wondered what people on the end of the line would think if they could see me soaked in sweat.

We didn't know about propane refrigerators at the time, so we improvised with what we had by turning the freezer into an ice box. We layered the bottom with water-filled plastic packets that I got from my uncle, then plugged the freezer into the generator and froze the packets overnight. The ice kept our food cold for a couple of days at a time.

We hadn't traveled far from the confluence with the Mississippi when Friends of the Illinois River called to let me know they were having cleanups, too. I thought that was good news because there was certainly plenty of garbage. They asked me to help with a cleanup in Florence, Illinois, which was 50 miles upriver.

When we arrived, we found a couple of men and a half-dozen ladies sitting in the shade of a pavilion in the park. The river was on the other side of the levee. All I saw cleaning along the shoreline was a group of work-release prisoners. They didn't need us or our boats. Friends of the Illinois River did, however, want to give us a donation. They grandly presented me with a $100 check written on a large poster board. I stood with a bewildered expression as someone snapped a grip-and-grin picture. It seemed weird that they would make such a big deal out of a $100 donation. I wasn't expecting a financial contribution from them, but I thanked them for the gift. We appreciated everything that people could give to help the cause.

The summer season progressed into June as we made our way up the Illinois River. We had to run the freezer more often as the weather got hotter. It was miserable in my bunk, but I didn't have a choice. We had to have the ice. The forests transformed into a palette of green and the understory produced a thick crop of poison ivy and stinging nettle. It was a bad year for mosquitoes, too. I took a photo of Heidi with her skin covered by an ivy rash, lacerated by switchgrass blades, and peppered with dozens of welts from mosquito bites.

The brutal conditions caught up with Tony and Cliff Dawg. One time, they went out as a two-man team. Heat waves shimmered over the mud-flats as they sank to their knees in the black ooze. Their sweat-drenched clothes stuck to their bodies and mosquitoes whined around their ears and buzzed their eyes. The sticky mud trapped Cliff's boot as they were digging out a barrel, and he stumbled barefoot into the hot muck. He never complained, but he started to yell at Tony and Tony yelled back. They went at it, screaming at the top of their lungs.

As a river cleanup veteran, Tony took a leadership role on the project. He shouted, "Do you want to get paid? Do you want to get paid?"

Cliff Dawg shouted back, "You couldn't pay me enough to do this work! You couldn't pay me enough!"

Of course, no one was in it for the money. I paid $1,000 per month plus free room and board. That didn't add up to much—about $32 for a long workday and a cramped bunk on a crowded boat with lots of pre-packaged meals. Making matters worse, Cliff was a vegan. Many times for lunch, he ate ketchup sandwiches with nutritional yeast sprinkled on top. Often he put his sandwiches in the boat box, where they would bake in the hot sun. The rest of us thought they were gross, but he'd chow down on them when he was hungry. I just hoped I never got that hungry.

The Illinois River was much smaller than the Mississippi, even though it ran through a valley scaled for a much larger waterway. That's because the ancient Mississippi had scoured the lower half of the Illinois River valley and deposited rich soil in the bottoms. For 60,000 years, the ice sheets of the Wisconsinian glaciation pushed the Mississippi west onto its present course. Then the glaciers receded 12,000 years ago, and the Illinois River took the ancient Mississippi's place through central Illinois.

I really liked working on the Illinois—it was squeezed by levees and channelized so the water was more confined than in the Mississippi. The garbage was more confined, too; it didn't spread out for hundreds of yards on the floodplain. The trash accumulated in pockets, and when we finished an area, it looked totally clean.

We also had more company. The towns were oriented to the river with numerous commercial fishermen, recreational boaters, and a thriving barge industry. The townspeople talked about the river in the cafés and bars, and the towns staged fishing tournaments and river festivals.

We were hopping upriver in July from town to town when Friends of the Illinois River called again to ask for our help at a cleanup in Meredosia. They told me there would be tons of people there. Although less than enthusiastic, we shuttled our two workboats the day before the cleanup to scout for garbage and then stayed in a local motel so we could get a good night's sleep.

When we rolled up to the cleanup site the next day, no one was there. We waited an hour and nobody ever showed up—not even the organizer. We finally went ahead and cleaned up our prescouted sites, but we were mystified by the no-show event.

The trip up the Illinois River opened new territory for us. We didn't know what lay around the next bend. We worked out a pattern where we would establish a base at a boat ramp in a town and then clean up for ten miles in each direction. We piled the garbage next to the ramp, and then took it to a recycling center or landfill when we left for the next town. Although this process sounded simple and easy, it wasn't. Every location required dozens of phone calls and meetings for us to set everything up.

We also worked through some remote places where there were no boat ramps. In the middle of July, Rodney and Tony made a giant trash pile on the shore where a farm road dead-ended. They were driving the truck to remove the trash when the farmer saw them kicking up a cloud of dust as they crossed the road through his fields. He jumped off his tractor and sprinted full-speed toward them. He yelled, "What the hell are you doing?" Rodney smiled and tried to explain, but the farmer remained furious at them. After 20 minutes of a tense face-off, the farmer finally understood that Rodney and Tony were taking the garbage away and not leaving it there.

This incident really showed me how inefficient we were. We got garbage by the boatload and hauled it away with a little truck. We spent more

than half our time finding places to stockpile and dispose of the garbage, not to mention that we were moving the junk manually too many
times. Usually people were happy that we were cleaning the river, but
sometimes, like with the farmer, there were tense moments. We needed
to make friends, but our piles of garbage sometimes created misunder-
standings. I thought, "There's got to be a better way."

I started thinking about barges. If we had a flat-deck barge, we could
stockpile all the garbage for weeks or months and then haul it away in
one fell swoop. The barge could serve as a floating recycling center.
On deck we could put a skid-steer or a small front-end loader to help
unload the garbage from our workboats and to move the junk around
and stack it really high for storage. And beyond its practicality, a barge
could also serve a higher purpose in making a mammoth statement
about the amount of garbage there was in the river. When I was 13, the
New York City garbage barge that couldn't find a legal place to dump
had made a big impression on me, and I knew that a lot of people still
remembered it. I thought, "Wow, a garbage barge could serve as a great
focus for the organization."

People were already amazed when they saw our giant piles of garbage
next to the boat ramps. They couldn't believe the variety of stuff or even
the sheer bulk of it. The sight of that much trash disgusted them, too.
Usually, they thanked us for getting it out of the river, and they often
asked how they could help. I figured if we took the garbage that we piled
at one ramp, multiplied it by 20 and stockpiled it on a barge, then we
would really have some gigantic results to show people.

In early August, we made a side trip back to the Mississippi River to
nourish our roots there. I had spoken the previous year to the Burlington
Rotary Club, and its president, Len Williams, really wanted to conduct
a cleanup. He called me persistently and told me that he could bring 35
Rotarians to a cleanup. At that point, we were less than 100 miles over-
land to the Mississippi, so we shuttled two boats to Burlington and started
to get ready for a cleanup that weekend.

We arrived on Friday to scout for trash, and Rodney was launching a boat when the game warden who issued me a ticket in 1998 for the feather pulled up to the boat ramp. He said, "Whose boat is this?"

Rodney rolled his eyes and said, "You already know whose boat this is. That's why you're waiting here."

The warden walked all around the boat inspecting it closely. Finally, he found an infraction—he couldn't read the numbers on our starboard registration sticker. Rodney explained that we launched our boats several times a day when we were unloading garbage and the numbers had rubbed off. We showed him our registration papers and told him that we didn't have enough time to get replacement decals before tomorrow's cleanup.

"No," the warden said. "If you put that boat in the water then I'm definitely going to give you a ticket."

It was raining the next day and more than 30 people from the Rotary Club came out for the cleanup. I considered Rotarians to be pillars of the community, and it was great to take them out on the river to pick up garbage. They didn't mind getting muddy and they removed a lot of trash. They had fun, too, even though we could only shuttle a dozen people at a time out on the river while the rest of them had to wait on shore in the rain for the boat to come back. That's because we could only launch one plate boat—the other one sat in the parking lot all day because of the scratched numbers on the hull.

On the same trip, we also took our boats to the Quad Cities, where the Living Lands & Waters' river cleanup project had been named by the *Quad City Times* as one of five QC2K community-building projects. The newspaper provided a lot of free publicity for our cleanup that summer.

During the planning phase, the *Quad City Times* had said they wanted to do a kids' cleanup, but I told them we weren't set up for taking a lot of children in our boats. A city councilperson then suggested that the kids could clean up Duck Creek, one of the streams that runs through Davenport and Bettendorf, and everyone else could clean up the Mississippi with Living Lands & Waters. I thought it was a good idea to include more young people and to clean up one of the tributaries that would ultimately contribute its load of litter to the Mississippi waste stream.

A hundred people met us at the Marquette Street Landing, and still more volunteers and children went to the Duck Creek site. It was the first time we branched out to do a small tributary stream, and it was our first "satellite" site where we didn't have oversight of the operation. It had rained the night before the cleanup and the water rose high in Duck Creek. The kids had to stay back from the stream but still cleaned out a lot of trash. Despite the fact that the rain continued falling hard during the cleanup, nobody cared. The hard-core volunteers came out and just tore into it. Everybody got muddy, but nobody complained.

I was getting so many calls from people who wanted to get involved with a cleanup that I was feeling a little frustrated. I wanted to involve more people but could only be in one place at a time. As I was driving down the road after taking a call from someone who wanted to help, I saw an Adopt-a-Highway sign, and I thought, "All these people are calling me; what if we just had an 'Adopt-a-Mississippi-River-Mile' program? It seems pretty simple—they pick a mile, we mark it on the map, and send them a free sign."

We wouldn't charge anything to join the program. The people who adopted the river could do the cleanups as needed—it would be their decision. That was a way to ensure perpetual maintenance on the river and to expand the cleanup project. It would be good for the river and good for the cause.

I also figured it might help prevent people from trashing the river. In a small town, everybody knew each other, so if people saw a neighbor's name on an "Adopt-a-Mississippi-River-Mile" sign next to the boat ramp, they might be less likely to litter or dump in the river.

We kicked off the program in August, and I convinced my parents to adopt the mile along the riverfront by their house. By the end of the cleanup season, we had garnered 15 Adopt-a-Mississippi-River-Mile participants.

When we returned to the Illinois River, Cliff Dawg left the crew to go back home to Kansas. We were headed to Peoria, Illinois, where the mayor wanted to have a big event on their newly restored riverfront in conjunction with our cleanup, including a benefit concert. The concert was staged in a brand-new amphitheater on the riverfront in downtown Peoria, and included Vince Welnick (from the Grateful Dead), Brother Jed, ekoostik Hookah, and several other acts.

As we kept moving upstream, we found posters from Friends of the Illinois River plastered around the towns we were approaching. The posters announced the Friends as a new group working for the river, and the fliers highlighted their intentions to do river cleanups. When we arrived in these towns, the townspeople were confused, thinking we were the Friends. When I asked for money, I found that the Friends had been there a week before asking for support. I started to worry that we would go broke if this pattern continued. Everybody on the crew was angry, and the poster campaign torpedoed their morale.

In September, Heidi left *The Miracle* in Chillicothe and went back to college in Oregon. About the same time, I got an unusual call. A soccer mom who lived in Short Hills, New Jersey, had seen the CNN segment about the cleanup in 1997 and had become a river cleanup supporter. She sent us money and cookies every so often, but more important, she adopted the Rahway River in New Jersey and started to clean it up. She wanted to meet me and introduce me to her family. She offered me an airline ticket back East. I agreed to come but said I'd like to go by Amtrak because I'd never taken a train before. This was a real step forward in our outreach.

While I was in New Jersey, we went to hear Robert F. Kennedy Jr. talk about Riverkeeper—an organization he had helped start for people to monitor and protect their local rivers. I met him and his assistant after the speech and gave them my card. The next day, they called to invite me to a Riverkeeper conference and offered to fly me to the Hamptons on New York's Long Island. I was honored and excited by the invitation.

A few weeks later, they flew me back for the conference. Several dozen Riverkeepers had gathered from all over the country. It was one of the fastest-growing environmental organizations in the country. It has since become Waterkeepers, to include freshwater lakes and saltwater estuaries, sounds, and bays, in addition to rivers.

I thought they wanted me to become a Riverkeeper, which I felt would be a great honor, but at the same time I thought it was better to be on my own and to contribute to the cause in my own way.

I was moving in high circles. One day at the conference, we went out to a party on Billy Joel's yacht. I went below with a Riverkeeper and found our host alone behind the bar pouring himself a beer. The Riverkeeper was really nervous and said, "So is it Bill or Billy?"

But Billy Joel is a seasoned celebrity and replied, "Call me whatever you want."

The guy nervously tried to make conversation and asked, "So, where're you from, Billy?"

I jumped in and said, "Dude, he's from Allentown, don't you know that? Don't you listen?" Billy just rolled his eyes and laughed. One of his most famous hits is titled "Allentown."

When I returned to Illinois, I attended the governor's conference on the Illinois River Watershed. It was scheduled in October in a brand-new conference center on the riverfront in Peoria. It was a big conference with hundreds attending, and I put up a booth for Living Lands & Waters. I covered the table with maps, photos, and found items from the river.

I wasn't too surprised when two ladies from Friends of the Illinois River came up to the booth while I was in the middle of a conversation. They were carrying an enlarged photo of me at the prisoner cleanup in Florence holding that poster-size check for $100, and asked me if they could put it on my table. I felt like they put me on the spot and I couldn't say no. Even worse, they put the photo dead center in my crowded display. The big photo visually dominated my booth and the gigantic check seemed so lame to me. Yet when they asked me to stay after the conference to attend a planning meeting about cleaning up the Illinois River in the next year, I agreed.

I had been invited to make the keynote speech at the conference—my first keynote address! Standing up in front of 300 people after dinner, I told some funny stories about my experiences cleaning up the river and got people laughing. I talked about what we were doing on the river and what we were going to do. I soon divulged to them my plan to use barges. I asked everybody to look around the big conference room with its high ceiling. I said a crew of six people could easily fill the room with garbage in a month. Given the tons of garbage on the river, our boats and trucks were far too small to handle that much junk. I explained the practical reasons for using barges and told them I was planning to get more community involvement, so I would have even more garbage to deal with.

"That's my plan, but the problem is I don't have any barges," I said. "I've called everyone I know who has barges and can't find any available."

I looked down at the front table and saw high-ranking officers from the Army Corps of Engineers sitting there—Col. Jim Mudd and Maj. Gen. Phillip Anderson. I said, "Colonel! Major General! You've got barges! I've seen your barges across the river from my parents' house. You've got whole fleets of them."

The crowd was laughing and looking at the officers for a response.

I put them on the spot and said, "Can I use some? I only need two of them."

Colonel Mudd was a great guy, and I met him the next morning walking with a big group of people. He said in front of everyone that I would be getting some barges from the Corps. I found out later that he provided the barges to us against the advice of his general counsel, but he was adamant about the cleanup being a project that the Corps needed to embrace. We worked out a lease over the winter for two barges the next year.

That afternoon, I went to the postconference meeting to plan for the next year. Friends of the Illinois River wanted to have a riverwide cleanup like the Ohio River Sweep. The people at the meeting were flipping

Cliff "Dawg" Anthony drives upriver near Grafton, Illinois, with the Piasa Bluffs rising behind at the confluence of the Mississippi and Illinois rivers.

through booklets, and the ladies started asking me detailed questions about cleanups: Where did I get the trash bags? Where did I get shovels? Who were my sponsors? Who were my contact people? I answered almost all their questions while they took notes, but I told them I didn't think my sponsors would want me to give out their contact information. At the end of this interrogation, they told me, "Okay, you can go now."

I was disappointed that I had agreed to stay, especially after I had postponed returning to the river for an entire day to attend this planning meeting. I had been in the meeting for ten minutes and they were showing me the exit door.

I realized this was the same pattern that had been repeated all summer—we saw how they plastered the towns with their posters to get their name out even though we didn't see much actual cleanup work getting done.

That was my first time trying to partner with another river organization. I felt like I did everything I could to help them and everything they asked of me. But they were walking all over us the whole time. The problem had reached the point where it damaged my crew's morale and threatened the project's finances. I knew that in the future, instead of letting problems build up, I would have to meet them as they arose. I also promised myself to choose partners more wisely and to watch out for those who would use us to grandstand.

I attended another important conference that fall—the annual meeting of the Midwest Area River Council 2000 (MARC 2000). This was a consortium of barge companies that formed in 1993 to advocate for the expansion of the locks on the Upper Mississippi. The lock-and-dam system had been built in the 1930s, and after 60 years it needed major maintenance work. The barge companies wanted to use the reconstruction as an opportunity to make the lockage system more efficient. They proposed doubling the length of the locks to 1,200 feet so long barge tows could use them more easily.

I was invited to speak for ten minutes and told an audience of a hundred or so stern-faced men about the river cleanup project. At the end, a man asked me about my political platform. Where did that question come from? I looked down at the podium and considered my answer for a second. The room was quiet and everyone was looking at me.

I said, "I don't know what the hell a political platform is. I'm just picking up tires and barrels."

The whole place just rolled with laughter. Out in the hallway people started handing me business cards, and I met a lot of important people, including Craig Philip, president of Ingram Barge Company; Royce Wilken, president of American River Transportation Company (ARTCO); Gerry Brown, president of a Cargill marine and terminal company; and Terry Becker of the Riverway Barge Company. They really liked me and the Living Lands & Waters project. They appreciated that we were results oriented and could work with all different kinds of people to clean up the river.

I was continuously hustling because I had to. I wasn't scared to go into anyone's office or to speak in front of any crowd to advance the cause. I was happy to talk to anybody who might be able to help. I was on a mission and had people who were counting on me to keep the project going.

I gained some momentum after the MARC 2000 conference. We worked up the river and parked at a Cargill facility in Spring Valley, Illinois. I got their employees to come out and help us clean up. Cargill gave us a donation, and the money came at a crucial time. It allowed us to finish the season and helped me pay back a personal loan I had taken out for the project. Nevertheless, we were still basically starving out there.

After Tony left in late fall and went back to Oregon, Rodney and I were the only ones left working on the project. I had to switch to planning and fund-raising for the next year, and that meant leaving Rodney on the river for several days at a time when I went on fund-raising trips—which was a long time to be staying alone in the middle of nowhere. I would come back after a few days and couldn't believe that Rodney hadn't quit. He was tough as hell.

I was becoming better at strategizing. Most of it was common sense. For example, I thought it would be a good idea to go to the governor's conference in Peoria because I was working on the Illinois River and figured there would be lots of people at the conference interested in the river. Likewise, I knew the MARC 2000 conference would be attended by people from the barge industry, so that's where I needed to go.

That fall, Charles Poole invited me to attend the Anheuser-Busch Environmental Partners meeting. That was a big-time affair. I walked into a large conference room at the Anheuser-Busch headquarters and saw all these environmental heavy-hitters in there—people from The Nature Conservancy, National Geographic Society, Rocky Mountain Elk Foundation, The Conservation Fund, National Fish and Wildlife Foundation, Ducks Unlimited, and several more. These were some of the biggest, most respected, and best-known organizations in the country, and here I was representing Living Lands & Waters. We didn't have memberships and databases; we had no newsletters or magazines. But we did have my mom—KeeKee aka the Keekinator.

Anheuser-Busch had convened the organizations to lay out their reasons for partnering. They also were setting up each organization with different A-B brands. They paired me with O'Doul's, a nonalcoholic beer, because I didn't look old enough to drink. I thought it was great because it promoted safe boating.

Everyone I met was very supportive of the river cleanup. Standing in such august company, I realized that every one of these organizations was started by somebody. They all had to begin somewhere. Maybe I was on the right track. I thought, "This is it. I think I've arrived. I think this thing is going to go somewhere."

One person in particular I met was Whitney Tilt from the National Fish and Wildlife Foundation. The next year the foundation would give me the Chuck Yeager Award. I was really honored to be chosen out of the entire country for this national recognition—plus a $15,000 prize accompanied the award! This also started a long-term relationship with the foundation.

Despite these encouraging developments, fall on the river was the toughest time. It was desolate compared to spring when everybody was charged up. By the time fall came, we had been working for seven solid months, almost every day without a break, and we were tired. The weather turned rainy and cold, and the days grew short. The houseboat was chilly and damp. The leaves changed and that was inspiring, but then a few windstorms blasted through and blew the leaves away. It was barren then and lonely. We didn't see anybody on the river. And there was still tons of garbage.

We were collecting huge amounts of junk but nobody was seeing it. I realized we weren't making as big an impact as we could when we worked in a vacuum like that. Sure, we were getting the garbage out, but unless people knew that someone was making a conscious effort to clean up the river, then the same people who threw the stuff in there in the first place would continue doing so. People had to *see* the garbage to make change happen.

We continued to work up toward Harborside Marina and felt good that we had completed the journey back to Wilmington from the confluence of the Mississippi. As we drew closer to Chicago, the scenery changed from a natural to an industrial landscape.

When we reached the place where the Chicago Sanitary and Ship Canal comes into the river, my jaw dropped when I saw all the garbage. There were barrels and tires as far as the eye could see. This area had been heavily polluted for a long time, and when we pulled tires out of the bank oil oozed out of the mud. The garbage was disgusting, topped off by tons of tampon applicators and condoms. After that, Rodney and I renamed it the "Chicago Sanitary and Shit Canal." We also picked up a prosthetic leg and a plastic lounge chair made to look like an open hand. The middle finger was missing, and the way the hand stuck out of the bank, it looked like a giant man was buried in the mud.

The last five-mile stretch of our cleanup season was the worst place I had ever seen. It seemed like we found where all the garbage had been coming from. It was overwhelming, and I was really discouraged.

It was cold and gray when Rodney and I drove the houseboat back to Harborside Marina. They pulled *The Miracle* out with their cranes and parked it for the winter at no charge.

A freezing rain fell the last night we were on *The Miracle*. We could hear it dripping as we stuffed all our clothes into garbage bags to take home with us. It was three days before Christmas, and I had already sent out holiday cards. It wasn't a typical family portrait with people smiling in the snow. Our card showed a stark picture of barrels and tires as far as the eye could see, and it read, "Thank you for making this scene clean ... Merry Christmas."

Rodney and I went back to living in my parents' house and sleeping on their couches. We knew we'd be going back on the river in just a few months, and it was hard to rent a place for a short period. Also, we were essentially broke.

As I reviewed the past year, I decided I had really liked working on the Illinois River. It was smaller than the Mississippi, and we could see our results more easily. I liked the fact that we had a reliable houseboat that didn't cost $500 every time we started the engines. It was good to have some experienced crew members who returned from the previous year, and the fact that Rodney was on board gave me tons of confidence. The Living Lands & Waters organization was growing, too, with a part-time office worker and a volunteer board of directors.

We also made big strides in reaching out to new sponsors and communities. We now had good contacts in the Army Corps of Engineers, and the barge industry, and we would need their support to be effective in our efforts, because their influence was pervasive and far-reaching on all navigable rivers in the United States.

I learned that it was ineffective to try to raise money on the fly as we went from town to town, and I learned to be watchful when choosing allies in the cause. The season had been tough and discouraging at times. It was difficult to keep up morale when you realized how much garbage there was. But if cleaning up the river was easy and cheap, it would have been done a long time ago.

I was recognizing that our cleanup system was too small to be efficient. After seeing the massive amounts of garbage coming out of Chicago's industrial core, I realized that we had to adopt an industrial-size approach to cleaning up our rivers. Next year, I wanted to return to the Mississippi River, but this time we would have barges. I was sure that we were going to make a big impact.

That winter, Rodney and I took a month off and drove out to Oregon with Heidi. She had been back on Christmas break from school and we left right after Christmas Day. That wasn't my favorite trip. We crossed the Rocky Mountains and high plains with no heat in the truck. I got sick and lay down wrapped in five sleeping bags while Rodney drove 32 hours straight through to Eugene—he drank 30 cups of coffee to stay awake. While we were there, we visited Tony and Rachael. I also was able to do a lot of snowboarding.

In January, midway through my trip, I had to fly back for Bald Eagle Days and ended up staying in the Quad Cities an extra week because of a lot of Living Lands & Waters business. That was always my first priority.

I flew to Oregon to finish my vacation and then returned with Rodney in late January. We started right away to get ready for the upcoming season. Rodney repaired the engines, trailers, and equipment while I spent most of my time on the phone trying to raise money for our cleanup season. I knew that barges were going to improve our efficiency and the project's impact on the public, so I needed a visual prop to show sponsors my concept. My dad made a line drawing of a barge loaded with barrels, tires, and garbage bags. He showed a skid-steer on the deck and drew a banner printed with the name of the project and company sponsors—a version of "your logo here."

When I visited sponsors, I told them I planned to go back to the Mississippi River to do community cleanups. To build up momentum, we would return to all the river towns with the barge and use its accumulation of garbage as a focus. The banner would tell people who we were and what we were doing. It also would show who our sponsors were. People were always asking if the government paid for the project, and they were usually surprised to learn that our funding came from private sponsors.

My efforts took a big step forward by some timely questioning. Every day on the Mississippi River behind my parents' house I had seen a towboat from Moline Consumers Company (now Riverstone) pushing sand barges. They went upstream empty in the morning and came back full in the afternoon. I called Bob Emler, a manager, and explained the cleanup project to him. I asked if they had any barges that we could use or have. He said it was an amazing coincidence that I had called because the owner had just decided to retire four barges and scrap them out. Emler called the owner about my request and was told to pick the best barge and give it to the project.

I was really excited by this unexpected boon, but when I drove down to look at the barge, I realized I didn't have a place to park it. I was hoping that he really hadn't given it to me but was just letting me use it. No, they informed me, it was all mine. That led me to scrambling to find a winter home for it. My first thought was to park it in front of my parents' house and tie it to their dock. But that didn't work out so well. In the end, I worked with Blackhawk Fleet to move the barge and park it near Buffalo, Iowa, until the cleanup season started.

I was so happy to get the sand barge and to have leases on two Corps barges that I never considered the need for a boat to tow the barges. That was simply poor planning.

I started calling around to see how realistic it would be to get rides from fleeting services. All along a navigable river there are designated places where barges are tied to the shore as if in a parking lot—these are called fleets. Small towboats then move the barges short distances to terminals, dry docks, or wharfs—and this is called a fleeting service. Unfortunately, there weren't that many services on the river and none in a lot of the places we would be cleaning.

Rodney reminded me about an army surplus boat we had seen the year before at Harborside Marina when we were working on *The Miracle*. The marina had used it for pushing docks around and was refurbishing it for sale—redoing the bottom of the hull and overhauling the engines. The boat was built in the 1960s with a riveted aluminum hull and was 25 feet long and 7 feet wide. Two 90-horsepower Detroit diesel engines powered the boat with through-the-hull twin propellers, and it was steered with two huge semicircular rudders. It was a Vietnam War–era vessel originally designed for building bridges. We needed a boat capable of pushing barges, and this tough army veteran with faded camouflage-green paint looked like it could do the job.

I called Ron at Harborside Marina to check into buying this army surplus boat, and asked him if he thought it could push a line of barges that was 360 feet long, 30 feet wide, and loaded with garbage. I said we'd be working on the Mississippi River. There was a pause while he consulted with his mechanics, and I could hear laughter in the background. When Ron got back on the phone he said, "Yeah, well, it'll push you downstream pretty good, but I don't know about upstream."

"Perfect!" I said. "We'll take it!"

We called this vessel the "Nam boat" or *Nammy*. It came with a specialized steel cradle to hold it but didn't have a trailer. A crane at Harborside Marina placed the boat in its cradle on my dad's flatbed trailer. We had determined that the cradle needed to be installed backwards on the trailer to keep the weight balanced over the trailer's wheels. We also learned that the trailer had to be completely submerged to launch or load the boat. For that reason, the boat's bow stuck out the back of the trailer. It looked weird, but it worked.

On another boat front, Alcoa donated a stack of aluminum plate, and we traded it straight up for a used 28-foot plate boat to add to our cleanup fleet.

By February, Rodney and I started to worry that we didn't have a crew yet and wanted to start the new season in March. At that time it was hard to recruit people for the project, but by the end of the month we did have some signed up. We talked to four people—Mike Scott, Lisa Hoffmann, Eric Wilson, and Jen Anderson—who we were really excited about it.

I knew Mike from high school and ran into him that winter at a concert. I warned him that it was a lot of nonstop work for very few rewards, but he really wanted in. He was short, stocky, and strong. He also played guitar like Ted Nugent, which would help crew morale in the evenings.

I had known Lisa for several years, and she had come out to help with cleanups in the past. She was really excited about the opportunity of joining the crew, but she could not start until her semester at Southern Illinois University ended in mid-May. She was an extrovert and was very fit.

Eric and Jen came aboard as a couple. They were sick of the daily grind and wanted to do something adventurous and meaningful. Eric was the ex-drummer in Burnt Melba Toast—Rodney's defunct band. He was about five-foot-six and had a real outgoing personality. Jen, with long blonde hair, was attractive, intelligent, and soft-spoken, the type of person who thought things through and made a lot of sense.

Rodney and I went out to dinner with them and discussed the project. I said we were getting barges and didn't know much about working with them. I also told them the cleanup work was hard and long for little pay and no benefits. My frankness didn't deter them. They didn't expect to make much money working on the project—just enough to live and pay their existing bills. In the conversation, Eric and Jen informed me that they would have to bring Jimbay, their black Labrador retriever. I said that would be perfect because I was bringing my dog, Indie.

In early March, Rodney loaded our gear in *The Miracle* at Harborside Marina and drove the houseboat down the Illinois River to the Mississippi where we set up our first base on Bolters Island. I trailered the *Nammy* down to Grafton and parked it there while we were waiting for the barges to arrive.

We launched the army surplus boat at the Grafton boat ramp. Rodney and I climbed down into the *Nammy*'s cockpit and fired up its noisy engines. We pulled away from the dock in Grafton and drove full speed into the mild current. The engines throbbed with power but the boat felt like it was crawling on the four-mile voyage to Bolters Island. When the sand barge arrived, our plan was to attach the tow boat to the barge—a procedure known as "facing up."

None of us had experience driving such an unusual vessel, and we learned quickly that it was built for work, not for comfort. The boat rode low despite its relatively shallow draft, and the engines were actually below the waterline. The hull was shallow and narrow, and it had a top speed of six mph. The exhaust pipes ran along the bottom of the cockpit on both sides of the driver, and there was no seat. When the engines ran, the heat and smell from the exhaust became nauseating and the noise unbearable. But the *Nammy* had heavy-duty brackets on the bow—called "tow knees" in the marine industry—and the squat boat was made for pushing.

We started working on the river as a crew on March 15. It was great to be back in this area again, and we went out every day to pick up garbage. It was a little easier than the first time in 1998 because we were more familiar with the setup. We reconnected with the people in Grafton, and we knew where to shop for equipment and supplies. I remembered where the garbage tended to collect, and I knew the areas we had missed the first time. In a month, we had piled up a mountain of trash on the same spot as before on Bolters Island. By the time our first barge arrived in the middle of April, we had collected enough trash to almost fill its 3,000-square-foot deck.

I called Gerry Brown at Cargill, and he arranged for one of their contracted towboats from the Marquette Transportation Company to deliver our sand barge as it went downriver. These 15-barge tows don't stop for any reason because "time is money" in the barge business—a 15-barge cargo of grain could be worth $4 million. A standard "tow" on the Upper

Mississippi River consists of three rows of barges with five barges in each line. The barges are lashed tightly together in dozens of places with inch-thick wire cables and chains. The three barges abreast usually span a width of no more than 105 feet to be able to fit into a 110-foot-wide lock chamber. The five rows of barges in a tow can reach a length of 1,500 feet—longer than an aircraft carrier or an ocean liner. The barges are essentially floating warehouses or platforms and have no power themselves. They require a large towboat of 5,000- to 10,000-horsepower that is lashed tightly to the hindmost barges to push them up and down the river.

When I got the word that our barge was coming, I was on the road, so I called Rodney to let him know that it was slated to arrive at Bolters Island between 4 p.m. and 4 a.m. The towboat captain couldn't be more precise because of potential delays when he locked-through the dams.

A 15-barge tow had to break into two sections to fit into the 600-foot-long lock chambers on the Upper Mississippi. This took several hours for each tow. Sometimes several tows had to wait in line as they took turns locking-through a dam—a river version of a traffic jam.

The Marquette tow arrived later rather than sooner. It was raining hard at 2 a.m. when the towboat captain hailed Rodney on the radio to pick up our sand barge—a 100-foot-by-30-foot steel behemoth. When the tow coming downriver arrived at Bolters Island, the captain pushed the front end of his tow up on shore and held the barges at an oblique angle. His deckhands untied our sand barge, which was lashed near the back end of their tow.

Rodney and Eric brought their boat alongside the line of barges, and Rodney lashed the bow of his boat to the stern of our sand barge. When he was finished, Eric grabbed a barge line and jumped up on the sand barge to be ready to tie it off to a tree on shore.

Rodney backed out and let the current swing the untied barge away from the tow. When the sand barge was floating freely, Rodney rammed his boat into it, gave the engine full throttle, and pushed our barge into the bank. Eric jumped nine feet down to the ground with a three-inch barge line in his hands, scrambled up to the edge of the woods, and tied the barge to the biggest tree.

When I returned to Grafton, I jumped into a plate boat and headed to Bolters Island. I was excited to finally be able to see the sand barge and the Nam boat together. As I rounded the final bend, I spotted the crew on our newly arrived barge. They stopped what they were doing and started waving and cheering. I pumped my fists and hooted back at them.

This was an auspicious moment—finally we would pick up garbage by the barge load instead of the boatload. We would be free of the burden of hauling garbage in small amounts and moving it numerous times to recycling centers, scrap yards, and landfills.

But I stopped laughing as I got closer. I sized up the barge and then the *Nammy*, and I thought to myself, "Oh shit!" The low-riding *Nammy* was mismatched with the high-sided barge. Our sand barge had rake ends—meaning the bow and stern curved like the front end of a flat-bottom boat or skiff. A barge with a rake moved more efficiently in the river compared to a box-end barge with a square bow and stern. However, if we had tried to push the barge, the bow of the Nam boat would have slipped under the barge's rake. I felt like a moron for buying a push-boat that didn't fit the barge.

We weren't deflated for long, though. After some configuring, we used handheld ratchets called come-alongs to pull up the bow end of the *Nammy* to meet the flat part of the barge. Once it was faced up, we used logging chains and chain binders to hold it in place. We salvaged a length of cable from an old half-collapsed oil boom designed to contain oil spills and used it as a lashing. Once the Nam boat's steel-pipe tow knees lined up with the top edge of the barge, we were able to push it around fairly easily. In fact, the *Nammy* handled better and was more stable when faced up to the barge.

But we still had a huge problem due again to my lack of forethought. The towboat rode so low in the water that the driver couldn't see over the barge. We had to figure out a way to build a pilothouse about ten feet tall. I was dismayed by this obstacle because the whole cleanup season depended on barges, and they were useless if we couldn't move them. I discussed all sorts of solutions with the crew, but nothing feasible came to mind.

Later, I was driving up to Jerseyville, Illinois, to buy supplies and was thinking about the pilothouse problem. Rodney and I had considered building a tower out of sheet metal but realized it would make the Nam boat top-heavy and too tippy. As I drove up through the steep, wooded hills and out on the flat, agricultural plains, I noticed a farmer in a field driving a John Deere tractor. He was sitting up high in a glass cab that looked like it was fairly lightweight. I thought, "That's it! We'll get a tractor cab, put it on six-foot stilts, and bolt it to the Nam boat."

I called John Deere to find out if they had any scratch-and-dent tractor cabs. They put me in touch with McLaughlin Body, who made the cabs, and I drove up to the Quad Cities to check out what they had. I was expecting to see some discarded cabs behind their factory but they took me to a field that was filled with them. They said, "Take your pick."

Showing true ingenuity, Rodney designed and built a tower and control room for the tractor cab. His father and grandfather came down from the Quad Cities to help him. Rodney built the steering wheel, shaft, and bearings for the pilothouse. He welded motorcycle sprockets to the steering shafts—one on the boat and the other in the pilothouse—and connected them with a nine-foot loop of bicycle chain. Next, he made a platform for the throttle levers, bought longer cables to reach the diesel engines, and wired the pilothouse for a marine radio. Rodney called it "hillbilly engineering."

I scavenged some aluminum straps and bars from a salvage yard and Rodney designed a pilothouse tower. He built it with the aluminum pieces and we bolted it to the boat. The driver had to climb an aluminum ladder to get into the cab/pilothouse and sit on a five-gallon plastic bucket. The Nam boat with its jury-rigged pilothouse was tippy as hell, but when faced up to the barge, it was actually quite stable and steady. I was hugely relieved and thought, "Problem solved, next problem."

Rodney Shaw drives the army surplus boat Nammy in the pilothouse he built from scrap materials. A bicycle chain connects the steering wheels.

But the last laugh was on me—we soon found out that when the barge was loaded with garbage, you couldn't see over the pile even with the raised pilothouse. We would have needed a 30-foot tower! We solved that problem by buying two-way radios and sending someone to stand watch at the front of the barge and call back to the driver in the pilothouse.

I had worked over the winter with the Caterpillar Corporation in Peoria and the Altorfer dealership in the Quad Cities to get a skid-steer to help unload our workboats and move materials on the barge. My parents picked up the skid-steer and brought it down on their trailer. They weaved their way around the back roads of Calhoun County, Illinois, looking for our base camp across the river on Bolters Island. I had made arrangements with a landowner to use the sandbar along his riverfront property to load the skid-steer on the barge.

The sand barge had a four-foot railing made of steel plate surrounding its flat deck on three sides—this is called a "coaming" on a barge—and Rodney used a cutting torch to make a space at the front end for the skid-steer to pass through. He then used the *Nammy* to push the barge to the Illinois side and ram it into the sandbar. We didn't have a crane to pick up the skid-steer so we used what we had—garbage. We built a bridgelike ramp by piling refrigerators and huge Styrofoam blocks in front of the barge. Some of the foam blocks were ten feet long and four feet square. We decked the 35-foot ramp with plywood boards. When the landowner saw what we were doing he got really nervous and started to dip into the two cases of Budweiser I gave him for using his property. He said, "You're not going to sue me, are you?"

I asked Rodney if he wanted to drive the skid-steer, but he said I should do it since he didn't want to be responsible when it flipped off the ramp. That gave me pause. We talked it over and decided it would be safest to drive backwards up the ramp. I climbed inside the caged cockpit and slowly drove toward the foot of the ramp. I spun a half-circle in front of it and started to drive in reverse up the ramp, with the reverse-warning horn sounding a beep-beep-beep that echoed across the river.

By this time, a small crowd of neighbors had gathered to watch the spectacle while drinking the landowner's free beer.

I had driven a skid-steer only a few times, and it wobbled back and forth as I eased it up the makeshift ramp. My heart skipped a beat, but I straightened out the skid-steer and crept up toward the top of the barge. By that point, my head was 15 feet above the river's edge.

Rodney, afraid the ramp would crumble or fall over, yelled for me to give it the gas, "You're there, man! Go! Go! Go!"

I accelerated up the last ten feet of the ramp and the skid-steer roared onto the barge. It rocked back and forth like a bucking bronco on the work platform between the coaming and the leading edge of the hull. I rammed the skid-steer into the steel plate of the coaming. This was where Rodney was unable to completely cut out the steel plate and it was still attached by a sliver to the barge. I had to crash three times into the coaming before the steel plate finally fell flat on the deck. All of us cheered and the landowner took a final big draw on his brew.

We dismantled the ramshackle ramp and loaded the pieces back onto the barge, and Rodney drove it like a pro back to Bolters Island. He spent the next few days welding two-inch pipe to the coaming so we could insert ten-foot poles to attach wire fencing around the barge. This created a cage to keep loose litter from blowing into the river.

I called Gerry Brown at Cargill again to arrange for towboats to deliver the two Corps barges to the Grafton area. One barge was up the Mississippi River and the other was up the Illinois, so it was perfect that we were working at the confluence of the two rivers. I called Rodney and asked him to move the sand barge four miles south, downstream from Bolters Island, to a deepwater cut between two islands across from Grafton. This new location would put us in a good position to pick up the Corps barges.

The first army deck barge arrived in Grafton at 2 a.m. By now, Rodney knew the maneuver to retrieve a barge from a tow and peeled it off the tow as smooth as silk. We received the other barge a couple of days later.

When the Marquette towboat captain saw Rodney trying to use logging chains and come-alongs to lash the barge, he said, "Hey, don't you have any rigging? Let my first mate set you up." The first mate came aboard and wired the barge tight with professional rigging—harnesses made of wire loops and linked with chain to a heavy-duty ratchet. He twisted the ratchet with a "cheater" bar—a five-foot steel rod that provided the leverage to really apply torque to the ratchet, tightening the wire like he was tuning a piano. The proper rigging held the towboat and barge together rigidly, and this made a huge difference in how it handled—the whole tow drove like a single-hulled boat. If we had known the advantages of proper rigging, we would have bought it much sooner. After that, Rodney and I went to a marine supply store in Alton and dropped about $3,000 on rigging supplies, navigation lights, and safety equipment.

With all our boats and barges assembled, we had an impressive fleet of vessels. I was pretty pumped up. I had predicted when I was 16 that I would work with barges someday, and here I was doing it.

The garbage barges attracted a lot of attention, just as I had hoped. Recreational boaters would speed by the island until they saw the barges. Then they would slow down and usually came alongside to get a closer look. They would ask us what we were doing and where all the garbage came from.

Although the barges were working for gaining attention, I still didn't like the jury-rigged way we were doing things with them. They weighed tons and could easily kill or maim people. I knew full well that situations on the river could spiral out of control quickly. The Mighty Mississippi was not timid, and a storm could whip it into a raging torrent. We needed help!

Mike Hanlin, the director of my dad's vocational school, who lived two doors away from my parents, had worked on barges when he was younger. He had just retired from the school district and had renewed his Coast Guard master's license to operate 100,000-ton vessels. He planned to drive corporate VIP boats and yachts for wealthy clients.

Mike had had an interesting past. He played football in college and worked on barges during the summer. His father was a famous river pilot who worked for the Federal Barge Line in the 1930s and then for private barge companies until he retired. Mike grew up in Keokuk and, as a kid, visited his dad a lot on the towboats. He could splice rope by the time he was eight and lied about his age so he could work as a deckhand at 17. He earned his master's license, but decided to make a career in education. His brother and nephew became river pilots, while Mike got a job as a teacher and football coach. Later, he became a school administrator.

I asked him to consider helping us. At six foot three, Mike was in great shape, with a shock of white hair. In the first week of May, he came down to Grafton to look at our fleet. When he saw the makeshift pilothouse on the *Nammy* and the barges filled with garbage, he knew he was in for an adventure. "What a rush!" he said, and signed up to be our captain. From then on, he was Captain Mike.

We had done a good job of picking up garbage in the pool above the Melvin Price Dam at Alton, but it was time to move on. Underpowered, the Nam boat could make only six mph at full throttle. We could walk faster than the *Nammy* could push our barges. We needed to hitch a ride upstream with a big towboat—a so-called line boat.

I didn't know how to go about catching rides with towboats on the river. I wondered if it was like hitchhiking—could a captain just pull over and pick somebody up? If so, I would need to cut out a giant outline of a hitchhiker's thumb and set it up on the barge. I ended up calling Royce Wilken at ARTCO, the barge line owned by Archer Daniels Midland, and telling him about our situation. He offered us a ride on one of the ARTCO tows.

That meant we needed to face up our barges and be ready for the tow when it arrived. We knew next to nothing about rigging barges, and even though we had the right stuff, we just didn't know how to use it. Captain Mike had the knowledge we needed but hadn't worked on barges for decades. It took him a lot of trial-and-error to remember the art of rigging. Plus, he also was used to working with barges that matched up. Our unusual assortment of barges presented a unique puzzle. Patiently yet gruffly, he showed us how to make straps using loops of wire, links of chain, and heavy-duty ratchets.

He figured out the best way to wrap the straps around the steel fittings, and we leaned back on the cheater bars to tighten the wires.

Captain Mike also taught us the vocabulary of barges—steel deck fittings were "timberheads" and "cavels"; cables were "wires"; clevis hooks were "shackles"; manhole covers were "hatches"; floors were "decks"; walls were "bulkheads"; and front and back became "forward" and "aft."

To get ready for our upriver tow, Rodney and I worked a 20-hour day—a full 10-hour shift picking up garbage and then another shift rigging the barges. We finished at 3:30 in the morning. Even though I was dead tired, I slept in the truck so I could see the ARTCO tow coming upstream.

When the *Sierra Dawn* came for us, the tow had a "notch" on the starboard side—an empty space in the outside line of barges for us to insert our barges. Captain Mike pulled out of the cut and into the channel with the *Nammy* pushing our three barges. Luckily, the river was wide there. Captain Mike told us to use our plate boats as "bow thrusters" to push the barges at the front end to help turn them. The *Sierra Dawn* stopped and held in the current while Captain Mike brought our tow alongside. He made the maneuver look easy as he gently steered into the notch. The ARTCO deckhands wired us in tight to their barges, and we rode about 60 miles and locked-through two dams on our way north to Louisiana, Missouri.

I let the crew take this time off since they had been working for several months without a break. First, they had to drive *The Miracle* and plate boats to Louisiana because the ARTCO line boat could not take our small boats along with the garbage barges. Mike Scott left the crew at that point, and Rodney told me that Heidi was pregnant. After that, Rodney started drifting away from the project. She was due in December, and he spent a lot of time talking to her on long-distance phone calls to Oregon.

Although this was my first trip on a line boat, I was too exhausted to check it out and slept for 13 hours straight. We arrived in Louisiana late in the day, and Captain Mike peeled off our barges from the ARTCO tow. I drove the plate boat as a bow thruster, and the maneuver couldn't have been any smoother. We found a great spot on an island to tie up. Captain Mike then went home to East Moline, I went away to attend some meetings, and the cleanup fleet stood vacant for a couple of days.

Captain Mike's presence on the project gave me a strong sense of relief. He possessed knowledge about barges and had experience on the river. He could take command of our fleet when we were under way, and that released me to work on other vital business associated with the project.

We cleaned up in Louisiana, and then Captain Mike pushed the barges with the *Nammy* on little hops upriver. The springtime high waters had subsided, and we cruised slowly upstream, just picking garbage and piling it on the barge. This time around was so much easier. We weren't restricted to a boat ramp to store the trash and didn't have to hustle around for permission. We could pile up a mountain of trash on the barges rather than hauling countless small loads to the landfills.

We subsequently hitched a ride 40 miles to Quincy, Illinois, and cleaned up there for a week. Then we hitched a 50-mile ride to Fort Madison, Iowa. That last ride came from Captain Mike's nephew, a towboat pilot, who held his tow in the channel while Captain Mike brought our barges up alongside, barely moving. Again, I drove a plate boat as a bow thruster. I pushed a little bit and the captain turned a little bit and we repeated that maneuver over and over for 400 yards while we inched sideways into the notch. Captain Mike had learned the *Nammy* well and he was a good driver.

We tied the barges to an island upstream from the railroad lift bridge in Fort Madison and dropped two anchors to keep *The Miracle* in the deep cut between the mainland and the island. That led to an unusual mishap. Rodney was sick one afternoon and fell asleep on the houseboat. He woke up feeling *The Miracle* oddly adrift and sprinted up on deck in his underwear. He saw the houseboat was just about to collide with the bridge pier! He jumped into the plate boat, started the engine, and pushed *The Miracle* out of danger. When Rodney looked back on shore, he saw a small crowd at the boat ramp watching his crazy antics. Looking back upriver, he saw the aft end of a big towboat churning away upstream. He gulped deeply, realizing that the tow must have passed him floating by in the channel while he was sleeping off his fever below.

We determined later that *The Miracle* had drifted because the anchors had pulled each other out of the mud. The wind had spun the boat around the anchors, twisting the anchor lines together and consequently pulling the anchors from the bottom. After that incident, we never used two anchors again.

It was early June by this time, and we had scheduled our first community cleanup for the year in Dubuque, Iowa. My main goal for the year was motivating people to clean the river with us. Therefore, we really needed to be there to start promoting the cleanups and recruiting volunteers. I heard on the marine radio that an Ingram Barge Company tow was moving upstream, so I called Steve Crowley at one of their corporate offices in Paducah. I told him what we were doing and where we were going and said, "Hey, I was wondering if we could hop a ride."

He had his computer on while we were talking and surfed the Internet to find Living Lands & Waters. We had a simple Web site with some pictures of our garbage barges and our schedule. He liked what we were doing and asked his bosses at Ingram if their line boat could help us out. The tow arrived an hour later and we hitched a ride 140 miles up to Dubuque.

In 1998, we had cleaned the river in Dubuque, so people remembered reading or hearing about the project. Early June was the start of the main boating season, and a number of boaters eyed our barges and the banner we put up. We overheard them saying, "Oh, they're cleaning up. They must have pulled that stuff out of the river." When they saw us, they gave us a thumbs-up and thanked us for cleaning the river. The garbage barge was working as a visual statement like I'd hoped.

We had a big cleanup in Dubuque; lots of people came out and we picked up tons of garbage. We were still off-loading our boats the next morning when we started driving our tow downstream to Bellevue, Iowa, about 20 miles away. We planned to head south doing ten major cleanups in cities along the way. As always, there was so much garbage that it blocked the view from the *Nammy*'s tower. Captain Mike stood on the bow where he could see better and radioed commands to the person operating the controls—half turn to starboard, three-quarters throttle on the right shifter, all stop, half throttle back, quarter turn to port, and like that. A trained monkey could have driven the tow. Captain Mike would say each order twice and the operator would repeat it.

As our tow went downstream, we had limited ability to back up, and it even took a long time to stop because the current was pushing us. We slowed to a stop when we got near Bellevue. This was our first time locking-through a dam on our own, and we convened a powwow to talk about it.

In the 1930s, the Army Corps of Engineers built Lock-and-Dam Number 12 in Bellevue as one of a series of 29 lock-and-dams on the Upper Mississippi. The dams create pools that maintain a navigation channel at least nine feet deep, while the locks allow vessels to pass through the dams. The Bellevue dam controls the river level in Pool 12 with steel cylindrical roller gates built into the dam's concrete structure. The gates are lifted to let water flow underneath or lowered to hold the water back. Boats and barges travel from pool to pool in stair-step fashion as they navigate the river. The vessels are raised in the locks going upstream and lowered going downstream.

The locks are huge concrete chambers with swinging double gates at both the upper and lower ends. When closed, these gates are strong enough to hold back the entire river behind the dam. Lock Number 12 is like a gigantic swimming pool 600 feet long and 110 feet wide. The lock chambers are filled with water by gravity from the upriver pool using a system of pipes and valves. When a boat or barge pulls into the chamber, the water is emptied from it into the lower pool using a system of drains. The boat or barge then pulls out into the lower pool.

Captain Mike said it was a difficult lock-through because of the current's strength and decided to drive the boat from the pilothouse rather than relay commands from the bow. I had the walkie-talkie and stood forward to report our location to him—so many feet off the wall and so many feet back from the gates. Captain Mike told me he didn't want to hear any sputtering, stuttering, or "ummm's." He needed to know the distances in feet and wanted me to stay focused on that.

The Bellevue lock was located "river right," or on the right side going downstream. It consisted of two parallel concrete walls 110 feet apart—a long wall, called the "guide wall," on the river-right shore and a short wall abutting the dam in the river. The short wall had rounded ends called "bull noses" painted bright yellow. Our tow was 30 feet wide and roughly 360 feet long, and we fit in the lock easily even with the 42-foot houseboat and the 24- and 28 foot plate boats tied alongside.

Like a normal lock-through, our plan was to nose up against the guide wall and to slowly slip our entire tow into the lock chamber. Then we would tie up to the steel fittings in the lock and, once secure on the long wall, the lockmaster would close the upstream gates to hold back the river in Pool 12 and then drain the water out of the lock. Once we were lowered to the level of Pool 13, the lockmaster would open the downstream gates and we'd proceed downriver.

Although we had devised a good plan, the situation was destined to unravel quickly. We noticed right away that the strong current above the dam drew our vessels toward the roller gates and away from the lock. Captain Mike said our tow had to enter the lock chamber with the length of the barges almost parallel to the long wall. If the current swung our stern away from shore we could get sucked under the dam. He put Rodney in *The Miracle* and Eric in a plate boat to act as thrusters to keep our barges tight against the long wall.

Captain Mike radioed the lockmaster and got permission to enter. We didn't have an official name, so the lockmaster registered us as "River Cleanup." I stood on the bow and talked us in, except that I didn't know what I was doing. As we approached the lock, I was intimidated by the raging water above the dam.

Captain Mike asked me, "How far from the wall?"

I said, "One hundred fifty feet."

Then I corrected myself, "Maybe 135. No, it's actually 150 feet."

I didn't know. I had never really judged distances before. He asked me again how far off the wall. I thought, "Does he mean the end of the wall?" I was getting confused.

Captain Mike asked me a new question, "How far off the bull nose?"

What the hell was a bull nose? He had told us but I didn't remember. I was getting flustered. I asked him what he meant.

His voice started to get intense, "How far off the wall are we?"

I thought, "Does he mean straight forward or from the side?"

We crept up to the long wall and started sliding into the lock. The worker on the long wall was watching us and told me to throw him a line. The captain hadn't given me the command, so I called on the walkie-talkie and said, "Cap'n, the guy here told me to throw him a line."

Captain Mike didn't respond; maybe he hadn't heard me. The worker yelled, "Throw me a line! Throw me a line right now!"

I threw him a line and he tied it to a steel fitting on the wall. The line drew tight and the barge bumped hard against the wall. Our bow was now stuck tight to the shore and our stern started to drift very quickly toward the roller gates in the dam. As the barges swung out into the river, the current pushed against more of the hull area, and we drifted faster with every foot the barges twisted away from shore. Our first lock-through had become a collective nightmare, one that was accelerating into fast motion.

The barge crashed into the bull nose, twisted, and nearly snapped the wires. We were pinned on the bull nose by the powerful current as the water rushed toward the dam. The collision nearly sandwiched *The Miracle*, and the houseboat almost crushed the plate boats. Our stern was hanging precariously above the dam, and the bowline was the only thing preventing us from getting sucked through the roller gates. We all knew we were perched merely 100 feet from death.

Everybody on the barge sprang instantly into action. The captain steered us back toward the long wall, then pushed full throttle, but the barges wouldn't budge. Rodney wielded a machete to cut his lines on *The Miracle*. He hammered the twin Hondas full throttle and T-boned the side of the barge with such force that it smashed the houseboat's bow. Eric, too, slammed the plate boat into the barge and twisted the handle to full throttle. Five of our six engines roared, and the combined thrust slowly started to relieve the pressure on the bull nose. I ran back to fire up the other plate boat. Everybody on our barge was yelling and scrambling frantically.

At last, our tow began to nudge back toward the long wall—at about a foot per minute. It took a long time, but we eventually got lined up with the long wall and slid into the lock chamber. We throttled the motors down and released a collective sigh of relief. The upper lock gate closed behind us, the lockmaster opened the valves, and the water started draining.

Everybody was in shock and stressed out. The captain was concerned and upset. I was nervous and practically shaking.

We dropped 26 feet in the lock, and the downstream gate opened up. Happy to be alive, we motored out into the channel into the bright sunlight. Captain Mike decided that from now on he would drive the tow while sitting on the forward barge. He would use three radios: A marine radio to talk to lockmasters and towboat captains, a walkie-talkie to talk to the operator in the *Nammy*, and another walkie-talkie to talk to the drivers in the thruster boats.

The river flowed faster below the lock-and-dam than in the pool above it, and we were slipping and sliding in the current as we went downstream. We ran over some navigation markers, and the captain called "All stop" until we cleared the buoys and their anchor wires. We could hear the metal buoys scraping underneath, and when they bounced up behind us, Captain Mike said, "Ahead full throttle."

Our next obstacle was a railroad bridge in Sabula, Iowa—the only town in the state located on an island. This swing bridge had a narrow opening with tricky currents, and tows often waited in line to pass through. Because we had fairly low horsepower, Captain Mike resurrected an old-time technique from the steamboat days to maneuver through the bridge. Boats handle better when they face upstream and push against the current. So, as we approached the bridge in Sabula, Captain Mike spun our tow 180 degrees by using the plate boats as thrusters. One boat pushed the bow one way and the other boat pushed the stern in the opposite direction. Our tow pivoted around and spun practically in place. Once we were lined up above the bridge, the current backed us through the opening slick as a whistle. Captain Mike steered by adjusting the throttles on the twin engines. When we cleared the bridge downstream, he spun another 180 and away we went.

A quarter-mile below the Sabula railroad bridge, a belt broke on the *Nammy*'s starboard engine and Captain Mike limped our tow to an island where other towboats had nosed up on the beach to wait their turn to pass through the bridge. It was a fortunate place to break down because we had staged a truck in Sabula, and we needed to buy food, water, and supplies anyway. Rodney had recruited a friend to join the crew—Kevin Boyd was yet another former band member in Burnt Melba Toast—and he came aboard here for the first time. We left Kevin alone on *The Miracle* while everyone else went ashore to run errands and track down parts to fix the *Nammy*.

Kevin was a huge guy and looked like he'd been lifting weights for years. He walked around our barges until he got bored and then went into the houseboat to read a magazine. After a while, he happened to casually glance out the window—and dropped the magazine to the floor. He saw a massive steel wall—the first three barges of an enormous tow—about 20 feet from the Nam boat and creeping slowly toward our barges. The captain of that towboat had pushed the nose of his tow onto the bank while he was waiting for another one to pass through the bridge. He was headed upstream, idling into the bank while he awaited his turn, but his engines were making him creep up the bank at about a foot a minute. There was a crew change at this time and the new pilot couldn't see us because the island curved and there were some overhanging trees blocking the view along the shore.

Kevin jumped up and grabbed a radio. He had been aboard less than an hour and didn't know how to use the radios, but he tried to hail the towboat. He could see serial numbers painted on the front barge and he flipped frantically through the channels shouting into the mike, "X-Y-Z, one-two-three, come back!"

The towboat captain responded but thought someone was messing with him. He said, "Yeah, what the hell do you want?"

Kevin shouted back, "You are about to hit our boat! You're up on our boat! Stop! Stop!"

The captain didn't believe him and said, "I don't know what you're talking about. I haven't hit anything in 32 years."

Kevin saw the barges grinding into the *Nammy* and slowly smashing the makeshift pilothouse. He begged, "You've got to send some guys. You've got to stop. You're moving up on our boat."

Receiving the captain's orders, a few deckhands walked the fifth-of-a-mile distance along the barges, taking their time. When they reached the bow, they saw the wreckage of the Nam boat and could see their tow starting to slide up on our barges. The deckhands radioed back to the pilothouse, "Captain, pull back right now! Pull back! You are up on them, pull back!"

The chastened towboat captain backed off and held on the shore until I returned. As I drove up, I could see the tow really close to us, and then I saw the smashed *Nammy*. I had only been on shore for an hour—what the hell happened? When I boarded *The Miracle*, Kevin told me the story and said the towboat captain wanted to see me. I smiled wryly and told Kevin, "Welcome to river cleanup!"

The towboat captain had called his company and was talking on the phone as I went up to the towboat. He was near panic and pacing back and forth when I walked into the pilothouse. I heard him say, "What should I do? Do I need to pack up and get off the towboat?"

I tried to tell him not to worry about it. "Sir, it's not a big deal. I've got a welder and can fix it. We've got time to get where we're going. I'm not going to sweat it."

But he was so nervous that he didn't hear me. He kept pacing laps around the pilothouse and talking on the phone. I must have asked him five times to let me take the phone. Finally, he gave it to me. "Listen," I said to the person at the other end, "I'm not even worried about this; it's not a big deal. We'll get it fixed, welded, whatever. Just get on your way; we don't want to slow you down because I understand that time is money for you guys."

We had broken down in the wrong place at the wrong time. The chances were slim that a collision would occur under those circumstances, but shit happens on the river. For a little while, we considered changing the name *Nammy* to *Shit Happens*, but we didn't.

We took the *Nammy* to the Island City Harbor in Sabula, and they put a full crew onto repairing it. The welding shop fixed our boat in record time, finishing the next day just before a news team arrived from *The Des Moines Register*. The reporters never knew about the collision. Plus, Island City sent us on our way without charging a dime.

Kevin stayed aboard after his dramatic introduction to life on the river. It was great for morale to have the musicians on board—Kevin played guitar, Rodney bass, and Eric drums. They were phenomenal musicians, and it was fun to hang out and listen to them play after working all day.

With Kevin, our crew now consisted of six people. Lisa Hoffmann had joined the crew earlier in mid-May. She was a student at Southern Illinois University and had signed up for the project between semesters. She was slim and athletic, and knew how to work hard. We also were joined from time to time by my girlfriend, Lisa Eno. She was really smart and helped us keep track of our garbage lists. She also cooked for us when she was aboard.

We pressed on downriver to Clinton, Iowa, and conducted a big volunteer cleanup with the Clinton County Area Solid Waste Agency and the Soaring Eagle Nature Center. We concentrated on Beaver Island where there were about 15 cabins, some of them abandoned, with huge trash piles in the backyards. We found so much stuff that we filled half a barge in one day. Among the debris, we extracted a 1958 International Harvester truck from a pile of rubble. We placed this wreck on the bow of the forward barge and then covered it with a tarp for shade. From this new pilothouse, Captain Mike sat in a lawn chair looking out with cop-style sunglasses. He ripped the bottom off a shirt and made a big headband with it. He looked like the craziest dude out there, just smiling.

Captain Mike really enjoyed his time on the cleanup project. He stayed overnight only when we were traveling and pitched a tent on the barge. I'm not sure how pleasant that was when the steel deck got broiling hot in the sun. One night, a storm flattened the tent on top of him and he retreated to sleep in *The Miracle*. Even with a few mishaps along the way, he told me numerous times that he was having the time of his life.

We soon reached Lock-and-Dam 14, which was across the river from my parents' house. We had a good rigging system by then, even though some of the arrangements were unconventional. For example, we used wooden shovel handles to prevent the ratchets from twisting loose instead of the steel "toothpicks" used on the line barges. Also, we wore life jackets, but they were the regular $10 variety, all different colors, some of which were a mishmash we had found on the river or beside the road. Our unusual setups may have singled us out to the lockmaster at Number 14.

We slipped our tow handsomely into the lock this time, and the upper gate closed behind us. With the gate holding back the river in the upper pool, the lockmaster drained the water out of the lock and lowered us to the level of Pool 15. When the downstream lock gate opened, though, we were surprised to see a tow tied up just below the exit. We barely had enough room to maneuver around it.

We swung into action. The Nam boat pushed our barges out of the lock chamber, and Rodney and I drove our plate boats to work as bow thrusters. Captain Mike ordered a turn, and our tow rolled out into the rushing current below the dam. I had to keep the motor on full throttle to prevent the river from pushing us into the barges tied up on the long wall below us. Rodney drove the other plate boat and pulled on the forward end of our tow. We twisted our barge out into the current and away we went downriver. Because we had practiced these maneuvers, we made it look easy.

About a half-hour after leaving the lock at Dam 14, I got a phone call from the Coast Guard. At first, the caller said he knew about the river cleanups from newspaper articles and praised us for what we were doing. But then he

Rodney Shaw and Kevin Boyd taking a "test ride" in the 1950s pickup truck found while cleaning Beaver Island in the Mississippi River.

said the lockmaster reported that we were running an unsafe operation. The guardsman asked, "Do you feel unsafe?"

I told him our captain had a master's license and that I had bought everything the captain instructed us to get for a safe operation. The Coast Guardsman accepted my answer and wished us the best. He said to give him a call if we ever needed anything. This was the beginning of a good relationship with the Coast Guard. After that, we started saving the loose navigation buoys we found and turning them back in to their shore-based facilities. On a few occasions, their buoy tender would pull up next to us in the river and lift the buoys off our barge with a crane.

We continued to Davenport, Iowa, where we had been building momentum for the last three years. While we were scouting for trash, we had a hard time finding enough places to take a hundred volunteers. The river was becoming cleaner. Nevertheless, we had a great community cleanup in the morning with more people than ever. We hosted a river festival in the afternoon at Buffalo Beach in Buffalo, Iowa. We set up our barge as a stage and five different bands performed, including Rodney, Eric, and Kevin. Several dignitaries spoke to the crowd about the Mississippi River and the importance of what we were doing, including congressmen Jim Leach and Lane Evans, Roger Bollman from the Corps of Engineers, and Jon Duyvejonck from the U.S. Fish and Wildlife Service. Part of the audience had participated in the cleanup, but most just came for the music and the party.

The festival was a huge headache because of the logistics involved with setting it up and breaking it down. On the lighter side, I hired a few college students to do security at the event. I had seen them on the river that morning and gave them a temporary job. They were coming downriver from Prairie du Chien, Wisconsin, on a homemade raft built out of plastic barrels. They claimed to have stolen the barrels from their college's boiler room. They put up a screened-in porch and outfitted it with sleeping cots. I needed the help, so I hired them on the spot.

We had accumulated mountains of garbage on the way down from Dubuque. Our cleanups had been so successful that one of the 150-by-30-foot Corps barges was completely loaded after the Quad Cities cleanup. We parked it across the river from Buffalo Beach near Andalusia, Illinois, then pushed on downriver with two garbage barges toward our next stop in Burlington, Iowa. The Nam boat could handle only so much weight, and I doubt that such a small towboat had ever pushed anything so big.

At Burlington, the Rotary Club and the United Way organized the cleanup and had planned it meticulously, compared to our free-form way of doing things. It was one of the smoothest and most effective cleanups we did that year.

We kept on staging cleanups in the towns as we proceeded. We put out fliers and contacted newspapers, and I did some radio interviews. If I knew people from our cleanups in 1998, I would call them. We had a good turnout of volunteers in some places but not in others. I never got discouraged, though, because the cleanup project was growing and in most places it was a brand-new concept. I didn't have any expectations, so I couldn't be disappointed. Whether two people participated in a cleanup or 200, this year was better than last year and next year would be better yet.

After Burlington, we cruised down toward Fort Madison under calm skies in the 47-mile pool above Lock-and-Dam 19 at Keokuk, Iowa, one of the longest pools on the Mississippi River. The river was wide near Dallas City, Illinois, and it broadened on each side into shallow stump fields. The surface was glassy smooth and reflected a white thundercloud billowing over the green hills.

I should have known the calm was deceptive. The clouds rushed toward us and darkened as they came. All of a sudden, a blast of freak wind roared out of the clouds and slapped our tow on its high, broad side. Loose life jackets scattered across the deck, lightweight garbage started flying away, and dust whisked across the barge and into the air like smoke. The squall kicked up waves instantly, splashing into the plate boats and threatening to swamp them. The violent turbulence blew us toward the shallows studded with sunken stumps. These hidden hazards could punch holes in any of our vessels. *The Miracle*'s fiberglass hull was particularly susceptible to getting holed, and our barges were thin-skinned and ready to be retired—that's why they were given to us in the first place—and an impaled barge would present an especially difficult salvage problem. Springing into action, Captain Mike ordered the Nam boat operator to turn directly into the gusts to reduce the windage on the barges. A stinging rain whipped us for about 15 minutes, and then the storm passed as quickly as it came.

Sobered by this sudden display of nature's power, we returned to Fort Madison and did another cleanup there. The number of volunteers was so-so, but I continued to look at these events as building momentum.

On the way down to Quincy, we passed a line boat and tow heading upriver, and Captain Mike hailed the other captain on the marine radio. The towboat captain saw our strange conglomeration of garbage barges with *The Miracle* and the plate boats sticking out from the side. Then, as the tows approached each other, he spotted the Nam boat with a John Deere combine cab on top of a makeshift tower. All he could say was, "*River Cleanup*. Whoa, quite a rig you got there."

As we passed in the channel and got several hundred feet downstream, our tow suddenly started to spin sideways in his wake. The bicycle chain had slipped off the steering-shaft sprocket and Kevin lost control of the helm. Luckily, the river was wide there and Kevin was able to climb down to put the chain back on the sprocket before we ran aground.

The towboat captain called, "*River Cleanup*. Are you guys all right back there?"

Captain Mike came back, "Oh yeah, we're okay. Our bike chain just popped off."

A long moment of radio silence followed and then the towboat captain said, "Bike chain, huh? What kind of operation are you running there?"

Kevin fixed the chain with a piece of wire and a socket to make a roller for it like a chain tightener. And away we went down the river.

At Quincy, Illinois, we parked on the floodwall at the riverfront park. The next morning, a wedding party came to the park so the photographer could take their portraits with the Mississippi as a backdrop. I don't think they were too happy to see us parked there with a barge load of garbage.

Nor was the cleanup at Quincy well attended. Only two people came to it, and they drove from far away. I couldn't figure out what happened. We had high expectations for Quincy because it was a big town and there were lots of boaters there.

Disappointed, we moved on to Hannibal, where we had scheduled a big cleanup. The mayor of Hannibal liked what we were doing and planned to have a big celebration after we were finished. He had another motive as well. He had read my opinion of Hannibal as one of the dirtiest towns on the Mississippi, and the newspapers had written, "Look at what an outsider sees." After that, the town made a concerted effort to clean up, and the progress definitely showed.

Another harrowing experience awaited us in Hannibal. I had gone to New Orleans to attend some meetings and promotional events with the Delta Queen Steamboat Company and had to miss the cleanup. I arranged my flights to get back in time for the mayor's party but missed my connecting flight in Chicago. I talked to a random couple who had missed the flight, too, and we rented a car for the two-hour drive to Bloomington, Illinois, our final destination. Once there, it took me another three hours to drive my truck to Hannibal.

Eric called while I was on the road and left a message: "We've got big problems here! Call me!" I tried calling immediately but couldn't get through to anybody. That was not unusual because we often didn't have cell phone coverage on the river. My mind started racing as I wondered what could have happened.

Eric had made similar "mystery calls" to me. He left a message once that said, "Chad, strong winds from the west! Trees getting ripped down, maybe a tornado! We're securing boats!" And then he just hung up without any explanation or follow-up. His call stressed me out wondering what had happened, but it turned out to be just another summer storm. Everything was fine.

Meanwhile, it was growing dark and I was still 90 minutes from Hannibal when Eric finally called back. He reported that one of the plate boats had sunk five hours earlier. He said they were still searching but couldn't find it. That was really bad news.

After the volunteers in Hannibal had left the cleanup, our crew was hauling the garbage to the barges. We always were tempted to fill up the boats as much as possible, because the bigger the loads, the fewer the trips that were needed. It was easy to load too much in the forward end because the boats are nosed into shore to keep the motors out in the deep water. We've all done that when loading garbage after a volunteer cleanup.

Jen and Kevin were driving bow-heavy when the tour boat *Mark Twain Riverboat* pulled away from the dock across the river, spawning big waves. The plate boat drove up the first wave, teetered over the crest, and slid down the backside, but then it promptly nose-dived into the following wave. The motor powered the boat straight to the bottom of the river like a submarine on an emergency dive. Jen and Kevin were wearing life jackets, fortunately, because the boat dropped out from under them in a split second. They instantly found themselves floating in the river amidst all the buoyant garbage. Everything else disappeared under the bubbling wake of the plate boat. The scrap metal on board pinned the boat to the bottom in 18 feet of water.

An unlikely hero known as Wild Bill was sitting on a nearby island when the plate boat foundered. He jumped into his motorboat and rescued Jen and Kevin. Wild Bill was like a homeless dude with a boat. We had first seen him in the Quad Cities. Short and wiry with a long beard and buzz-cut hair, he wore earrings, his nipples were pierced, and his body was covered with tattoos. Bill wandered the river with no visible means of support, camping on islands. He acted crazy, and we could sometimes hear him getting drunk by himself at his campsite, yelling and howling in the night. He tried to tag along and we tried to lose him, because we didn't want people to think he worked for us. When we got to Hannibal, he set up his campsite right by us.

The boat sank in the middle of the channel around 2 p.m. and nobody knew where it went down. The crew stopped picking up the garbage and everybody started looking for the boat. One boat crew dragged anchors and the other poked along the bottom with a boat hook—a 20-foot aluminum pole designed to grab barge lines and boats. Wild Bill searched the area with his depth-finder. It was like looking for a needle in a haystack.

Everybody worked until the sun set. They had given up any hope of celebrating with the mayor in Hannibal. They were also starting to lose hope of ever finding the sunken boat when a 15-barge tow came upriver and the turbulence from its propellers dislodged the boat off the bottom. The buoyant bow popped up in the towboat's wake but the weight of the Honda motor on the stern started to sink it again. Rodney's boat drove over, and they grabbed the tip of the bow as it bobbed on the surface. They fastened a line to the boat so they could tow it and then accelerated to spill the water over the transom. Rodney jumped into the swamped boat and bailed it with a five-gallon plastic bucket. Finally they trailered the boat and pulled the drain plug, letting gravity empty the remaining water.

As he had done with our earlier sunken boat, Rodney changed the oil in the Honda—twice—and removed the spark plugs to blow the water out of the cylinders. It fired up and ran fine after he serviced the motor.

I arrived in Hannibal around 11 p.m. just as Rodney finished working on the motor. I went to the party to apologize to the mayor but everybody had left. Our crew was bummed about missing the mayor's celebration but the sunken boat had to take first priority. The next day, we finished picking up the garbage from the cleanup and headed down to Grafton, where we had started this adventure-filled year.

Now that we had completed a circle, I had new challenges to face. For several months, I had been interested in the Ohio River. I knew we would be taking our barge south to the Ohio for the winter to avoid ice on the Upper Mississippi, so I sent a garbage-scouting team of Brent and his friend Mike Havlis to drive plate boats from Pittsburgh, Pennsylvania, to Louisville, Kentucky.

A *Time* magazine article came out in July about the project, and we received an email from an organization on the Ohio River called ORSANCO. They had read in *Time* that I someday wanted to clean up the Ohio, and they informed me that they had been cleaning it for 12 years. Their annual cleanup event was called the Ohio River Sweep and it was one of the most successful efforts in the country. Ironically, I had first learned about it from Friends of the Illinois River. I interpreted ORSANCO's email message to mean that the Ohio was their river and they didn't want us stepping into their territory. I had thought there was plenty of garbage on the Ohio River and that an allied river group would be more complimentary to our efforts on the Mississippi and welcoming to us on the Ohio.

As we worked our way back to the St. Louis area, I became involved in an issue closer to my home in East Moline. I had been keeping track all year of a controversy concerning barges and fleeting services on the Upper Mississippi. The Army Corps of Engineers was responsible for managing barge operations and issued permits for fleeting barges on the river. The Corps held public hearings to gather input about various fleeting proposals. Two companies in the Quad Cities area were jostling for fleeting rights. One wanted to park barges directly across from Buffalo, Iowa, in front of three sandy areas where people camped and near a slough where people water-skied. I had stayed there many times myself and, in the summer, I had seen countless recreational boaters using that area on busy days.

Blackhawk Fleet asked me to attend one of the public meetings and, although I agreed to go, I felt really awkward. I tried to avoid taking a position because I knew that no matter what I said, I was going to make somebody mad. I needed to be able to work with a broad spectrum of people, and my philosophy was to include everybody. But my high profile as a river steward put me on the spot. I had to express an opinion.

At the meeting, I said, "Look, I'm not against barges at all—commerce is good and that's fine. But there's a place for everybody—a place for barges and a place for recreation—and that's not a good place for barges."

I wasn't opposed to fleeting barges because, after all, Living Lands & Waters needed a place to park our barges, too. So I got together with Blackhawk Fleet to suggest that we work on a joint project that would promote goodwill among all parties.

An abandoned barge on the beach at Buffalo had become a focal point of discontent in the local area. This derelict vessel was actually a half-barge about 55 feet long, 25 feet wide, and 8 feet tall. Originally it was intended to be the floating base of a supply store for towboats passing on the river, but the store never opened and the barge got twisted up, foundered, and filled with mud. For years, it sat half-buried on Buffalo's popular recreational beach. It was tagged with graffiti, and people wrote editorials complaining about the ugly hulk. Several organizations were trying to figure out how to remove the wreck.

In the past several years, people had sent me newspaper clips about this derelict barge, but I realized that all the articles in the world were not going to remove the eyesore. I didn't know exactly how to do it, but I suggested to Blackhawk Fleet that we work together to remove it. I also talked to people in Buffalo and the mayor and city council. Everybody was very excited by the idea.

Of course, any project on the river requires permission from some agency or other. I told the mayor that we would remove the barge if he would get the permits, and it took a lot of work to get the necessary approval from the Iowa Department of Natural Resources.

By then, we were cleaning up more than 200 miles south, near the mouth of the Illinois River. When the mayor finally received the permits, I shut down our operations and arranged to moor the houseboat for a couple of weeks at a marina near Grafton. We parked the garbage barge in a slough below the bluffs at the confluence of the Illinois and Mississippi rivers.

By this time, Kevin had left the project and Lisa Hoffmann had returned to college. I took the remaining crew of Rodney, Jen, and Eric to Buffalo, Iowa. For starters, we set in hand-digging mud out of the derelict barge with shovels and wheelbarrows. We couldn't use our skid-steer because it would sink in the sand and mud. Also, the barge was settled too low in the mud for the skid-steer to enter, and the barge's interior was obstructed with reinforcing cross-braces and steel ribs on the floor. We had to cut that metal out before we could drive into the barge.

Once inside the dank atmosphere of the wreck, we had to resort to working with hand tools like old-time coal miners. The sweat poured out of us in the 95-degree heat, dripping off our noses and chins as we dug the mud out by hand. Each shovelful was a wrestling match—the mud's suction made the shovel stick in the ground, the waterlogged mud was extremely heavy, and it had to be scraped off the blade into the wheelbarrow. We had to remove all the mud before we could dismantle the barge because cutting torches wouldn't work until we got down to bare metal. We squinted against the brightness every time we stumbled out of the barge's darkened interior, and the air almost felt cool. We looked like trolls slogging back and forth across the glaring beach in single file. The hot sand gripped at the wheelbarrows and held them back. We dumped the mud next to the railroad tracks on the other side of a low, sandy berm—just the most god-awful work.

This backbreaking job took so much time and effort that we knew within the first day, "Holy shit! We are screwed."

I wanted to cut holes in the hull and let the Buffalo Fire Department blast the mud out with their hoses. It would have been easy. But the permit required us to remove the mud from the river to prevent it from contaminating the water. That didn't make much sense to me. The Corps already had plans to dredge the river bottom, and the dredge spoils would have covered up the mud.

Yet our work would not go unrewarded. Local people were so happy to see us removing this huge eyesore that someone called the media. All the TV stations sent camera crews.

I wore a blue shirt during the interviews and the rusty brown barge filled up the screen behind me. We were still working that evening when the broadcast aired on Channel 6. We missed seeing the news segment— and the editors also missed something: Their broadcast clearly showed graffiti on the barge that included, "fuck you" and "ass whale."

Back at the barge the next morning, I turned on the radio to listen to Dwyer and Michael's morning talk show and people were calling to talk about the TV news coverage. We heard a woman say, "My eight-year-old son was watching TV as I was cooking and he's saying, 'Mom, fuck you. Mom, ass whale.'" People called in for an hour with similar stories, and I felt kind of bad for Channel 6, but it was funny. We got a big kick from all the attention.

As we kept digging, the Blackhawk fleeting service stepped in to join the effort. They hired temporary workers to help us and rented two skid-steers with tracks that were capable of maneuvering in the sand and mud. That eased our work considerably. We just scooped the mud into the buckets on the skid-steers and they whisked it away.

Lafarge operated a cement plant close to Buffalo and became a major sponsor for Living Lands & Waters. The manager of the plant, Alain Pfaff, later became chairman of our board of directors. The company also provided workers who started dismantling the crossbars with cutting torches so we could move farther inside the barge. They cut out the other end so we could attack the hulk from both sides. The *Quad City Times* covered the demolition, and the front-page photo pictured a Lafarge worker operating a cutting torch with white sparks showering the dark hull plates. I liked the picture so much, I had it framed and hung on my wall.

However, I had grossly underestimated the time it would take to finish this job. After two weeks, the Grafton marina needed the houseboat's slip back so a different boat could park there. I sent two crew members to move *The Miracle* over to the garbage barge that was tied to the island near the confluence with the Illinois River. I wanted them to continue picking up garbage down there and to make sure the barge didn't sink—even a small hole or crack would allow water to fill the barge. The rest of us kept digging out and cutting up the barge on Buffalo Beach.

Four days after the two crew members left for Grafton, I drove back to the office in East Moline. My mother, who was working for free as my part-time office manager, told me about a recent email exchange. A man from Grafton had written to ask us to remove the garbage barge. He said he could see it from his house on the bluff and it was "unsightly."

My mom answered by saying we'd be moving the barge very soon. Her message was a bit jabby and she went on to say how hard I worked every day to make the river cleaner.

He countered by saying he was going to contact my sponsors because he thought they would like to know that, from what he could see, I didn't work at all. He accused me of using the sponsors' money to live a life of luxury.

My mother told me flatly, "This guy is absolutely nuts. Don't even call him."

But it dawned on me that he must have thought that I was living on the boat right then. I imagined that the scenario on the houseboat was pretty kick-back—it was late in the season, and they were probably taking it a little easy trying to recover from busting up the barge in Buffalo. The email correspondent lived on the bluff and could see all the activity—or lack of it—on the river below his house. I tried calling the houseboat to get their side of the story, but the reception was bad and all I heard was a crackling sound.

I got the man's address and phone number and called him. He definitely had an ax to grind. He told me that he had kept track of the activity on the houseboat—he even recorded the times and dates. Their general pattern was to get up at 10 a.m., feed the dog, and then go back inside. They would come out again at 3 p.m. and maybe clean garbage on the river for a couple of hours. In the evening, they would go ashore for a few hours and then return to the houseboat to sleep.

I thanked him for his report. Then I said that I was calling from the Quad Cities and had not been on the houseboat for several weeks. I explained we had been hand-digging a wrecked barge out of the sand and I would send him newspaper articles to prove it. I offered to meet him when I had finished the barge-removal task and he accepted.

Once I finally got phone reception with the houseboat, I told them about the guy on the bluff. They were mad at him for spying on them, but I told them that he was just looking out his window and couldn't help seeing what was happening on the river.

I don't like confrontation but I was extremely angry at them. I chewed them out—big time. They were representing the project, and if one person thought of us as lazy slackers then other people would think the same thing. That mistaken impression would smear our reputation.

I guess I couldn't blame them for taking it easy—I might have done the same thing. We had taken hardly any breaks all year, and the Buffalo Beach barge job was grueling.

When I returned to Grafton a few weeks later, I met the man who had complained about our inactivity. I talked to him about our operation and showed him articles about what we had been doing up in Buffalo. After that, he turned completely around and became a sponsor of the project. Reaching out to him proved to be very beneficial. His foundation sent us a check every year, and I could visit his house—a huge mansion, really—and take select guests up there on clear days to see the Illinois, Mississippi, and Missouri rivers.

Blackhawk Fleet brought a crane barge to Buffalo beach to pick up the last huge sections of the wrecked hulk. The barge was partially submerged, so we couldn't cut it up, and the sections were heavy. On one section, the operator revved the engine for more power, and black smoke jetted from the exhaust. The ragged piece rose from the river and dripped with mud and water as the crane operator arced it slowly toward the barge where he was loading it. There were a dozen of us on shore and we all cheered, but our exultation was premature. The cable snapped and the massive piece of metal clipped the edge of the barge as it dropped back into the river. The crane rocked wildly and we stood there with gaping mouths as the impact waves rolled up on the beach.

They repositioned the crane and loaded it on the second try. When the last of the barge was gone, we discovered the hull of a sunken towboat. We ended up removing that as well.

This industrial-strength cleanup effort spawned an extensive movement to remove nine other barges that had foundered in the area. Most of them had been abandoned for at least 30 years. The Army Corps of Engineers established a policy of granting fleeting permits with the condition that the companies remove the derelict barges. The impact was tremendous. Where there used to be a virtual graveyard of rusting hulks on that reach of the river, now you can't see a single one. The Corps also ensured that recreational uses were separated from some of the fleeting areas—the Corps couldn't make everybody happy, but they did a good job trying.

Done at last, we all returned to the houseboat in Grafton and kept cleaning up in that area. I arranged for the loaded garbage barge in Andalusia to be brought downriver to meet us. The Corps needed their two deck barges back; one had to go up the Illinois River and the other up the Mississippi. We needed to unload them and get them shipshape before returning them.

While we were waiting, we worked on a special project to remove a vintage tractor from a big island at the confluence of the Illinois and Mississippi rivers. Quite a few people in Grafton had been asking us since we first started in 1998 if we were going to remove this wreck.

The enormous old tractor was used decades ago to work the fields on an island and had been laid to rest at the edge of a field. The banks subsequently eroded and the entire tractor fell into the river and tipped over into the mud. The tractor had been there a long time because the silver maple trees and sycamores had grown to be 50 feet tall in the old farm fields on the island. The tractor was encrusted with Zebra mussels when we saw it.

I decided that we should remove the tractor before going south for the winter—a last hurrah in Grafton. We planned to raise the tractor's rear end nine feet up on the dirt cliff and then lift the front end high enough to lean it on the barge. Then we could drag it on deck with the skid-steer.

Our two come-alongs and logging chains weren't adequate, so we needed reinforcements. I recruited two local brothers who had been commercial fishermen. They provided their plate boats and a bunch of heavy-duty winches and cables. I bought some extra equipment, too, and we went to work—on another very hot day—to move the tractor.

I climbed up in a big maple tree and attached the come-alongs to the high branches so we could lift the tractor like it was doing a wheelie. It took us nearly all of a day's labor and some brain-numbing engineering but we got the tractor poised on top of the steep, muddy bank. All we needed now was the barge.

It was tied up on the other side of the island just 500 feet away yet it took us about an hour to go around the island. As we rounded the corner on our return, we noticed that the tractor had fallen back in the water on the river's edge.

I called Ted, one of the fisherman who was helping us, and he came out in his boat. We couldn't figure out what happened at first, and then we saw that someone had cut the five-ton strap that was tied to the silver maple tree and held the tractor up. That wasn't all. Someone had stolen all the winches and cables. Whoever did it moved really fast because we were gone less than an hour.

We figured they had been spying on us and must still be close. We cruised out in search of the guilty low-lifes, and found a guy out on the river that Ted knew as a bully who had ripped off other people. We pulled up to his boat and Ted asked if he'd seen anybody. When the dumb-ass said no, Ted asked if we could look around in his boat. Of course, the guy said no. There was nothing we could do. We couldn't see anything in plain sight, but he had a cubby in the bow of his boat that could have hidden his loot. Or he could've just ditched it in the weeds.

I had never been robbed like that on the river. We'd had stuff stolen on shore but never on the water by a river person. People on the river had been the very opposite of thieves. They were always trying to give us stuff and help us out.

In any case, I had to drive up to Jerseyville to buy new gear. It hurt, because money was tight at the end of the year. The fishermen had loaned us heavy-duty, American-made winches worth $160 each, and we replaced them with new ones.

We went back to the tractor and raised it up again. It was easier this time since we'd done it before, and it took us only half a day. We removed the tractor from the island and loaded it onto the barge.

The local people were excited and most of them said, "Hey, great job! You got the tractor out of there." But one big, drunk guy complained to me about it. He said, "You took a landmark of Grafton."

All I could say was, "Dude, why don't you have another one?"

On a positive note, I had been getting peppered with calls for more than a year from a freelance videographer from Missouri. He had seen a TV segment on the *Missouri Outdoors* program about the river cleanup. He wanted to start a cleanup project on the Missouri River and was asking us to come up to mid-Missouri to help. I agreed that we would do a cleanup with them the following fall.

In September, we went down to the Gateway Arch in St. Louis to clean with Anheuser-Busch employees. It was our first big company cleanup, and everyone from managers to groundskeepers came out to help us. It was scheduled in the afternoon, too, and they served beer when it was over. Several executives came out to give speeches, and I cobbled together a makeshift podium from a blue plastic barrel and a piece of bent pipe that I found in the river. As a joke, we duct taped a microphone to the pipe even though it wasn't attached to anything. I started the speeches by saying, "Test check," and tapping the microphone as a joke. Everyone followed suit by talking into the mike when addressing the crowd. It was hilarious.

After that rousing success, I arranged for a tow to bring us the Corps's barge that we had left in Andalusia. When we had our three garbage barges together, we took all of them to Alton to be unloaded. The scrap metal was removed at Azcon, where they used a crane on railroad tracks with a huge electromagnet to pick up the iron and steel.

Tim Wall from CNN arrived at this point and videotaped us as we unloaded the garbage we had been collecting all year. The project had taken a quantum leap in 2000. Formerly we measured success by the boatload, now we measured it by the barge load.

MEMCO Barge Line was helping us significantly at this point. I had worked out a large sponsorship with Mark Knoy, the president of MEMCO, and he also offered to take the Corps's barge up the Illinois River for us. Pressed for time, we worked for 24 hours straight to unload and clean the Corps's barges, using our gas-powered water pump to hose the decks and then sweeping every crevice and corner until the barges were immaculate. We were absolutely exhausted by the end, and I slept in my truck with the marine radio next to me because I was afraid I would still be asleep at 6 a.m. when the tow was scheduled to arrive.

I got the call at 7 a.m. and the tow came a half-hour later. For this coupling, I had to drive the barge because Captain Mike wasn't there. My bleary eyes could hardly focus, but the adrenaline racing through my bloodstream brought me fully awake. I started the *Nammy* in the thin light of dawn and pushed the barge out in the river. The line boat stopped the tow for me and I brought the Corps's barge alongside and slipped it into the notch in the line of barges. The maneuver was smooth and I couldn't have done it any better. Yet once it was in place, the deckhands realized it didn't fit, so I had to pull it out and wait for the next tow coming up river. It was pretty discouraging and exhausting after we had just worked all day and night to get ready for this tow. But at least the barges were ready to go, and we sent them on their way in short order.

By now, it was October and time to head south to a warmer climate on the Ohio River. Our fleet was reduced to *The Miracle*, the Nam boat, two plate boats, and the yellow sand barge with the coaming and the ten-foot fence. Nevertheless, our single barge had plenty of storage capacity for a month's worth of garbage. Captain Mike was driving, and the crew had dwindled to Eric Wilson and my brother.

Jen was packing up to go to graduate school. She had worked the whole season on the project while studying in her "spare time" for her graduate entrance exams. I was also studying at the time to finish my two-year degree. The crowded bedlam inside *The Miracle* served as our study hall.

Rodney—my right-hand man—went to be with Heidi in Oregon where she was going to college. Their baby was due in December (she had a midwife and home delivery, and they named their son River). I was extremely happy for them but Rodney's absence was a huge loss for the project and for me personally. I had depended on him every day for the past three years, and he had worked just as hard as I had. I was sad to see him go and also nervous to be pressing on without him. But I had to.

A young woman named Nancy who used to rally as a volunteer for an environmental organization joined the crew in St. Louis. She had learned about the project in a magazine and had visited earlier that summer to check us out. She wanted to join for the rest of the season and, since it was hard at that time of year to find people to work on the project, I told her to come out. We picked her up at the St. Louis airport.

A terribly violent thunderstorm blew through the area her first night on *The Miracle*—standard weather fare in the Midwest. Yet, it was bad enough that Captain Mike and the crew struggled to park our fleet in a protected spot. Nancy tried to sleep in the cramped interior while waves rocked the boat and wind screamed outside through the railings. Lightning flashed like strobes and made the night even blacker. Heavy sheets of rain pounded a loud drumbeat on the thin fiberglass roof. Anybody would feel pretty fragile and exposed on the river under those conditions.

The next day she emerged from the houseboat looking shell-shocked. She asked Captain Mike if he thought working on the project was dangerous. He told her that it could be, and she quit the project after that one night. Jen drove her and her baggage to the Arch, where she had arranged for a cab to meet her. She was flying back home to Virginia and then on to Kazakhstan. I thought, "If you can't make it out here for more than one day then good luck over there." After that, we would tell each other, "Don't be a Nancy Pants" when we wanted to encourage someone to be tough.

She wasn't the first to drop out. Some people who worked with us on the river lasted only an hour or two. Maybe they saw the project on TV and it looked noble, but then they were out in the middle of nowhere and wrestling a barrel all alone—they had no idea what they were getting into. Or people came out for three weeks and quit all of a sudden after I expected them to stick it out the whole season. You couldn't always tell if someone could handle the river cleanup.

With the bare-bones winter crew, the Nam boat pushed our fleet down the Mississippi to the confluence with the Ohio River at Cairo, Illinois. I met them near Olmsted, Illinois, at Lock-and-Dam 53 where the Corps was building a new dam with an expanded lock system. At a cost of more than $1 billion, the project would extend the lock to a length of 1,200 feet.

I didn't have permission to park anywhere, but asked Captain Mike to push our fleet below the new dam at Olmsted, near some big piers on the Kentucky side far away from the active construction. We tied up to some trees and nestled in the slack water behind the pier. At that point, Captain Mike returned to the Quad Cities.

This was my first time on the lower Ohio River. I was amazed at how big it was—a lot wider than the Upper Mississippi—and it kicked up huge waves in a strong wind. The current was fast, powerful, and confusing. I was to learn, too, that the river level fluctuated wildly. The Ohio could rise ten feet overnight and then drop out just as fast.

My brother told me a million things that I didn't always listen to. This time, he said, "Make sure you pull your barge off the bank every night, because it'll get stuck. It's not the water going up you've got to worry about, it's when the water goes down."

I replied, "Whatever, dude. I've been working with barges for seven months now and I know what it's all about. You don't know anything about barges."

Yet he was right. The next morning the damned barge was tilted on the bank with half of it high and dry because the river had dropped out from under it.

In one way, though, this was good because it gave me a chance to fix a small hole in the barge. The hole was the size of a quarter and didn't seem big compared to a 100-foot barge. However, it allowed the water to pour in continuously and would fill the hull very fast unless it was fixed. The hole was perfectly round and hard to plug with cedar shingles so I needed to weld it shut.

Now I really missed Rodney, because he had done all the welding on the project. I had watched him but didn't know how to do it myself. With some trepidation, I pulled the welder out and fired up the generator to practice a little bit.

Once I'd gained some confidence about using the welder, I dug out some mud to expose the hole. I crawled into the mucky depression next to the barge—careful to avoid touching puddles of water while I was attached to the electric generator with the welding equipment. I stuck a bolt in the hole and welded a bead around it. I got really skudgy crawling in the mud and my first barge patch was a little sketchy, but I felt really proud—it was a good job.

I crossed the river in the plate boat to find help getting the barge off the shore. I approached two guys working a small towboat used in construction and told them about the cleanup. After that brief introduction, I mentioned that our barge was grounded.

They looked at me with expressions that said, "Yeah, it's stuck, jackass. The water has been dropping for the last two days."

That didn't slow me down. I gave them T-shirts and talked them into helping us. They came over and we got out our barge lines. They pulled for a half-hour with their 600-horsepower engines—the barge was small compared to their towboat but it was pretty far up on the bank—and it took ten hard yanks to float the barge. We were wiser about the up-and-down ways of the Ohio River when we parked the barge again.

A week later, the weather got really dreary—the temperature dropped and the rain began to fall. I got sick and crawled into bed for three days. I had a hard time recovering since the houseboat was so damp and very cold. It seemed to get smaller every day. I reached an emotional low-point and questioned what I was doing with my life. I didn't feel good, there was nothing to eat, and I was in the boondocks far from my friends who were back at home having a good time.

"What am I doing down here?" I asked. "Am I really on the right path?"

I couldn't answer those questions but I knew in my heart I was doing something good. I just knew I had to keep going.

My brother lived in a small town near Carbondale, Illinois, only 35 miles from the Ohio River. Eric and I were the only two living on the barge, but sometimes Brent came to help during the day and went home at night. It was good to have him out there even though we argued a lot. For one thing, he was my brother and gave me confidence. He also was better on the Ohio River because he had spent months fishing commercially on it and on the Mississippi—both big rivers bordering southern Illinois.

Brent often brought people he thought would be interested in the project, and we needed the help. There was so much garbage, just tons of it. I could not have imagined it before I started collecting it. We didn't bother picking up small cans and bottles. We would hardly reach down for an antifreeze container or a milk jug. We just went for the big stuff—propane tanks, diesel drums, barrels, TVs, and appliances—not to mention the thousands of tires that could be found everywhere.

The Ohio River drains a sizable area of the industrial states in the central and southern Midwest. The Ohio proper starts in Pittsburgh at the conjunction of the Allegheny and Monongahela rivers and flows along Ohio, Indiana, and Illinois on its northern shore and West Virginia and Kentucky on its southern shore. The cumulative garbage from this area floats to where we were based in southern Illinois. We also were working below the mouths of the Tennessee and Cumberland rivers. These major waterways drain parts of North Carolina, Tennessee, and Alabama. As a result, the Ohio River below Paducah, Kentucky, was a river seething with garbage.

When the river came up, the high water floated the stuff off the shore and sent it downstream like an armada of trash. We would take all three of our boats and cruise back and forth in line in the same place, never touching the shore, and let the garbage float down to us. Most of the time, we could barely keep up with the onslaught.

The banks were steep and tall due to the river's scouring action, and the fluctuating levels kept the weeds down. Once the river dropped, the garbage landed on shore, where it was exposed.

If the river flooded over its banks, the trash could float miles into the floodplain before settling out. For example, I drove over the Interstate 24 bridge and saw a white refrigerator standing upright in a green wheat field and four barrels piled up a mile from the river in a field of corn stubble. The floodplains were covered with brightly colored trash—yellow oil containers, blue detergent bottles, red anti-freeze jugs, aluminum cans, and plastic bottles. I was sure those farmers had to remove the big debris every year to work their fields and probably just plowed the small stuff into the soil.

When we piled the garbage on the barge, we had to keep a watchful eye on the river levels. If the barge tilted when the river dropped, the garbage would slide to the downward side.

During the month of November, we worked our way from Olmsted to Metropolis, Illinois—a river town that claims to be the "home of Superman" and a great place to buy Superman memorabilia. It was getting late in the season and we tied up at a huge coal dock. It was shut down and we parked there for weeks without getting permission. Nobody said a word.

Even with supplemental help from Brent's friends in the Carbondale area, I was short on manpower. I could have kept an army of people busy for years cleaning all the garbage confronting us. I remembered the guys on the raft I met earlier in the summer on their way from the source of the Mississippi River at Lake Itasca, Minnesota, to New Orleans. I figured they had finished their journey a long time earlier and called to ask them to work with us. I was surprised to learn that they had just completed their trip and were driving back home from New Orleans to Muscatine, Iowa. They didn't have jobs so they came down to Metropolis with their two dogs to help us. With my dog, Indie, it was like we were running a small kennel on *The Miracle*.

We were tied up in a treacherous spot below Lock-and-Dam 52 near Metropolis. I had learned that the lock-and-dams on the Ohio River were different from the ones I knew well on the Upper Mississippi. Many of the Ohio dams were old-school structures that were built between 1910 and 1929 with upgrades completed in 1973. These dams included regular locks on one side like the dams on the Mississippi River. The old Ohio River dams did not have the massive, steel rollers to control the water level, though. Instead, the dam was built with a series of movable, concrete sections called "wickets," and the river flowed over the top of the structure. Under high-water conditions, a Corps workboat could lower the concrete wickets so vessels could drive right over the top of the dam, thus avoiding the time-consuming procedure of locking-through.

The weather really started to get cold, and an ice storm blew in while I was picking up garbage about a mile from our small fleet next to the dam. I drove back through the highest waves I'd ever seen on the river, holding my hand in front of my face to keep the sleet from blinding me. I had to keep a wide stance and crouch low to maintain my balance in the pitching boat. Opening up the throttle, I went as fast as I could under the savage conditions. But to my dismay, the motor started dying every time I went up a wave—there must have been water in the gas—and this stop-and-go action slowed my progress. The wind picked up speed and the sleet turned into freezing rain.

I finally reached the barge and found our fleet getting pummeled by the winds and waves. The Nam boat was tipping so hard from side to side that I barely made it into the cab. My knuckles turned white while grabbing the icy ladder, and I was scared that the violently tossing boat would fling me into the frigid water. Still, the boat had to be secured. I fired up the engines, backed the boat in the frothy water, and drove full speed up on the bank between two concrete cylinders. The *Nammy* was stuck in the mud, but I didn't care—at least it wouldn't sink.

Meanwhile, the storm was thrashing my next objective. The freezing rain iced *The Miracle*'s superstructure, and the metal fittings started snapping off due to the violent rolling caused by the waves. I fired up the engines, floored the throttle, and jammed *The Miracle* on shore next to the Nam boat. Then I did the same thing with the plate boats. Our boats were secured from sinking, but I was still worried about the barge. I checked the lines but that was all I could do.

That night truly fit the description of harrowing. The plate boats didn't run, so I was stranded on the river. There was no food on board so I went hungry that night. The houseboat didn't have heat and it was very cold. At least I had blankets. Outside, the storm continued to kick up the biggest waves I had ever seen, and they pounded the boats all night long. Fortunately, we had built shelters for the dogs using 55-gallon barrels and wood we had found in the river.

The next day, the storm abated but it was still freezing cold. The drain holes on the outboard motors were iced up and all our rain gear and ropes were frozen solid. Eric came out and we had to use hammers to break off the ice that coated *The Miracle* and the *Nammy*. Once we got everything in order, I checked us into a motel so we could thaw out our gear. A fringe benefit was the opportunity to take a hot shower.

We worked for another few weeks in an absolutely desolate and lonely place. The days grew shorter and the trees lost their leaves. It was the end of the season and morale slumped with the falling temperature. I again reached the point where I questioned what I was doing and whether the project would continue to grow. There was so much overwhelming garbage that we could hardly make a dent in it. Where was the project going?

That's when I thought back to all the people I had met in the summertime who told me the project was great. They had encouraged me to keep this thing going. I really appreciated their excitement and said that I would remember them when it was cold and barren on the river. And that's what kept me going—all the people who had supported and encouraged us. We could only try as hard as we could, and even if we made but a small difference, we were still helping to clean up our great rivers.

At last, the end of the season arrived. We packed up and the rest of the crew went home. I parked the barge for the winter in Metropolis at the TECO Barge Line. I worked out a sponsorship with them, and their employees offered to keep an eye on the barge and periodically pump any water out of it.

I made arrangements with a marina on Lake Barkley in Kentucky to store *The Miracle* and the Nam boat over the winter. These last steps would prove to be dangerous ones. I had to take them about nine miles up the Ohio River and then 20 miles up the Tennessee River, passing two dams on the way. The lock at the Kentucky Lake dam had a lift of 55 feet—the highest in the United States.

The Nam boat was top-heavy with the tractor cab attached to the tower above the cockpit, and it made for a tippy ride when the *Nammy* wasn't lashed to the barge. As I drove up the Ohio, I saw a line boat with barges coming toward me below the old-style Ohio River dam. I hailed the pilot on the marine radio to ask about the route over the dam. He said to stay to the right and I thought I understood his directions.

The river grew really turbulent as I approached the dam. The water looked brown and cold as it boiled with whirlpools and cross-currents. The *Nammy* started rolling, twisting, and practically spinning in the weird currents. I felt like I was riding on top of a bowling pin. There were no waves but the boat was close to capsizing. I kept a white-knuckled grip on the steering wheel as I tried to maintain control of the boat and my mind. The treacherous water scared me and I could feel my heart beating.

The dam loomed ahead in my windshield as I tried to remember the barge pilot's instructions. I had thought I knew what he meant but now I was confused. As I approached the dam, I was thinking in my head, "Did he mean the right side going up to the dam or the right side of the river as you descend?"

A million ideas raced through my mind. The darkest one was probably, "I'm way out in the river and the water is freezing—I bet I'm seriously going to die if I hit something right here." I knew the dam could punch a hole in the hull and I'd sink, or rip the rudder off and I'd capsize. But I couldn't turn the boat around because the crazy currents would tip me over. I had never felt my heart beat so fast.

I just hammered straight ahead—there was nothing else to do. I pushed the throttle full ahead, the engines roared, and the boat blasted above the dam where the water suddenly became calmer. I had survived the gauntlet.

I continued up to the Tennessee River, locked-through to Kentucky Lake, and made my way through a canal to Lake Barkley. It was really cold in the cab without a heater, a fact I hadn't noticed before with all the excitement. I found the marina I was looking for and pulled in.

The barge and Nam boat were "put to bed" for the winter. That left the houseboat as the last boat to go. I recruited Brent and his friend Mike Havlis to help me take *The Miracle* to the marina. We drove the same route up the Ohio and Tennessee rivers, and I cleared the Ohio River dam with no problems. But this time we had to face down Old Man Winter himself.

On the last night, the temperature dropped to nearly zero degrees and it started to snow. Everything on the boat was freezing and the cookstove was our only source of heat. We cranked up the stove, but the propane heat created moisture in the air. All the windows fogged up and we constantly had to wipe them down to see where we were going.

We locked through to Kentucky Lake. It was a huge body of water—184 miles long and 4 miles wide—scalloped with hundreds of coves and bays. The level was lower than when I had brought up the Nam boat because the man-made lakes, both Kentucky and Barkley, were used for flood-control purposes and the reservoirs were drawn down each year to accommodate the volume of rain over the winter. The Tennessee Valley Authority had dropped the lakes, exposing the tops of flooded hills, and the hilltops appeared as islands.

As night fell, we drove into unfamiliar waters with newly created shallows all around us. The snowstorm strengthened as the light faded. The wind picked up and whitecaps began rolling across the surface. *The Miracle* started to toss and pitch as the snow fell faster and thicker. We cruised into the blizzard and visibility faded to nearly white-out conditions. It was fully dark, and we couldn't see a light in any direction.

We had no idea where we were going, and then we started bumping off the bottom of the lake. The hull was fiberglass and could easily be holed— you talk about scared! If we hit a stump or sharp rock, we would sink out there at night in a blizzard with no small boat with which to abandon ship and escape. Brent and Mike kept wiping off the condensation and I squinted ahead as I steered into the waves—bumping, bumping, bumping. I was simply looking for anyplace to park but had no idea where to find shelter. I shivered, but it wasn't from the cold.

At last, Brent saw a faint white light in the distance and I aimed the boat in that direction. I wanted to get there quickly but didn't want to drive fast with the boat hitting the bottom. The light turned out to be a marina and we tied up there for the night. We woke up early the next morning, the weather had cleared, and we cruised to the marina on Lake Barkley where *The Miracle* was going to stay all winter.

I had no sooner returned home than I started setting up for the next year. It was my intention to do more of the same we'd accomplished this year. We had returned to the Mississippi and conducted ten community cleanups as well as working every day as a crew. We had upgraded our equipment base with a skid-steer, the Nam boat, and barges. We gained knowledge and experience about towboats and barges; we had hired a captain with a master's license and moved on to the Ohio for first time. And on a personal note, I had finally completed my associate's degree from Black Hawk College.

Our biggest step had been moving from just using our workboats and a truck to using barges. And the barges did exactly what I thought they would. Because we had barges, we could spend more time cleaning the river instead of hauling garbage; they served as a great visual focus for the mission. The barge made its own powerful statement about the neglect of the river without us having to say a word.

The project had reached a new pinnacle. I wanted to continue to build on the momentum for a cleaner river. I once heard a quote that change was like a freight train—it was slow to get going, but once going it was hard to stop. And in our case, change was like a garbage barge.

The garbage barge had been so successful in 2000 that I wanted to get two more. The Corps had leased two barges to us the year before, but we had had to return them at the end of the season. We were much more efficient with the barges, and the floating mountain of garbage moving from town to town became an attraction that people discussed. The barges naturally raised people's awareness about the neglect of our rivers.

The *Nammy* had proved barely adequate and would be woefully inadequate if we procured more barges. I needed to obtain a real towboat. I had been eyeing towboats since the year before at Olmsted, Illinois, when we first got out on the Ohio River. I asked Gerry Brown at Cargill to keep his ear to the ground, and over the winter we started casting about for prospects in the barge industry. After a few leads, I drove up to Minneapolis in February to see an old towboat sitting up on blocks in a foot of snow on the shore of the Mississippi River.

At 36 feet long and 18 feet wide, it was fairly small for a towboat but would be perfect for pushing the garbage barges. I was told it had sunk in Lake Pontchartrain, Louisiana. It had been raised off the bottom, and

Upper River Services in Minneapolis had bought it. When I first checked it out, the boat looked like a disaster—it was rusty, the hull was banged up, the windows were busted out, the sponson tubes on the sides were smashed in, the tow knees were crooked, the engines didn't work, the rails and stairways were twisted, there was seven inches of oil and grease in the bilge, and the putrid light-green paint was flaking off to reveal five layers of old paint underneath.

So what did I say? "This is awesome! That's the one. I want it."

The people who came with me didn't know much about towboats, but this one looked so obviously bad that they thought I was nuts to consider buying it. I took pictures of it to show my board of directors so I could illustrate how we could restore the towboat. They needed to approve such a major capital improvement.

The board now had 12 members who served three-year terms. All of them were volunteers, and, after naming family and friends as the initial board in 1998, I had been seeking to diversify the board with people who both approved of our cleanup mission and represented a wide range of professional experience. For example, when I was a clammer, I had worked with Kevin Duncalf at the credit union to obtain a loan for a boat and motor. I knew that someone on the board should possess banking expertise, so I asked him and he agreed to serve. We filled out the board with a variety of people who knew law, business, marketing, and so on, and I met with them monthly to chart the course of the organization.

An anonymous woman (I'll call her Mary) gave us a handsome donation, and we bought the towboat for $30,000. Upper River Services offered to fix it up for us, and they ultimately donated $30,000 in labor and materials. Upper River Services assigned one of their mechanics to work on the towboat almost full-time, and it turns out that the man's father had owned the boat in the past. The guy had grown up around this towboat and was really stoked to be restoring it.

The boat was named *Francis* when we bought it, and we changed it unofficially to *Thank You Mary*. Later, it officially became *River Cleanup*.

Our newly refurbished towboat pushes our first two barges with The Miracle *tied alongside toward the Missouri River for a community cleanup.*

I asked other sponsors to help us outfit the boat—Caterpillar donated two 185-horsepower diesel engines, Twin Disc donated the transmissions, and Kahlenberg Brothers donated the shafts and wheels (towboat propellers are called "wheels" by rivermen, a term harking back to paddlewheel steamboat days). As a result, the engine room became an engineer's puzzle with all these different pieces to put together. I was told the towboat would be ready in June.

Fund-raising was easier going into 2001 because more people had become aware of our efforts. We were covered by CNN for a second time; there were articles in *People*, *Reader's Digest*, and *Time* magazines; and countless newspaper articles, most of them front-page; and we even received coverage overseas. When I called to talk about the project, people would listen. Many of them said no because the river was not necessarily their priority, but I gained increased support during this sponsor drive.

During this time, I also gained a valuable worker. I knew a guy who managed Rampage, the skateboard park I had been going to for ten years. He was a big, burly guy and a fantastic skateboarder. With his curly red hair, he looked like a Viking, and everyone called him Yam. I didn't know him really well but liked him. He knew me as the guy who came in just before closing and thereby got in free. I asked him to go on a snowboarding trip to Colorado, and when we were driving home after ten days traveling together, I turned to him somewhere in Nebraska and asked him, "Dude, what's your name? I don't even know your real name."

His name was Eric Louck, and he informed me that he was quitting Rampage. I asked if he wanted to join the crew. At first he was reluctant, and I suggested that he just try it out. I said, "Think of it as a ten-day camping trip."

That was the start of recruiting for that year's crew. Rodney and Heidi had a baby, so obviously they weren't coming back. Yam was going to try out for the crew and my brother's friend Mike Havlis wanted to sign up for a season. He had helped us out sometimes on the Ohio River the year before. Another possible crew member came to try out, too. Dave Maasberg was staying in a youth hostel in North Carolina and read about us in the *Time* article. He really wanted to work on the project and called me up. I invited him to try it for three days. He came out and ultimately stayed on the crew. Lisa Eno would volunteer her help sometimes, and Lisa Hoffmann planned to join us in May at the end of her college semester.

We started the cleanup season on February 15 in Paducah, Kentucky, near the confluence of the Tennessee and Ohio rivers. Driving trucks with our boats on trailers, I convoyed down there with Yam. We left late and pulled off the road around 2 a.m. in southern Illinois because his truck had thrown a spark plug. The engine sounded like a machine gun, and we parked until morning behind a random strip mall in the middle of nowhere. Yam tried to sleep but couldn't because it was so cold. The next morning when we woke up, I realized that Yam had just finished his first full day on the job and told him, "Welcome to river cleanup!"

The two Mississippi River rafters from last year were going to rejoin the crew and were bringing their dogs. Kevin and his dog dropped out before we started, but Brad joined us for a second season with his dog. In late fall, he bought the *Shanty* from my brother because he wanted his own living quarters, and I couldn't blame him. I warned him that the *Shanty* was unpredictable, however. I said, "Dude, that thing is a head-ache, and it's going to cost you and me money." The framed quote on the *Shanty*'s wall said it all, "A houseboat is nothing but a hole in the water into which one pours money."

Brad had been working on the *Shanty* over the winter. In February, Brent put the houseboat in the water for Brad at a marina on the Ohio River. Brad barely knew how to drive it, though. He turned the key and it wouldn't start. When it finally fired up, the throttle was stuck wide open and the boat bolted like a frightened horse. Luckily the houseboat was pointing outbound, since it tore off at full speed with the docks rocking in the huge waves. We could see him inside fran-tically trying to get the boat under control. When the *Shanty* got out on the Ohio River, it turned upstream with the engine screaming. We all stood on the dock laughing until our guts hurt, yelling "Go! Go! Go!"

The amount of garbage on the Ohio River was still unbelievable—I could not begin to express how much stuff had accumulated there, and more was still coming downstream. The Ohio made the Mississippi look pristine. We started grabbing big items like propane tanks, refrigerators, barrels, and tires, separating the junk into piles on our barges. We hardly even bothered with the little pieces of trash.

Ingram Barge Company loaned us a 200-foot jumbo deck barge to go with our 100-foot sand barge. These flat-topped barges were pretty rare on the river, since most commercial barges were "jumbo hoppers" with open holds that can be filled with grain, coal, cement, and other bulk materials. They said they'd need the barge back in June.

The first time we tried to move the jumbo deck barge with the Nam boat, it was a real risky maneuver. The barge was just a monster. We couldn't move it very far, and definitely not upstream. We hopped a ride with MEMCO Barge Line up to Cave-in-Rock State Park in Illinois, where we parked our barges. The park had a 50-foot limestone outcropping that dropped to the Ohio with a cavernous opening in it. The mouth of the cave was 20 feet tall and 50 feet wide, and the cave went back 40 feet into the rock. When the river levels were high enough, you could drive a plate boat inside the cave. Folklore from the keelboat days told of people finding shelter in the cave—they sold liquor and food, there was prostitution and gambling, and people were said to have been killed there. It was an infamous lair for river pirates.

In a six-week period, we collected more than a hundred refrigerators—between Golconda, Illinois, and Cave-in-Rock—about 20 river miles. We stacked this huge pile of appliances like the stone blocks of an Egyptian pyramid, except they were colorful—pink ones, green ones, yellow ones, brown ones, and, of course, a lot of white ones. We tipped the topmost refrigerator on its back, filled it with dirt, and transplanted a six-foot-tall sycamore tree that had eroded from the riverbank. That tree kept growing up there and looked like a funny kind of symbol of something organic. Then, after a while, it died.

While we were working around the Cave-in-Rock area, a woman from SCI Real Estate Investments in Philadelphia called to invite me to ride the *Mississippi Queen* on a theme voyage from New Orleans to Natchez, Mississippi. She had read about the cleanup project in *Time* magazine and asked me to speak on the trip. I gladly accepted the invitation. Oddly enough, when I boarded the steamboat, they checked me into a stateroom named Cave-in-Rock.

The journey was a great experience. I had never seen the Lower Mississippi, and the river down there is much wider. I saw the numerous shipyards and unloading terminals between New Orleans and Baton Rouge, Louisiana, I figured out where all the barges on the Illinois, Ohio, and Mississippi rivers actually went. I stood by the boat's rail at night and was amazed by the passing scene—the elevators, towers, and cranes looked like something out of a science-fiction movie. The welders on narrow scaffoldings were working 90 feet in the air—their carbon arcs crackling like blue lightning and sparks falling in yellow-white curtains. The constantly changing industrial scenery scrolled by slowly as the paddlewheel churned.

When I returned, we moved on from Cave-in-Rock. The month of June came upon us fast, and Ingram needed their barge back. I got word that our towboat in Minneapolis wasn't ready like we thought it would be, so I had to figure out another way to move our garbage fleet around.

We pushed the sand barge with the Nam boat up to Shawneetown, Illinois, where we were able to park in a fleet of barges. We got permission to tie the *Nammy* to a sand dredge anchored in the middle of the river, and our crew lived on a big, high-banked island just downstream in *The Miracle* and the *Shanty*.

While we were stationed there, I saw an old crane behind the IMI Concrete Company's building. They had detached it from an old navy ship and used it on one of their dredges. I could see that they weren't using it now, so I asked them if we could have it. They were happy to give it to river cleanup, and now we had a crane.

We started cleaning in the Shawneetown area and found tons of garbage, as we had expected. We would load our barge at the fleeting service, and then return to the island to eat and sleep. All was going well until we came back to work one morning and the *Nammy* was gone. I pulled the plate boat right up to the Nam boat's mooring, trying to understand what had happened. It couldn't have been stolen and it didn't slip loose in the night. All of a sudden, I glimpsed the white top of the tractor cab about six inches below the surface of the muddy water. I announced, "It sank."

We were dumbfounded. The Nam boat was sitting on the bottom of the river. We went to visit the harbor workers in their office, told them what happened, and asked if we could hire them to rescue the *Nammy*. There wasn't much business right then, lucky for us. They said they would come out that afternoon.

Around 1 p.m., the workers came out in their 800-horsepower towboat, and they brought a bunch of their buddies to hang out and watch. I wasn't exactly having a good day, and it didn't help to have a towboat with a bunch of gawkers onboard.

First, they wanted to lift it with their winches, so I free-dove down and hooked it up. The Nam boat was small but heavy, and it sat in about 12 feet of water. They tried but couldn't budge it. By now I had some knowledge of rescuing sunken boats, so I suggested another plan. The river bottom was sandy and flat, and I pointed out that they could just drag it as far as possible toward shore.

They said, "Well, yeah, we can do that. We can do anything you want."

I was paying them by the hour, so we adopted my plan. I dove down and hooked up to a strong fitting on the *Nammy*. They pulled the sunken boat underwater almost all the way to shore where the river got shallow and their towboat started churning sand.

The last step was the hardest. We had collected a number of lost barge lines while we were cleaning up the Ohio River. The fast current must have snapped them. We had huge piles of these three-inch-diameter ropes in a range of colors—red, yellow, blue, brown, white, orange, tan. Tying them all together, we made one long rope that looked like a trick handkerchief from a clown's act. We attached the knotted line to the towboat and stretched it around a tall willow tree on shore. Then I dove down and lashed the other end to the Nam boat. The towboat throttled up and dragged the sunken boat toward the shore. When the *Nammy* rose out of the water, though, the resistance increased and pulled one of the knots apart. We retied the knots but the rope kept coming apart every time we tried to pull the boat up on the beach. Finally, we ended up hand-digging a shallow trench with shovels. It was a big headache, and the dragging broke off the rudder and bent some of the bottom sections of the Nam boat.

Once the *Nammy* was resting on the beach, we pumped out the water. We couldn't find a hole or crack, and we couldn't figure out why it sank. It was a mystery. But the engines obviously had to be taken apart and rebuilt, the rudder had to be fixed, and the bottom repaired. The harbor workers suggested we take the boat to a mechanic who owned a shop in Shawneetown.

Shawneetown is located just downstream from the mouth of the Wabash River. It used to be the major city in Illinois during early settlement years. Shawneetown had the first bank in the territory, back when Chicago was a small, upstart town. Chicagoans applied for a loan from that bank to help build the new town's infrastructure, but the bankers in Shawneetown thought that Chicago would never grow because it was too far from the Ohio River. Ironically, Shawneetown was wiped out in the flood of 1937 and only a few buildings are left there, including the original bank that denied the loan. Most of the town consists of trailers on stilts—it's just a forgotten kind of place. We had a lot of our stuff ripped off there. The thieves took everything out of the truck box, including bags of dirty laundry, a bunch of tools, and the brass portholes from the towboat.

We pumped out the *Nammy* and towed it to the boat ramp. Loading the boat on a trailer was difficult because it had to be put on backwards, and the little *Nammy* had a fairly deep draft. We had to back the truck all the way down until the cab was nearly underwater and then winch the boat onto the trailer by hand. The process was physically tiring and mentally stressful.

We took the boat to the mechanic's shop, and he agreed to fix it for us. I assigned two crew members to help him so the job would go faster and cost less. He was a great mechanic and a nice guy. He also was a combat veteran and enjoyed showing his collection of war photos.

All the same, the mechanic rebuilt the engines and repaired the boat at a very fair price. We caught a ride with a towboat to take all our boats and barges up to Mt. Vernon, Indiana. As we moved upstream, there was no way to clean all the garbage covering the shores, so we focused on getting the big stuff. It didn't matter where you went, garbage was everywhere.

I decided to split the crew and take some of them with me to Minneapolis to paint the new towboat and get it ready for installing the new equipment. I took Yam and Dave Maasberg with me to Minneapolis, while Brad and some helpers from Carbondale kept cleaning up the Ohio River. Lisa Hoffmann had finished the semester at SIU and rejoined us for the summer.

In Minnesota, we lived for three weeks in a youth hostel because it was cheap. We met some interesting people there including a Swedish girl who helped us paint the towboat. We went to the towboat every day to work on it and clean it out. I spent time on the phone arranging for Caterpillar, Twin Disk, and Kahlenberg to prepare the engines, transmissions, shafts, and propellers for it. Upper River Services was going to oversee the installation of the engines and drive train. I was told the towboat would be ready in July.

While we were working on the towboat, I often saw a woman driving back and forth on the river in a small boat. She kept staring at us, and I asked the guys at Upper River Services if there was a "river patrol" person because I kept seeing this woman in a boat. They told me she was Anne Hunt and lived in a houseboat with her two dogs. She had been a local resident for years and had befriended nearly everyone on the river. She had never seen us before, so she was curious.

The next time she motored by, I flagged her to shore. After I explained the project and what we were doing with the towboat, I asked her to take me downriver to look for garbage. On that boat trip, we started talking about doing a cleanup in the Minneapolis–St. Paul reach of the river. She knew the local boaters, the marinas, and the towboat personnel. She had organized big outdoor events and knew the city officials, the civic groups, and the environmental community. I thought she would be perfect as a local coordinator for a cleanup, and we started talking about planning something for the next year. She was very enthusiastic about it.

Yam, Dave, and I headed back to the Ohio River, and I stopped at my house in the Quad Cities to meet with my office assistant, Sheila Bosworth, and catch up on business. In early 2001, I had hired Sheila, who worked for the local chapter of the Sierra Club, to manage payroll and correspondence for Living Lands & Waters. We had established an office in the apartment above my parents' garage, but she worked part-time for us out of her house in Princeton, Iowa.

I stayed overnight and slept on the floor in the Living Lands & Waters office. The phone rang at 6 a.m., and I heard a voice on the answering machine, "Chad, if you're there, pick up, man, pick up."

I answered the phone and it was Brad. "Hey, dude, the houseboat is half underwater right now, and it's sinking fast. It's going down as we speak."

I heard loud noices in the background that became louder as the water reached the exhaust vents, poured into the hull, and—whoosh—quickly sucked the boat underwater. Luckily we had used strong ropes to tie the boat to trees on shore, but I was still worried because the deck fittings were weak. Brad reported that *The Miracle* was tilting down the steep bank with only eight feet of the bow and roof exposed. The rest of the 42-foot boat was completely underwater. The bank dropped off steeply, and I was afraid the deck fittings would rip out. If that happened, the boat would slide down and disappear into the dark water. I told them to get some big barge lines to reinforce the lashings.

"I'm leaving right now," I told Brad. "I'll be down there in seven and a half hours. Just get what you can out of *The Miracle*."

Brad had awakened early that morning and boarded *The Miracle* to make coffee because his houseboat's stove didn't work. He glanced back toward my room and saw a glare, but he was groggy and didn't think much of it. A few minutes later he looked again and realized that there was a foot and a half of water in the stern of the boat. He stomped on the floor and started yelling, "Get up! Get up! The boat is sinking!"

Maasberg and Yam had just returned from Minneapolis the night before and were asleep in the "Hole"—a very small space in the bottom of the boat that you entered through a narrow passageway. You could lie down in the Hole but you couldn't sit up without tilting your head to the side.

The shouting woke Yam, but he thought Brad was making a joke. If the boat was sinking then surely he would be the first to know it down in the Hole. Brad kept yelling and finally rousted everyone. When they saw the water filling up the boat, everybody ran topside and scurried to the back of the boat, where they leaned over the stern to see what was happening. Their combined weight made the boat sink even faster, so they all sprinted to the front. They huddled on the bow and tried to decide who would call me with the bad news. Brad got on the phone, and the houseboat sank in the midst of our conversation.

Everyone got busy reinforcing the mooring lines and salvaging my notebooks, phone lists, business cards, and the rest of my paperwork floating inside the steeply tilted boat.

I immediately started driving and worked the phones along the way. I called the crane service on the river and a trucking company that specialized in moving big boats. I called my brother because he had the hookah rig and all the dive equipment, and I knew a diver would have to go underwater to put straps around the hull to lift the boat. We also needed big timbers long enough to use as spreader bars, because the straps would crush the hull if the crane tried to pick up the boat without them. I told the crew to get the wood we needed to make the spreader bars. It was a long drive, and the trip was consumed by all the arrangements I had to make.

The next morning, we set up everything to raise the houseboat. The crane barge came around noon, and Brent used the hookah rig to dive down with the straps. Up top, the crew set out the spreader bars. The job went smoothly, and the crane lifted the boat high enough to start pumping out the water. When it was empty and floating free, the crew used the plate boats to tow *The Miracle* to the boat ramp. The houseboat was awkward to steer with no motors because it didn't turn smartly without the use of the two propellers in forward and reverse.

I went ashore to meet the semi-truck driver and noticed that there were actually two boat ramps on the river about four blocks apart. One of the ramps was closer to the main road and had a big parking lot. The ramp was less steep there, so I directed the driver to use that one.

We had just pulled the houseboat on the trailer up the ramp when a black Dodge Dakota pickup truck roared into the parking lot and screeched to a stop next to the semi. A wiry, middle-aged guy jumped out of the Dodge and slammed the door, screaming at the top of his lungs. I recognized the man from earlier in the season when he had pulled our sunken plate boat out of the river with his tow truck, and thought he was joking with me.

I spread out my arms and said, "Hey, how's my old college roommate?"

But he was not kidding around at all. He yelled, "No! No! No! I'm going to have you arrested right now."

His private boat club had just built the boat ramp and spent $100,000 to have the concrete poured. Someone had called him about the truck on the new ramp, and he was scared that it would crack the pavement. I tried to explain our situation but he was angry as a hornet.

I said, "Hey, we didn't know about the ramp. But, look, the houseboat's already out, so why don't we just pull it away?"

The veins stuck out on his red face, and he yelled, "Get out of here!"

So we got out of there and I never saw that guy again. The semi driver had to be wondering what kind of situation he had just stepped into. I rode with him back to the Quad Cities. *The Miracle* was an oversize load so we had to go around construction areas and take special routes. The trip took 11 hours overall.

A crane raises a plate boat from the depths. We've experienced many sinkings and learned our boats can submerge in a split second.

The driver dropped off the houseboat near Sunset Marina in Rock Island, right where I worked on the first year of the project in 1997. We set *The Miracle* down on some Styrofoam blocks and used electric fans to dry it out. Then we removed the outboard motors and took them to the Honda Marine shop. The original hole that we had patched when we first salvaged *The Miracle* had worn through again, and that's what had caused the houseboat to sink. The fiberglass and wood were rotten, and when the boat hit bottom, the impact punched an even bigger hole in the stern.

It was the middle of summer, and I had scheduled cleanups in July on the Upper Mississippi River. It was important to me to keep building our momentum. I was able to arrange for the garbage barge to get a ride with American Commercial Barge Line (ACBL), but our crew had to trailer the rest of the boats over the road.

We regrouped in the Quad Cities and, while we were waiting for the garbage barge to arrive, I gained a new crew member in an unusual fashion. A guy in Kentucky who worked on barges had called to ask for a job with the cleanup project. A crew member had met him in a Paducah bar and given him one of my business cards. Nobody on the crew except Captain Mike had experience on barges, and I thought it might be good to have someone aboard with deckhand experience. His name was Shane Walraven and I asked him to send me a résumé and a list of previous employers. I told him I'd call him back after I checked his references.

A few days later, I returned to my office and Sheila told me that Shane had called from an interstate rest stop about a mile from the office. I had forgotten all about him, but she reminded me he had called about a job. She said he had mailed in a résumé already. I thought, "This guy really wants a job." I felt like it showed a certain kind of integrity and purpose— he was definitely going for it.

I told Shane how to get to the office and he showed up in an open-air Jeep with a camouflaged canoe strapped on top, a huge American flag flying off the back, and a little Border collie named Foxy. He jumped out and said, "Hey man, what's up?"

Shane was a tall, ripped ex-Marine with tattoos and a goatee, just an animal. I said, "Dude, I said I'd call you."

But he told me that he only had a dollar left and was there ready to work. I asked him if he had carpentry skills and he pulled out a tool belt from a giant ammo crate in the back of the Jeep. I told him the houseboat needed to be gutted out and fixed up. We went to the hardware and paint stores, and I bought everything he needed. I took him to the boat and showed him what I wanted done.

That was his job interview. I told him he could stay in the office and sleep on the floor. That's how we hired Shane.

The garbage barge came up to the Quad Cities, and we got *The Miracle* patched, the motors working, and put it back in the water. I needed to get the show back on the road and start picking up trash again. We launched the *Nammy* into the Mississippi and were scheduled to hitch a ride with a line boat up to Dubuque.

When I drove the Nam boat across the river, the engines died on me, and I had to paddle it into a fleet of barges tied to shore. I looked up the phone number of a roadside-assistance repair company that fixes diesel engines and, after 15 calls, talked to a mechanic who came out to fix the diesels.

While he worked on the engines, I found the leak that sank the boat on the Ohio River. When the *Nammy* tipped back and a passing boat kicked up waves, water would come in through the exhaust vents and run into the boat. If that continued long enough, the boat would settle in the river and eventually allow water to down-flood through the vents.

Although I had solved that mystery, the mechanic could not decipher the problem with the antique engines. I had to pull the boat out of the river, which required backing the truck nearly all the way underwater on the boat ramp again. There was a crowd at the ramp, and I inadvertently put on a show for them. I pulled the trailer out in four-wheel low and the rear wheels lifted up three feet in the air. I had no choice but to keep going. The truck crawled up the ramp on the front two wheels alone. I drove all the way across the parking lot like a monster truck. There was a steep hill on the far side, and I just backed up into the hill and pushed the boat onto the trailer. The truck dropped back down and I had all four tires on the ground. The people there just stared and thought, "What the hell?"

Now the Nam boat was sitting on the trailer and out of action, so I had to switch things up. We left the garbage barge tied to a fleet in the Quad Cities and took *The Miracle* and the plate boats to Dubuque for the cleanups. We went back to piling the garbage on shore and trucking it to landfills. It was inefficient work under the hot summer sun, and the crew got frustrated and short-tempered. People started arguing with each other—just flat-out screaming. Within a couple of days, Shane wanted to beat up Maasberg. "Let's go out to an island right now and I'll beat your ass. Do you want to?"

Though hardworking and trustworthy, Shane was a pretty intense dude. He was the type of guy you'd want to bring along to watch your back in a shady bar. Maasberg left for the season, but not because of the incident with Shane. Maasberg had been on the project all year—a tough year—and he said, "I can't take it anymore. I've got to go."

We worked our way downriver, cleaning as we went. Before long, we hooked back up with the garbage barge in the Quad Cities. In July, I had planned a massive community cleanup at Marquette Street Landing in Davenport, along with a river festival at the city beach in Buffalo, Iowa. I had arranged with Blackhawk Fleet to push the garbage barge down to Buffalo, where we tied up to shore and transformed its deck into a stage. Local congressmen and officers from the Army Corps of Engineers were going to give speeches, and Rodney Shaw's old band, Burnt Melba Toast, was scheduled to perform. It was going to be a big cleanup and a good celebration of the river.

That Friday dawned gray with a misty shroud of fog. It was cool but I could feel the sun burning off the overcast. A group of people from Missouri joined us on the scouting trip to see how we did community events. I had signed a contract with them to bring our barges, boats, and crew 170 miles up the Missouri River in the fall to help with their community cleanup and to haul away the garbage. The group was called Missouri River Relief, and our agreement with them marked Living Lands & Waters's first contract-for-services.

While I was feeling the pressure of so much to do before Saturday's events, somebody got stabbed late Friday night. Around midnight, a woman suddenly started screaming from an island on the other side of the river. We were camping on the beach when the commotion woke us up. Finally, a man landed in a boat and said, "I've been stabbed."

Brent got a flashlight and saw blood pumping out of the man's stomach with every heartbeat. Brent tried to calm him down and said, "It's all right, man. You're going to be all right. The ambulance is on its way."

The man was treated at the hospital, but I spent a sleepless night worrying. I felt a knot in my stomach when I realized the stabbing incident would be in the newspapers and people might associate our event at

Buffalo Beach with the knifing on the river. VIPs and dignitaries were coming the next day, and the incident had had nothing to do with us.

The cleanup and festival went well despite my worries. We passed a significant milestone by removing the last of the barrels near Sunset Marina that had initiated the cleanup project four years earlier. This year, hundreds of people showed up for the events. The speeches were great, the bands were fantastic, and even a full moon rose over the Mississippi River. Still, I was souring on the festival concept. We had to put out so much effort for so little reward. Most of the people at the beach party came to listen to a free show and didn't care about the river or cleaning it up.

We kept working in the Quad Cities area, and the Corps gave us a small deck barge to complement our bigger one. Blackhawk Fleet, ever helpful, welded the small hand-crank crane that IMI Concrete had given us onto the smaller barge. That barge subsequently became our work area to unload and sort garbage. We put in ramps to the big barge and that's where we piled the mountains of trash.

The new towboat was supposed to have been finished in June, and now it was August. We had a contract with Missouri River Relief for a cleanup on October 6 and had to move the barges up the Missouri River, which would take several weeks. I started to worry about getting there on time.

Finally, the towboat was completed in September. I had it brought down from Minneapolis, and Rodney came back on the project to serve as crew for the maiden voyage. The trip took four hard days to reach the Quad Cities. At last, we had a towboat—a real one this time—to face up to the barges with enough power to push them adequately. We would be more self-sufficient and would not have to depend so much on hitching rides with line boats. And unlike the Nam boat, the pilot could actually drive from the pilothouse—what a concept! We started pushing our barges downstream with *The Miracle* and a plate boat lashed on the side.

When we got to the Missouri River and turned upstream, the low-powered towboat could barely make forward progress. The current was so strong it was shoving big trees down the channel. We had barely gone five miles, and the river conditions looked too dangerous for the fiberglass-hulled houseboat. Yam and I took *The Miracle* back to a marina in Alton then drove our truck to the cleanup site where we met our tow.

The Missouri is a narrow, twisty river with a fast current. The first Corps of Engineers dam is located at Gavins Point on the Nebraska–South Dakota border, 800 miles upstream from the mouth of the river, and there are no locks on the main stem of the waterway. Even at low levels, the current flows at four to six miles per hour. Our tow had to make that much speed just to stay in one place. A couple of times in tight bends, the towboat could only make one mile per hour as it bulled the barges upriver.

Our tow made it to the cleanup site just one day prior to the event, after cruising 900 miles in three weeks from Minneapolis on its shakedown voyage. Since *The Miracle* didn't make it up the Missouri River, the crew stayed for the weekend in a river cabin called Club Medfly provided by one of the River Relief organizers.

On the day of the cleanup, the morning fog lifted and the sun lit up the red-and-gold forests that framed the white limestone bluffs along the river. It was a few weeks after the September 11 attacks, and people wanted to do something positive. Within an hour of opening the registration table, more than 400 people had signed up and boatloads of volunteers started motoring out to trash sites. The Missouri River Relief event was massive—the biggest cleanup we had ever done, and extremely well organized. The event coordinators had recruited eight boats from the Missouri Department of Conservation and two from the U.S. Fish and Wildlife Service to take the volunteers out to cleanup sites on the river. We had our four boats, and there were some local private boaters who helped out, too. In the afternoon, we used our plate boats to haul the garbage back to the barge and scrambled until nightfall to pile it on the barge. The Missouri cleanup was the start of a lasting relationship with a new river cleanup organization.

This was our last activity as a crew for the year. We took the barge to Alton and off-loaded all the garbage. We wintered our tow with the

Ingram Barge Line fleet in Paducah. People were burned out and took off to do other things. Lisa Hoffmann had already left the crew to go back to college but came back for the Missouri cleanup. Brad left the project to teach English in South Korea. Shane got off the barge in Missouri and moved into a tepee.

Yam and I took two boats to Omaha, Nebraska, and did a cleanup with some employees from Enron. They had donated a pickup truck to the project and gave us all the office equipment and furniture that we wanted. The Enron employees worked very hard with us and had terrific morale. I felt bad when Enron crashed, because the workers I had met in Omaha really loved their jobs and their company. It was a good cleanup, but it felt small after the big season we had completed.

While we were off-loading the last boatloads of garbage, I asked Yam how he had liked his "ten-day camping trip."

As I swung into fund-raising mode for the next season, I looked back with a sense of satisfaction that the "year of sinkings" was receding into the past. Both the *Nammy* and *The Miracle* had spent time underwater, and I had managed to sink one of our plate boats, too. These incidents, however, also marked the end of the makeshift way we had been operating. The *Nammy* was retired, and we had finally obtained a real towboat. We already owned the yellow sand barge and added a deck barge with an attached crane for lifting heavy loads. Our increasingly professional operations had landed us a contract-for-services to help with a cleanup on the Missouri River. I was already talking to Missouri River Relief organizers about bringing our industrial-strength cleanup operations back in 2002.

Living Lands & Waters had hired Sheila Bosworth as our first office worker, albeit on a part-time basis, and established a permanent office in a studio apartment above my parents' garage in East Moline (it was low overhead and had a panoramic view of the river). I also recruited a solid new crew member in Eric "Yam" Louck, whose ten-day camping trip had lasted the entire cleanup season with no end in sight. With most of the crew gone for the winter, I hired friends in the Quad Cities to help with the winter maintenance of our equipment. I wanted to get everything in order, because I was already looking forward to adding to the momentum we were building on the Mississippi, the Ohio, and the Missouri rivers—some of the mightiest waterways in the world.

The year 2002 would see expansion in a number of directions. On the local level, our trash collecting would be upgraded by the addition of another barge—but for living on rather than working on. Our reputation as hard workers doing good work would continue to grow, and I would receive a prestigious award in Washington, D.C., as well as an invitation to attend an environmental conference in South Africa. The idea of cleaning up our rivers was resonating everywhere, and this year would mark a turning point in our efforts.

We started the season in the middle of February in Paducah, Kentucky, with Mike Havlis, Dave Maasberg, and Yam Louck. We picked up *The Miracle* and broke out our two barges from the Ingram fleet. Kentucky was seven hours south of the Quad Cities, but the weather was still cold and gray when we got there. The days were growing longer, but the temperature could still drop, snow could fall, and the wind could blow right through us.

Gerry Brown from Cargill called and told me to set up a meeting with John Eckstein, who owned Marquette Transportation Company, a barge line based in Paducah. Gerry was great at opening doors for me in the barge industry. I called John a few times, but he didn't return my calls. When we finally did connect, he would prove to be very generous, but that didn't happen for several months.

We left Paducah and moved upriver toward Evansville, Indiana. Maasberg had grown up on the Ohio River near there and said we would find tons of garbage in that area. Evansville was 100 miles upstream from Paducah, so I arranged a ride on a tow.

Along the way, we parked near Henderson, Kentucky, and started cleaning up in that area. That's where a writer for *Outside* magazine caught up with us. After he left, we moved the barges ten miles upriver near Evansville.

I gained permission to tie up to giant 12-foot-wide cylindrical piers located on the outside of a sharp oxbow bend in the river. We tied the barges to the piers, and this arrangement created a little cove just outside the main channel where we moored our plate boats and *The Miracle*. The mooring between the piers provided protection from the strong current and the logs ripping downstream in the high water.

We had to keep a close eye on the river because it rose and fell so dramatically. Our boats and barges could break their deck fittings if the river dropped while they were tied up—and the Ohio could drop many feet overnight. Conversely, if the water rose, the boats could swamp and sink since they were tied securely to the piers. We constantly adjusted the lines, and someone had to stay with the boats all the time.

We went to work picking up garbage, but it was slow going. The river was rising and the current washed lots of wood and garbage downstream. The surface of the water became like a moving minefield of debris, including big fuel tanks, metal barrels, whole trees, refrigerators, and a plethora of large and small items. We had to drive slowly and thread our way carefully through the flotsam to avoid collisions. The fast current was especially treacherous because it was so pushy. When the boats angled to shore, the cross-currents and eddies could shove them off-course and into obstructions.

The powerful water made it difficult and dangerous to drive a heavily loaded boat. I kept a close watch to make sure we loaded the boats
evenly, since a front-loaded boat could knife into a wave and sink
like a rock. This had already happened to us two years earlier on the
Mississippi. I also made sure we didn't overload the boats, but that
was a difficult judgment call. Lighter loads were safer but also required
more trips. It created a tricky balancing act between lighter loads versus more trips. We almost always worked side-by-side in case anything happened.

The only way to learn how to drive a boat was to do it. With new drivers, I put them through drills—stop the motor, shift it to neutral, raise the
motor, put it down, turn it off. We practiced the drills until a new driver
was comfortable handling the motor. Then we started to teach about
reading the river—how to tell if the water was shallow, how to understand
the currents' movement around obstacles, how to steer over waves. They
had a lot to learn, and the hazards were not always obvious.

I also used the start of the season to try a new method of recruiting
crew members. People all around the country were hearing about us from
media reports, and I had received plenty of résumés over the winter. I
also gave talks to college groups, and students would come up afterward
to ask about summer jobs. I invited prospective applicants to "try out" by
working on the barge for three days. The trial period gave me a chance to
see what they knew and how they worked—and how well they lived with
other people. The project depended on a crew that could work and live
together under difficult conditions.

At one presentation at Western Illinois University in Macomb, a student named Margo Abts approached me and said she wanted to join the
crew. She was a tall, fit woman who was serious and smart. She came to
the barge for three days during her spring break, and I was impressed right
away that she would come in the cold weather when most other college
students were seeking warm climates. March was one of the worst times of
the year and offered some of the most difficult conditions for trying out.

A hard, cold rain pelted us on her first day. She was so pumped up to be on the river that she spent most of the day when she wasn't picking up garbage intensely sweeping the boats and barges. Finally it was getting dark, and I said, "You can stop and chill. We're done for the day." After her three-day trial period, I invited her to join the crew when she graduated.

In April, Larry Williams boarded *The Miracle* in Evansville for his three-day trial period. He had been writing me letters and emails for a couple of months. He started calling after I moved to the Ohio River. I knew by his persistence that he really wanted to work with us, so I invited him to try out, and he came aboard carrying a single duffel bag of clothes.

Larry was a big, quiet guy and incredibly strong. Because his parents were missionaries, he had grown up in Brazil and spoke English and Portuguese fluently. He worked hard during his trial period, but I wasn't 100 percent sure he would fit in with the crew. I wanted to think about it for a while, so I thanked him for his help and told him I would get back to him about a job.

But he was insistent. "I'm ready to work," he said. "I only bought a one-way bus ticket to get here. I've got all my clothes and stuff."

I was surprised, but I agreed, "Okay, it looks like you got a job, man. You're in."

The river kept rising until it was really raging. The current pushed between the cylindrical piers and continuously rocked our boats. The lines strained and loosened as the hulls tossed back and forth. The churning water bumped logs and debris on the bottom of *The Miracle*, and I was afraid a tree would punch a hole in the fiberglass hull. It was hard to relax enough to fall asleep knowing that Mike and Yam were bunking in the "Hole"—the confined space belowdecks.

While I was keeping a sharp eye on the rising river, Gerry Brown called again and asked about my meeting with John Eckstein of Marquette Transportation. I told him I had called John but hadn't heard back, so Gerry called him and said, "John, you really need to meet Chad. He's going to call you in one hour to set up a meeting and I want you at least to listen to what he's got to say."

As president of Cargill Marine, Gerry had a lot of clout in the barge industry. He said that if he could just get me into the room with people I could convince them to support the project. After all, everyone wanted a cleaner river.

After Gerry called him, John scheduled an appointment with me. It turned out to be a great stroke of luck. I went to his office and told him what I was doing on the river. He asked me if I wanted to go to lunch. Sure, I said—so we hopped in his Porsche and he blasted a Bob Marley reggae tune on his CD player. He drove fast to the restaurant, which was located in one of the buildings he owned in Paducah. After lunch he said he would make a substantial monetary contribution to the project.

John and I drove back to the Marquette headquarters and, before we entered the building, stopped to look out over the river. I noticed two unused barges tied up in the Marquette fleet—a deck barge and a barge with what looked like a broken-down motel on top. Flat-topped deck barges were in high demand, and I really needed a barge more than the money. I asked him what he was doing with the deck barge. He said he used it once in a blue moon and wanted to keep it. Then he pointed to the other barge and said that we could have it if we wanted it. It had been used as Marquette's headquarters before they moved their offices to a building on land. The floating office barge had been sitting there vacant for ten years. The roof had caved in, the floors buckled, and the rain gutters were bent off. The paint was peeling and the doors were wide open. The unused office barge had also been a target for vandals. It had 30 windows and 29 were busted out. Strangely, the biggest window was still intact. I wondered what kind of vandals did that—don't they always break the biggest window first?

Normally I jumped at an offer like this, but I knew the office barge would be a big restoration project and expensive, too. I hesitated and told John I would have to think about it. "I don't even know if my towboat will push this thing," I said.

I called Captain Mike, who was in Florida, and he stopped in Paducah a week later to look at the office barge on his way back to the Quad Cities. He said the towboat could handle it, no problem. Then I took Havlis and Yam with me to inspect it. It was 135 feet long and 27 1/2 feet wide, and the hull had been reskinned in the 1990s, which meant the bottom had new metal on it. The barge itself was built extra strong and had two separate basements for below-deck storage. The building on top was constructed in two sections separated by an open-air hallway. These structures were roofed and sheathed with metal, and they were divided into rooms and cubicles. None of the interior walls was weight-bearing, so we could gut it and rebuild rooms to meet our needs.

I went to the Living Lands & Waters board of directors to propose that we obtain the barge and renovate it as a floating dormitory and storage unit. It was going to need everything from septic and water systems to carpentry and wiring. Everything was expensive, and it would require hundreds of man-hours. We didn't have money to pay for renovating the barge, but the board thought it would be a good investment. I started to put out feelers to find funding sources.

Good fortune was smiling on us. A young woman and her husband in Colorado had read an article about the project, and she called my mother with an offer of financial assistance. The couple said their family had a private foundation and wanted to help us out with a capital project. I asked Mom to respond with a request for money to pay for the office-barge renovation. The woman told my mother to triple what we originally asked for, and we got a check for that amount less than a week later. That donation just came out of the blue.

Then John Eckstein straight-up donated the barge. He said it wasn't doing him any good and would cost him a lot of money to fix up for sale.

By the middle of April, the high water had become very dangerous, and I wanted to park the barge near the mouth of the Tennessee River where the high waters of the Ohio backed up, making a safe harbor. I called Captain Mike, and two days later we turned around and embarked downriver.

We parked right next to the office barge and started gutting it. We spent most of our time in Paducah renovating the office barge into a house barge. First, we had to strip it down to a bare frame. We tore down ceilings and chipped out tiles. We emptied the basement of old paperwork and boards. We had to grind through layers of old paint on the metal roof, siding, and deck and mill out the rusty spots everywhere. The steel rails around the outside edge had to be removed and ground down by hand. We took out all the windows that couldn't be repaired, tore down the interior walls, and ripped out the doors. It was handy to have a garbage barge parked alongside—we simply threw everything out the windows and onto the deck next door. There was an old railroad flatcar set up as a ramp to shore, and we could drive our truck right up on the barge.

We lived on *The Miracle* while we gutted the office barge and started reconstructing the new house barge. I moved off *The Miracle* as soon as we had a couple of rooms carpeted in the new barge and slept on some pieces of foam. I had been living in the confines of a houseboat for five years and was sick of it.

Havlis acted as our general contractor. He was experienced with home construction and was actually building his own house nearby in southern Illinois. Dave Maasberg was building a house in the mountains of Tennessee, so he brought a lot of knowledge, too. Yam and Larry knew how to work hard and did everything without complaint.

It was great to actually stay in one place for a few months while we were renovating the house barge. During that time, John Eckstein became a good friend. We all got to know the people working for Marquette Transportation, and it was helpful to have local contacts and allies.

We had to rebuild everything in the gutted shell—wiring, plumbing, cabinets, closets, windows, doors, vents, framing, paneling, ceiling tiles, light fixtures—you name it and we rebuilt it. In particular, the kitchen had accumulated 20 years of cigarette smoke, and it took four coats of paint to cover it.

We reconfigured the interior of the two buildings to meet our needs. The kitchen stayed in the smaller building, and we added a walk-in pantry and a dining table with wraparound bench seating. We put hinged tops on the benches to create more storage space. The smaller building also included a wide hallway with stairs to the basement and a furnace room that we turned into a tiny office.

In the main building, we refurbished four rooms for sleeping quarters and an office. We constructed plywood bed boxes with hinged lids under the mattresses so people could store clothing underneath. We made a mudroom entrance where the crew could hang foul-weather gear and take off their shoes before entering the living space. We tore out all the interior walls at the far end of the building. This large area became a living room with a bathroom in back and a stairwell to the basement. When I walked into the big empty space, it reminded me of a school classroom. I looked around and thought, "This space could be a classroom. We should probably have some classes."

That got me thinking about education—classes, students, teachers, field trips, and so on. What I remembered best in school were the field trips, and I started to wonder how we could start an educational program. I bought easy-care carpets and white ceiling tiles for the living room with the possibility of holding future classes in that space.

When we were fixing up the house barge, we had electricity from the shore, but we needed to decide about a power source for use while out on the river. We used a generator on *The Miracle*, but that was annoyingly loud, and when it broke down, we lost our electricity. The gas to run the generator could cost eight dollars a day. I started to think about a solar-energy system for the house barge. When I averaged the generator costs over a few years, it made the solar energy an economical choice. The sunlight off the water provided more solar energy than a land-based system and would free us to operate in remote areas. Solar energy implied "environmental,"

Long-time friend Dave "It's Just a Good Deal" Sparks strikes a King Tut pose while welding on the house barge in Paducah, Kentucky.

but more than anything it was practical. Mike Havlis had a friend in Carbondale named Aur Beck whose business specialized in designing and installing solar energy systems. He came to the house barge and put the whole system in for us.

We worked for nearly three months on the house barge. I felt we needed to finish it before moving on with our cleanup season. I wanted it to look nice, of course, but I mainly wanted to live there without knick-knacking the little details for the rest of the year.

Water was the one missing element on the house barge. We needed to install a large tank in the basement but couldn't get the materials before it was time to leave. The lack of a water system meant that we couldn't run our sinks, showers, and toilets. We would simply swim in the river to wash off, and we installed portable toilets on the barge's outside walkway. We'd been living like that for years, so we just kept going the same way.

In addition to Margo and Larry, all sorts of people came to try out for river cleanup. Most of them were disappointed because they expected to be out on the river every day instead of working on a reconstruction project. I responded by explaining, "This is what we're doing right now. We can't change our whole deal because you're here trying out."

One afternoon, I was out on the Ohio River trying to make arrangements to off-load 1,000 tires when my mother called me to let me know I had won the Jefferson Award for Public Service. I was one of four recipients selected that year; the others were Bill and Melinda Gates, Lilly Tartikoff, and Rudolf Giuliani. I won the award in the "young person" category for 2002, and Lance Armstrong had won it in 2001. Mom said I was supposed to go to a big presentation ceremony on May 17 in Washington, D.C.

I said, "Cool. Right on! But, hey, I've got to call you back because this guy is on the other line for these tires."

She made the travel arrangements. I was going with her, my dad, and a good friend, Tom Harper, who was a lawyer and board member for Living Lands & Waters. It was a formal affair, so I borrowed my uncle's suit because I didn't own one.

We flew into Reagan National Airport, and the first thing I noticed was all the garbage in the Potomac River. The tide was low, exposing tires and blue barrels out on the mud flats. As the plane descended close to the airport runway, I saw unbelievable amounts of litter on the riprap.

I was appalled. "This is the nation's capital? Are you kidding me?"

We visited memorials during the day and went to the Reagan Center for a big dinner that night. The place was crowded, and people were receiving regional awards. Lilly Tartikoff sat at the table behind us. I learned that she had been married to the president of NBC's entertainment division and had raised millions of dollars for cancer research.

I ordered the leg of lamb, and it came with the bone sticking out of the meat. I was really hungry, but it tasted so terrible that I could take only a few bites. I had never eaten leg of lamb and thought, "Man, is this what lamb tastes like?" I tried eating the rice, but that tasted horrible, too. I pushed my plate away and my mom asked me if I was going to eat dinner. I told her it didn't taste very good and made some excuse about being distracted by so much activity in the banquet room.

I woke up at 5 a.m. feeling sick. I started watching CNN on TV, and they were showing a 30th anniversary special about President Nixon and the Watergate scandal. I threw up about 5:30 a.m. and called my mom ten minutes later to tell her I was sick and didn't want to go to the awards ceremony. I thought maybe the lamb I tasted at dinner was spoiled.

She was very concerned but begged me to go. She reminded me how prestigious the award was and said the awards ceremony would be one of the biggest moments in her life.

I met the awards entourage at 7 a.m. to get on the bus. We went to a reception on the way to the ceremony, and I felt like throwing up again. I retreated to the bus and lay down on a seat, groaning and holding my stomach.

We drove to the awards ceremony and waited in line to get through security. I knew I was going to throw up again. I walked into the waiting area where there were a lot of movers and shakers and pretty powerful people. We were waiting to meet First Lady Laura Bush before the ceremony began.

I was feeling way too nauseous to stick around. I took off down a wood-paneled hallway with really high ceilings, found a bathroom, and threw up for five minutes. When I went to the sink to splash water on my face, I looked at myself in the mirror and saw my face as white as the marble countertops.

I took really small steps and held the wall with one hand when I walked out into the hallway. The hostess was looking for me and said, "Chad, where have you been?"

She led me briskly to these big, tall, double doors, and they swung open. Mrs. Bush stood there, so I walked in and we shook hands. We were talking but I tried not to get too close because I didn't have any breath mints. A photographer came up to take a picture and the camera flash blinded me. I thought that this wasn't exactly the best way to meet the First Lady, but what could I do?

Famous people filled the large room, and some of them talked to me. There was a guy named Peter who did the cover-album art for the Beatles, and there was a young guy who owned a big record company. I surreptitiously ate some of the hors d'oeuvres to cover up the bad taste in my mouth. Then everybody cleared out and we walked into a big room that was set up like a small auditorium with tables and chairs.

Right off the bat, everybody started singing "God Bless America." The room had great acoustics, and it sounded better than anything I had heard before. It was really moving with everyone singing together. Mrs. Bush came into the room through doors at the side of the stage and the audience clapped for a long time. She patted her hands down, like "Please, please," and the whole room got quiet. She talked about public service and how important it is. When she finished her speech, she walked back out through the side doors and the master of ceremonies started presenting the awards.

Everybody accepted their awards or had someone accept it for them. They were giving short speeches, and I realized during the third speech that I was last and would have to speak on the stage. Everyone had a prepared speech but me. I had no idea what I was going to say.

After a few minutes, I calmed down in my mind and thought about being in D.C. I had just visited the Vietnam and Korean War memorials, and the Korean War monument had an engraving on the side that read, "Freedom is not free." At the Vietnam Memorial, I saw the 58,000 names carved on the black granite wall. Those people gave everything for their country. That was the utmost in public service.

My name was called and everybody clapped as I walked up on the stage. I did the same hand movement as Mrs. Bush, "Please, please," and everybody started rolling with laughter. I said I didn't really know what to say. I had plenty of people praising me for cleaning the rivers, but I didn't know if I deserved the Jefferson Award. I was just getting started and hadn't been doing this all that long. Maybe I would deserve it in 25 years but not so much now. I said I really appreciated it and sure was sitting in good company.

Then I told them about visiting the war memorials. I said that I had read "Freedom isn't free" and saw all the names on the wall. I started to get emotional and said, "Those guys paid the ultimate price." I said there were many different ways to serve the country, and I felt like I was serving my country by doing what I could do. But my service was nothing compared to those who sacrificed everything. I was choked up, and I looked out into the audience and could see people with tears in their eyes. It turned out to be one of the best speeches I ever gave.

We went to a reception after the awards ceremony, and I saw Hillary Clinton, Tom Daschle, Paul Wellstone, and all these people from Washington, D.C., that you see on TV. The reception was in a Senate hearing room that had the tall U-shaped table where senators sit to question people sitting at the rectangular table on the floor. There was free food, and a chamber group with violins was playing music. We made up plates of food and I said, "Mom, let's go up there and sit at that table." I told her that this was probably where they interrogated Nixon back in the Watergate days, but she wasn't sure. I told her this had to be the place. I grabbed one of the many microphones and said, "So, Mr. Nixon, is it true that...?"

That's all I said because my voice was broadcast super loud, and the entire place froze and looked up at us. The violin player stopped his bow in mid-note and people held their forks in the air. The room was suddenly quiet, so I did what any respectable award winner would do—I instantly diverted the blame onto my mom by shaking my head and pointing at her while walking away. She sat frozen in her seat, absolutely horrified, and turned beet red.

Tom Harper had fun in D.C. pretending to be my security guard. He always wore a business suit and borrowed my sunglasses. He acted like he had a hidden microphone and talked into his arm. With the real security guards right there, he would say, "Chad has entered the building. Chad has entered the building."

When we left D.C., I saw more of the garbage in the Potomac River, which was such a stark contrast to the ultra-modern development complexes on the shorelines. I saw glass-tower office buildings in a place called Crystal City, and there were old town houses that had been restored in Alexandria, Virginia, while the river's banks were carpeted with plastic bottles and aluminum cans. Expensive condominiums overlooked the mudflats encrusted with rusty barrels and tires. It was disgusting.

I knew that people came from all over the United States and the world to visit Washington, D.C. It was disgraceful that the river running through our nation's capital looked so trashy. I thought, "What better place is there to do something positive for the country?" I also understood that powerful decision makers would see a cleanup in D.C. and that this would make a strong statement about all our rivers. As I flew back to the Midwest, I thought about how we could return and help clean up the Potomac River.

When I arrived back in Paducah, we only had a couple of weeks to finish the house barge and pack up for our season on the Mississippi River. The plan was to go up to Minneapolis for a ten-day campaign of nine back-to-back cleanups with hundreds of volunteers. Then we wanted to move downstream and concentrate on cleaning in some of the less populated areas. We had been concentrating on the bigger towns and hadn't focused enough on the smaller river towns. I had met many people from those towns who had driven to the bigger towns just to do the cleanups.

For example, we had one of our best cleanups in New Boston, Illinois, where it seemed like the whole town showed up to help. After the cleanup, the local conservation club hosted a dinner and bands played into the night. We liked it so much that we wanted to go back.

The Mississippi River came up in the spring of 2002 and the Corps was starting to issue high-water alerts. I was anxious to start moving upstream. We had scheduled several cleanups, and people were counting on us, but the house barge was holding us back. We couldn't move it until we removed the "spud" that anchored it in place. The spud was made from two pressurized railroad-car tanks that had been stuck upright in the bottom of the river. The house barge was welded to the spud, and it had to be cut out before we could get under way. The spud was so massive, however, that we needed a big crane to prevent it from falling over when the barge was removed.

I contracted with a crane company to do the job, but they kept postponing it. First it was due to high water and then low water, and then this and that. I was so frustrated. In the end, we were forced to leave the house barge in Paducah.

A crane at the National Maintenance & Repair marine terminal picked up *The Miracle* and put it on our barge. We blocked up the houseboat with Styrofoam chunks that we found in the river and strapped it down with chains and wires. Margo joined the crew for the season, and Captain Mike drove our tow down to Cairo, Illinois, at the confluence of the Ohio and Mississippi rivers. From there, we hitched a ride with the *John Paul Eckstein*, the biggest towboat in Marquette Transportation's fleet. Our towboat looked like a "mini" next to the giant one with its twin 5,000-horsepower engines, and our houseboat-on-a-barge arrangement looked really odd next to the massive jumbo-hopper barges in the tow.

The Marquette tow took us 850 miles up to Minneapolis in two weeks. When we arrived, we peeled our barges from the tow and took them to Upper River Services. They lifted the *The Miracle* with a crane and put it back in the water.

I had been working for a year with Anne Hunt to set up the cleanup campaign there. She was the first event coordinator I had hired for a project. We were calling it the Big River Cleanup and she was working with many organizations. Our main partner was the Audubon Society. Anne was the perfect local contact in the area because she knew so many people and organizations. She involved them all with the cleanup effort and lined up as many as ten boats to help take volunteers out on the river.

Minneapolis and St. Paul were progressive cities and kept their rivers clean. But as an urban area with a big population, there was still a lot of garbage. The Mississippi was narrow and fast as it ran through the city so most of the garbage floated downriver where the river widened out. Garbage also was captured by the bends in the river downstream.

We started the first cleanup on June 13. It was still early summer up north and the weeds weren't tall, so it was easy to find the garbage. We did nine massive cleanups in ten days, and they all went off great. A hundred people came out from the Cargill offices and everyone from executives to blue-collar workers picked up garbage together. The cleanup was Koch Industries's first service project and 150 of their employees chose to come out to the river. They had a ball. All the groups were extremely pumped because we were a new phenomenon with our garbage barges.

The Big River Cleanup campaign meant nonstop action for us. We woke up at 5:30 in the morning and went to bed at 11:00 at night just trying to keep up. There were 900 volunteers and 35 different groups, and they picked up an estimated 100 tons of garbage. Big groups of volunteers would come out each morning and pile the garbage on shore, and then we went back out and picked it all up, often working past dark. We hauled it to the barges and sorted it out into piles of scrap metal, tires, and garbage. We heaped three barges completely full. We could not have put another bag on the pile because the garbage was almost falling off the sides.

Mike Havlis said it was the hardest he had ever worked in his entire life—and he grew up working on construction crews in the Chicago area. It was the most intense day-in, day-out workload in the life of the project as well, but it also produced the most results. Not only did we fill the barges in a week and a half, but we emptied them on the 11th day. We took the barges to Upper River Services, and they off-loaded all of it with their crane for free. They also helped us with cutting up wrecked houseboats so we could remove them from the river.

We left Minneapolis on June 24 with completely cleared barges and a record-breaking 100 tons of garbage properly disposed of. We beelined straight back to the Quad Cities, where we met the house barge. It had finally been uncoupled from the spud in Paducah and brought up the Mississippi. We moved onto the house barge and started a whole new era of our life on the river.

Throughout July and August, we worked our way from the Quad Cities down to Fort Madison, Iowa. On Monday, August 19, we tied up the garbage barge late on a humid night in a backwater slough that the crew knew well near Fort Madison. We'd come back for another assault on the trash and debris that had been accumulating there for decades.

The permanent crew of seven had been pumped up for several weeks by the addition of two new members. Zach Loula was a thin, dark-haired teenager from West Branch, Iowa, a small town near Fort Madison. We also were joined by Woodson Spring, a 21-year-old native of Burlington, Iowa. We called him "Woody." He was the great-great-grandnephew of Aldo Leopold, the author of *A Sand County Almanac*. He first volunteered with us two years before as a member of an adventure scouting group. He had worked all day in the hot sun and loved it. The next year, he volunteered by himself and stayed on the barge for a few days. He was a really cool kid, slim but strong, and he was always very thankful. He didn't just stand around and wait to be told what to do, but looked for something that needed doing and did it. This year, Woody wanted to work with us for a few weeks before classes started at the University of Iowa.

We had scheduled a community cleanup in Fort Madison on Saturday, and I planned to stay busy all week using our four workboats and the permanent crew to clean up distant parts of the river. We couldn't take volunteers to those sites because of the long travel time involved with boating them there and back again.

This stretch of the river was extremely trashed and, in years past, I had not been able to spend adequate time cleaning it. This time, though, we had a full crew, all of the boats were working properly, and we could fill each boat with garbage once or twice a day.

We were also better at the art of collecting trash. Over the years, the Living Lands & Waters crews had developed several methods to efficiently clean the riverbanks and shoreline woods where high water deposited floating trash. Our system typically worked in a leapfrog fashion. One boat pulled in to shore and two people got out to work that area while another boat came in 100 yards above the first to work the next area. A third boat came in, did the same, and then when the first boat was done, it jumped ahead of the third boat. The pattern was repeated continually as we worked the bank in one direction, either upriver or downriver.

In other cases, an area would contain such large trash concentrations that all the boats pulled up to one spot and the crew worked as a team to pick up the garbage. In addition to loose, scattered trash, we often discovered old dumpsites where people used to get rid of their old appliances, vehicles, and garbage prior to the construction of public landfills and recycling centers.

When no volunteers were working with us, the Living Lands & Waters effort transformed itself into a focused, industrial-strength force. We dressed ready to get wet and dirty, usually wearing mud boots and work gloves. We packed the boats with hand tools such as shovels, pry bars, and sledgehammers to help remove deeply embedded debris. We brought chainsaws to cut up plastic barrels, and we relished the challenge of moving big tractor tires, mud-filled refrigerators, or sunken boats—the bigger the challenge, the greater the glory.

Competition was a great motivator. We would get stoked trying to outdo each other by extricating the toughest, gnarliest garbage. It was fun to razz each other. You'd get up in the morning and tell another crew member, "Dude, you're going down today!" Then you'd see people running to fill their boats with as much garbage as they could get. Every day it was, "Who's got the biggest boatload?" But some finds would "trump" a big load. A message-in-a-bottle would beat anything, and a refrigerator was also at the top of the list—if you found three refrigerators you could brag about it for days. Two bowling balls versus a refrigerator would definitely go to the judgment table where it would undergo greater scrutiny. Was it a swirled bowling ball that's engraved with a name like Juan or Betty? Or was the ball still in the bag? I came to the conclusion that there were a lot of pissed-off bowlers who threw their balls into the river after a bad game.

The crew had learned, too, that there was treasure in the trash—from water skis to upright pianos. I started a personal collection of bowling balls and motorcycle helmets found in the river, and the barge gradually became decorated with road signs and property markers found along the way. Anything you could think that was produced by American society ultimately ended up in the river—anything!

We unloaded the trash onto the flat-decked crane barge—a 25-by 80-foot barge rigged with a crane and an electric winch to lift heavy objects. This was the workspace where the crew sorted the trash and hauled most of it with a skid-steer to the larger barges where it was "warehoused" until the end of the season or until the barge became full, whichever came first.

The tires, appliances, and scrap metal were placed on the large, flat barge while the bagged trash or loose debris got stored on the sand barge, the one with the coaming and a ten-foot wire fence surrounding it to prevent trash from blowing out. We also placed a large container from a semi-trailer on this barge and used it as a secure storeroom and workshop.

While I operated the skid-steer, the rest of the crew unloaded the boats one at a time. Floodlights lit up the workspace as the crew worked past sunset and into the night. The "beep-beep-beep" of the skid-steer's reverse-warning horn rang out over the darkened river.

The deck crew wore hard hats while the skid-steer was in operation, and we all used a call-safety system to prevent accidents. When the operator lowered the bucket of the front-end loader, he or she would shout "Secure" or "Safe" before anyone approached the machine. Then after the deck crew had completely hand-loaded the bucket and stepped back, they would yell "Clear" to ensure that everyone was out of danger before the skid-steer operator moved the machine. The operator repeated "Clear" before moving. This routine calling became a habit that has saved a few crushed fingers and feet over the years.

When the first boat was completely empty, the boat operator motored to the other side of the barge and secured it there while a second boat tied up to the crane barge and the crew began to unload it.

We made a chilling discovery on Wednesday, August 21, when we were working in the Fort Madison area. The day started like any other crew-only cleanup effort. We went out in the morning, filled our boats, and unloaded them back at the barge. We ate lunch, did some maintenance on the barges and boats, and then headed back to where the Skunk River joins the Mississippi.

We started our leapfrogging technique with the boats to scour the trash upriver. As twilight descended, I was in the far upstream boat with a completely full load. I noticed the other boats were nearly full, too, and decided to send everyone back to the barge to unload the day's haul. I started driving back, and as I passed each boat on shore I shouted that it was time to go.

I began unloading the trash onto the flat-decked crane barge. The loud sounds of banging barrels and propane tanks and the muffled thud of refrigerators getting flipped onto the barge mingled with the hum and roar of the skid-steer's diesel engine. The sounds echoed off the 100-foot bluffs on the other side of the river. We proceeded unloading in order until the third boat, crewed by Margo and Zach, tied up to the barge and everyone started to off-load that boat. Suddenly, Zach yelled, "Hey, check out what I found—a human skull!"

He scrambled to the back of the plate boat, reached into a trash bag, and pulled out a skull—complete except for the jawbone. He assumed it came from an anatomy lab or science class. The rest of us weren't too sure about that. It looked like something we should notify the authorities about, so we put the skull in a cardboard box and called the cops. The police officer who came out took a brief report and said a detective would meet us in the morning to investigate further.

The next day, drizzle fell from the low, gray sky and the raindrops made millions of tiny circles on the water's calm surface. At 8:30 a.m., a detective called me to say that he wasn't able to come until later that day. Two detectives finally showed up around 3 p.m., and Zach and Woody took them in a boat to the site where Zach had found the skull. There was one problem—Zach wasn't sure of the exact location. At the time that he found the skull, he didn't realize it might be from a missing person, so he just placed it in a garbage bag and kept on working.

The detectives stayed seated in the boat while Woody searched the woods and Zach combed the beach where he had been cleaning the shoreline the previous day. He had seen a tooth in the sand and, when he dug it out, discovered the skull.

Zach checked the beach and the area didn't look right to him so he yelled at Woody to go. Woody was turning around to leave when he tripped over another part of the body—a skeleton with some fabric from the clothing still clinging to the bones.

The police detectives recovered the bones, and by the next day the coroner had determined the identity—a 19-year-old male who had been missing for more than a year. Apparently, he had committed suicide by jumping from a bridge spanning the Skunk River, which carried his body to the Mississippi. It turned out that Zach was acquainted with the guy through mutual friends in high school.

The next day, we conducted the Fort Madison community cleanup as scheduled, and afterward everyone shared a meal of hamburgers and fries at the marina's bar-restaurant. I was talking with a group of volunteers when a woman came up to me and introduced herself as the mother of the person whose body we'd found. She wanted to thank us personally for finding her son's remains and solving the mystery of his disappearance. She hugged us repeatedly, thanking us for giving her closure on her son's disappearance. It felt awkward, because we were surrounded by a

There are several barge terminals on the Mississippi and Ohio rivers where we unload the garbage. We recycle as much as we can.

small crowd and everyone was listening. Yet we felt compassion, too, and we were happy to help her in her grief.

We kept moving downriver and cleaning as we went. We eventually were poised to head up the Missouri River for a cleanup in September, but first I had to take a side trip.

In July, my office manager, Sheila, told me that a guy named Jeff Foote from Coca-Cola was trying to get in touch with me about the World Summit on Sustainable Development in South Africa. She gave him my cell phone number, and he called while I was driving near the Arch in St. Louis. I was towing a boat, fighting traffic, and trying to read the highway signs, so I was halfway talking to him and halfway trying to drive.

He said he had wanted to do something with me since 1997 when he first learned about what I was doing. He recently Googled "Mississippi garbage" and then clicked on my Web site. He asked me if I wanted to go to the environmental summit in Johannesburg, South Africa. He said the summit was scheduled from August 24 to September 4. I checked my calendar and said, "Perfect! I'll go. What do I have to do?"

He said all I had to do was show up in South Africa. He sent me information and a plane ticket, and I got my inoculations and a passport. I was excited about the upcoming trip but was so busy that I didn't think about it very much. I had so much going on that I had to miss the first week of the summit.

I packed a bag, got on a plane, and arrived in Johannesburg 19 hours later. Jeff sent someone to the airport who drove me to the youth hostel where the Coca-Cola contingent was staying.

Johannesburg reminded me of Los Angeles—a big, sprawling urban area. Right away, I noticed a stark contrast between rich and poor. It was like night and day. I saw a Maserati dealership on one side of the street and tons of poor people begging on the other side.

I arrived a week behind everybody else and was joining a group that Coca-Cola brought together for the summit—41 people from 33 countries who mostly were working for the environment in some capacity. The majority of us were in our twenties, and people came from all over the world—Bahrain, Fiji, Brazil, Scotland, Argentina, you name it. Within the first four days, a troop of drummers came to the hostel with a whole bunch of drums. The next thing I knew, I was beating a drum along with this huge group of people from all different cultures around the world, and we were all drumming to the same beat. It was bad-ass.

Coca-Cola did everything right and didn't spare any expense. They rented the entire youth hostel and hired security guards to make sure there were no problems. One night we went out without telling anyone. We were settling in at a bar when the security guard suddenly just showed up.

At the summit, we worked at the Mission Antarctica booth. Coke set up a big tent filled with lots of displays about Antarctica and had catered food. I worked almost every day at the booth answering questions about their project. They had sent a team to the scientific stations in Antarctica and cleaned up the garbage that had collected there for years. They brought their sailboat to their booth. It was named 2041—that's the year of an international conference to renew the treaty to keep the continent of Antarctica a world resource instead of letting individual countries own it. I gave tours of the 2041 to people attending the summit. The people with Mission Antarctica also built a maze out of garbage—big barrels all welded together—to show the variety of stuff they had removed.

Jeff Foote set up a stream-cleaning activity while we were there. Coca-Cola hooked us up with one of their partner organizations—a South African group that cleans rivers. Our cleanup was arranged by a local woman who looked like the actress Brigitte Nielsen. She was very blonde, incredibly fit, and extremely attractive. She was very enthusiastic about cleaning rivers.

On the van ride to the river, she talked to us about the cleanup—what we were trying to do and why it was important. My jaw dropped when I heard her speech in the van. I had developed a stump speech of my own on the importance of river cleanups and this South African woman was in a VW van telling my speech to a T. She was doing what I was doing on the other side of the world, and we were exactly on the same page. I realized that this movement for cleaner rivers was universal—not just in the Midwest or America but everywhere.

When I stepped into the river to start cleaning up, I was scared to death of tropical diseases. It was a small stream that you could easily wade across, but I was sure it had raw sewage in it. Even though we dressed in white Tyvek suits, rubber boots, and latex gloves, I felt like a total germaphobe freak.

The garbage there was so much different from that in America—it was stuff you just couldn't use anymore. We picked up little pieces of shredded plastic bags that absolutely could not be used for anything. Everybody was so poor that they kept every can and bottle unless it was broken.

After another 19-hour flight, I got off the plane in St. Louis and thought, "What just happened?" I was blown away to think that I could get a call from a stranger one day and then fly to the other side of the world six weeks later. I did not meet very many people from the United States at the summit and was honored to be a part of it.

I didn't dwell on my world travels very long because I had to plunge right back into work. We had a contract with Missouri River Relief (MRR) to help them with two big cleanups in September and October. We packed everything we needed for the expedition up the Missouri River, and I rode the house barge with a solid crew of trash-pickers. We had lost Woody and Lisa Hoffmann, who both returned to college, but we still had Yam, Mike Havlis, Zach Loula, Larry Williams, and Margo Abts.

Once we rounded the point at the mouth of the Missouri River, the towboat could barely make headway against the five-mph current. We were pushing a fleet of four barges with four plate boats tied alongside. At one time, Captain Mike measured our forward progress at less than one mph. The Missouri is a river pilot's worst-case scenario—narrow, fast, twisty, with a level that goes up and down quickly. We made the 150-mile trip to Hartsburg, Missouri, in a week.

The trip gave me some time to pursue another idea. We had lived and worked on the house barge all summer, but the living room was still unfurnished—just a big empty space. I hadn't had much time to think about getting it ready for the classes I envisioned. Yet when we arrived in Missouri I gave a tour of the house barge to the MRR people and they loved it. When I reached the living room, I explained that I wanted to make it into a classroom. I casually mentioned that we needed chairs.

One of the MRR board members, a local lawyer named Bill Rotts, said, "Do you need chairs? Well, get your guys right now and we'll go get you some chairs."

Bill told us to follow him and I chased his taillights for ten miles into the river hills on narrow gravel roads. He turned down a dirt road into a vacant farm where there was a pole barn with metal siding. It was totally dark, and we kept our headlights shining as we marched up to the door.

Bill unlocked the padlock, slid open two huge doors, and turned on the lights.

The barn was jammed full with furniture. There was every kind of chair stacked to the roof, hundreds of them, and he said, "Take your pick!"

We poked through the furniture and chose 30 blue upholstered chairs that stacked nicely together. They looked like expensive pieces. He told us that he got the chairs when he represented a firm that bought a hospital in Chicago. They were selling the medical equipment to another hospital in the Philippines, and the chairs and office furnishings were surplus. They were too good to throw away, so he was storing them in his barn. He later supplied a desk and chair from the hospital leftovers to every teacher in the Southern Boone County School District.

We loaded the chairs into the trucks and set them up the next day in the living room on the house barge. The rows of bright blue chairs instantly transformed that open space into a classroom. Now, all we needed was classes.

Of course, we also needed to get running water on the house barge. We were sick of bathing in the river and using Porta-Potties. I met a man at the cleanup site in Hartsburg who was a freelance welder and told him we needed a 1,500-gallon water tank built in our basement. I showed him the site and he took measurements. He threw me a bid to fabricate the tank on board and told me that if I could get the materials then he could give me a good price. I arranged to meet him a few weeks later in Alton. We hoped he could just drive his truck with the welder right onto the barge and build the tank while we were cruising to the Ohio River.

The day before the Hartsburg cleanup, MRR was hosting a learning festival on shore next to the barges. Bryan Hopkins, an education specialist with the Missouri Department of Natural Resources, arranged for 20 presenters from various agencies and organizations to set up learning stations for 200 elementary school kids. The classes broke up into small groups, which rotated from booth to booth. I gave a talk about the cleanup project to the entire group on the shores of the river next to the boat ramp. They could see the garbage piled on the barges. I stressed that if they saw a problem, then they could do something about it. The problem didn't have to be garbage in the river; it could be anything.

After the learning festival, I went for a boat ride with Bryan and we talked about using the river to create educational opportunities. I heard him at the learning festival, and his presentation was pretty powerful. He also was a fine musician and had built small wooden boats. I appreciated the fact that he had experience boating on the Missouri River.

We motored upstream and turned off the engine to let the boat drift in silence. I said, "Look, I'm setting up this education deal, and I want to work with you and your department to help us do it."

He told me the Department of Natural Resources had really liked the Missouri River Relief cleanup in 2001 and was enthusiastic about his work with the learning festivals. He thought his bosses would support a river education program. Bryan felt that our education workshops should be as interactive as possible and that we should get people out on the river. The classroom on the barge would be a good place for lectures and visual displays, but the in-class presentations should be backed up with real-world experiences on the islands and in the water. He said we could use our plate boats and barges to create a powerful learning experience.

The Hartsburg cleanup went well, and it was easy for us since MRR did all the local organizing. They arranged for live music during the cleanup, and a local bluegrass band set up on the house barge. Uncle Charlotte and the Swamp Rabbits entertained the volunteers as they off-loaded the trash onto the garbage barge. The weather was fantastic and it was great to be out in the fall season with the crisp air and colorful foliage.

Our next joint cleanup was scheduled for the following weekend in Saint Charles, Missouri, so we turned the barges around and headed back downstream. We rode the current and practically flew downriver—

at times we made 12 mph. Captain Mike kept us in the center of the channel but sometimes the current swept us radically close to the bank. In a sharp curve, he would anticipate the turn and line up our tow with the barges getting sideways as we floated into the bend. Once we were halfway through, he'd hammer forward to push us around the backside of the curve. It was nerve-wracking to watch, but he knew what he was doing. Given the strong current, it took everything we had to stop the barges in Saint Charles.

Later that week, we repositioned the barges for the cleanup. As we turned, the current swung our stern around and our rudder clipped the submerged rocks of a wing dike. The collision damaged the rudder, and we limped across the river and tied up to shore in preparation for the cleanup. I didn't like operating with only one rudder in these treacherous waters.

On Friday, MRR conducted another small learning festival in Saint Charles. Bryan was there, and we continued our discussion about river education. He said there were plenty of lesson plans and curricula that already had been developed, so there was no reason for us to reinvent the wheel. He suggested that we compile background materials about big rivers—their geology, biology, history, and economics—and then add existing lesson plans to the mix.

The Saint Charles cleanup attracted about 200 volunteers, including an old acquaintance of mine from college. I looked across the grassy area at Frontier Park and saw a tall, slim, athletic woman walking to the registration tent—it was Tammy Becker. I hadn't seen her in a couple of years.

Tammy's family lived nearby in Highland, Illinois, and she had just returned from Jamaica, where she had worked with the Peace Corps. She was between jobs and decided to come to the cleanup after seeing a report on the news. I remembered in 1999 that she and her friends came out to visit Rodney and me near Alton. They were the first people that we hosted on *The Miracle*. I also met Dave Gunn at the Saint Charles cleanup. He had worked as a mule driver in the Grand Canyon and was a really enthusiastic cleanup volunteer. He asked me if I had any job openings.

I was all for beefing up the crew and hiring fresh people before going down to the Ohio River. There was so much garbage down there that I could use an entire army to clean it up. I also knew morale slumped at the end of the season and new blood would help invigorate the entire crew. I asked Tammy and Dave to work on the project for the rest of the season, and three days later they joined the crew.

By that time, our barges were parked in a fleet near St. Louis to get the towboat rudder repaired and to fix a hole in the yellow barge. It took only one day for National Maintenance at Wood River, Illinois, to dry-dock our vessels and finish the repairs.

We went up to Alton to off-load the barges, and the freelance welder from Hartsburg met us there. We used our crane and skid-steer to lay down ramps, and he drove his truck aboard our small crane barge. It was a new Dodge pickup with a welder in the bed—his pride and joy—and he was wide-eyed with worry when he parked it on the barge. The scrap yard's magnetic crane loaded the metal plates for the water tank and we started cruising downriver to the Ohio.

During the day, the welder worked to fabricate the water tank, and at night, he drank whiskey. After a few nights, though, he ran out of whiskey, and there was no place to buy another bottle. He started to get salty on us and complained, "I haven't missed a day of whiskey in 23 years."

We were drawing near Cairo, Illinois, when he saw a boat ramp and told us to drop him off on shore. I reminded him that he hadn't finished installing baffles in the water tank. Without baffles, the water would slosh in the tank, and that could break the tank or spill water over the top. He didn't care, though, and demanded to get off the barge immediately. We couldn't get near the boat ramp, so we pushed our steel ramps onto the riprap, and he just drove his truck off the barge. It was really dangerous because we didn't have cross-braces on the ramps and didn't know the weight limits. When he got on shore, he just kept driving without shaking

Although our education workshops are geared toward teachers, this Buffalo (Iowa) Elementary School class took part in a program through a special grant.

hands or waving or even honking his horn to say good-bye. I didn't know if he had urgent problems at home to deal with or just couldn't wait to get a bottle of whiskey.

The people remaining on the house barge were my brother, Brent, Mike Havlis, Yam, Larry Williams, Margo Abts, Zach Loula, Tammy Becker, and Dave Gunn (and Jonas the dog, too). We received visits from Lisa Hoffmann and Lisa Eno, and other people got on here and there, so at times we had up to a dozen people on board.

Living on the house barge felt like paradise compared to *The Miracle*. The barge was spacious, while the houseboat was cramped. The barge had three bedrooms, two offices, a kitchen, a living room, and two big compartments down below. Both vessels lacked heat, so the living spaces were damp and cold, but *The Miracle* was a lot smellier.

As the weather turned cold, we hung out a lot in the kitchen, where we used the propane oven to heat the room. The windows would steam up and we couldn't see outside. When we slept, we would bundle in sleeping bags and cover them with blankets. We wore as much clothing as we could to stay warm while sleeping. Our breath came out in frosty clouds and froze on the bedroom windowpanes.

Mike installed plumbing, and we had a full bathroom with a hot shower, a sink, a toilet, and a urinal. The problem was that we couldn't run the septic system because the pipes would freeze in cold weather, so we continued to use portable toilets.

In November, we had started cleaning in the Owensboro, Kentucky, area when a camera crew from Minneapolis joined us. They were producing a documentary on waste in America, and the producer kept asking us, who were the bad guys trashing the river? I didn't really understand the point of his question. I told him I just picked up garbage and tried to set an example. But that wasn't the answer he was looking for. He wanted us to identify the evildoers. Finally, Mike Havlis exclaimed, "Me! I am the bad guy! I drink out of plastic bottles and I drive a car. We all are part of the problem."

Mike had said it best. Everybody in modern society benefits from industrial production and thereby contributes to the waste stream.

As we worked on the Ohio, I kept mulling over the idea of starting classes the next year. I first considered our limitations. Our classroom could hold only 30 people, and the barge was constrained to the river. I also knew we could make only so many stops. In order to make the biggest impact with our classes, I decided to focus on teachers. If we could get teachers excited about the river, then they could take it back to their classes and influence all their students. I also realized that I couldn't personally run the educational program. I was overwhelmed as it was with planning, fund-raising, and operational issues, not to mention crew dynamics.

I didn't know Tammy that well, but from living with her on the barge I knew she was an extremely positive person. I never saw her wake up in the morning without a huge smile and an enthusiastic "good morning" to everyone on the barge. She would push hard at full tilt all day and then fall asleep watching a video in the house barge's living room. Granted, she didn't know very much about educational programs or the river, but she had graduated cum laude from Western Illinois University and had experience in the Peace Corps. I thought she could do a fantastic job.

I don't always care whether people have the best skills as long as they're willing to work hard and can put their heart into the job. That's way more important to me than someone who has the right credentials. If you give people the freedom to do things on their own, then—nine times out of ten—they can do well.

I pulled Tammy aside, and we went out by the rail overlooking the water. I said, "Hey, next year I'm really thinking about having this educational program and I was wondering if you would be interested in running it. I'll up your pay, and you can work from your mom's house this winter half the week and come up to the Quad Cities the other half, so we can be on the same page throughout the off-season."

She agreed, and that was the start of our educational program. We would work together all winter with Bryan Hopkins setting it up; thinking about what we wanted to teach and who we wanted to participate. An important step was under way in expanding our mission for the river.

We cleaned the Ohio River into the second week of December before we turned back to Paducah. We wintered our boats with the fleet at Marquette Transportation. A winter blizzard nailed us the last day and covered the barge with snow. I enjoyed being on the river in a snowstorm. We cleared off the last of the garbage as the snow melted into a white slush. It was so beautiful and fun that we forgot about how cold our fingers and toes were.

The crew left the barge and most of them went home to their families for Christmas and then to Brazil for the New Year's celebration. Larry Williams had grown up in Brazil and had talked it up all year long—Brazil, Brazil, Brazil. Everyone was really psyched to go. I wanted to join them but just couldn't get away, especially since we were starting a new education program from scratch. This winter was an extremely busy period for me. Once again, I hired some local friends to do the maintenance and upkeep over the winter so we could start the next year with our equipment in tip-top condition.

I gave everyone who had completed the whole cleanup season a year-end bonus of one month's pay. I wanted to tide them over until we started working again in the middle of February. It was the first time I had ended the year with enough money to pay a bonus.

I felt like we were finally becoming an efficient river cleanup operation. We were running a towboat, four workboats, and four barges, including a house barge. The fact that we owned a towboat meant that we could increase our range up the Missouri River and all the way up the Mississippi. The towboat also freed us from depending on line boats to give us rides. The house barge was an exceptional addition to our fleet. Not only did it provide adequate crew quarters but it even had space for a classroom. This meant we could diversify and expand our mission into the field of education. Our improved fleet, equipment, and crews enabled us to best our own record for the number of volunteers and tons of garbage at the Big River Cleanup in the Twin Cities. We had our cleanup systems down pat. We also started to get flooded with résumés from people all over the country who wanted to join the project. We ended the year with a large crew in high spirits, and I hoped most of them would come back in 2003.

The Living Lands & Waters organization was becoming financially secure, and we hired our first full-time office worker, Laura Lopez. We were continuing to build momentum and were poised to start exciting new ventures.

hen I originally started cleaning up rivers, my goal was to find less garbage over time. Eventually, I hoped to work myself out of a job. I wanted to work on a clean river with little or no trash to pick up, and by 2003 that definitely was starting to be the case. Not only had we made a sizable dent in the amount of garbage in areas we had worked, but it didn't seem that people were trashing the river as they had in the past. Change for the positive was happening, but there was something else in the river environment that I had been noticing for years.

During my early years growing up on the river and later working as a shell-diver, I would occasionally see an oak tree and marvel at it because you didn't see many oaks growing along the river. The dominant tree species on the Mississippi was silver maple, especially in the backwater areas where I camped and shelled. I didn't know what a monoculture was back then, but that's what it was. I would see other species like sycamore with its smooth, white bark and cottonwood, which released flurries of fluffy white seeds in summer. Some cottonwoods were so big that it took four people with outstretched arms to circle the giant trunks. But in comparison to silver maples, the other species were few and far between. I thought of silver maples as junk trees, just big weeds.

I saw more wildlife than somebody in a city might, but when I considered the remoteness and vastness of some of the islands, I expected to see more animals and birds. I did see lots of great blue herons, belted kingfishers, cormorants, and egrets—the bird species that eat minnows and frogs. I often spotted different types of ducks and geese. But other wildlife was so rare that places like Andalusia amazed me. I saw a lot of deer, turkeys, and numerous other bird species there.

People were always asking me, "Don't you see tons of wildlife?" And the truthful answer was no, you don't.

Through the cleanup project I met foresters with the Army Corps of Engineers, biologists with the U.S. Fish and Wildlife Service, and game wardens with various state agencies. Through them, I soon learned why there weren't more kinds of wildlife: the animals don't have anything to eat. Ducks, turkeys, deer, squirrels, and geese all thrive in habitats with "mast" trees—the species that produce nuts and acorns. In many places on the Mississippi, those trees weren't growing, so the mast simply wasn't available for wildlife. The bottomland forest had become dominated by silver maples.

That wasn't always the case. In pre-settlement times, the forest was a diverse ecosystem with lots of oaks, hickories, and other nut-bearing trees. But these species were decimated when European and American settlers took over. They cut the trees to clear fields and to build barns and houses, but the majority of trees were felled for fuel. I was surprised to learn that most of the river-bottom trees had been cleared by the 1840s and that most of that wood had been burned to power the steamboats.

In 1823, the first steamboat voyage occurred on the Upper Mississippi from St. Louis to Minneapolis. The river soon became the major mode of transportation until railroads took over in the 1860s. Steamboats had voracious appetites for wood—a single steamboat could burn eight cords of wood a day. The trees close to the water were easiest to haul to the steamboats, so the forests on islands and shores were the first to go. Hardwoods burned hotter and longer than the softwoods, so the oaks, hickories, and walnuts were the preferred fuel. Virtually all the river hardwoods were wiped out in less than 25 years.

By the 1860s, the remaining steamboats operated on coal, and the bottomland trees started to return. As the forests grew back, they followed a natural progression. The first plants to sprout were fast-growing "pioneer species." The annual weeds germinated and then willow trees started to grow. The silver maples, cottonwoods, and sycamores followed in quick succession, but the silver maples grew fastest and shaded out everything else. The nut-bearing trees didn't have a chance. The ones that did survive were killed when the dams were constructed in the 1930s and changed the hydrology of the river. The water table rose and the mast trees couldn't survive with saturated roots. By now, the monoculture of silver maples had dominated the Mississippi Valley for more than a century. The mast trees would need a human hand to get a jump-start on natural succession and break the monocultural hold of silver maples.

I wanted to offer my hand to speed up the process. I envisioned planting a million trees. Instead of barges full of garbage, I imagined loading barges full of trees ready to be transplanted. We could reforest the bottomlands using volunteers, just like the cleanups. Instead of taking garbage out of the river environment, we would be putting trees back into it.

In the grand scheme of things, a million is really not that many. But even so, it was complicated because you couldn't just buy a bunch of little oak trees and plant them. Well, you could, but they wouldn't have a good chance of surviving long enough to produce acorns. The trees also needed to be suitable for the islands where we wanted them to grow.

First, we needed to find existing oak trees that had survived floods and collect the acorns from those trees. These lowland trees were adapted genetically to the river environment and to the local climate; therefore, I

Crew member Kim Erndt loads a plate boat to get ready for an education workshop and tree planting in Burlington, Iowa.

wanted to plant saplings within a hundred miles upriver or downriver of their parent trees.

Second, we needed to plant young trees that were tall enough to withstand flood conditions. Most tree nurseries provided "bare root" trees that were about 18 inches tall with a spindly root system. These little transplants would be killed by floods when the current knocked them down or when high water inundated the entire tree.

One of the Corps biologists told me about a tree nursery in Elsberry, Missouri, that could meet our requirements. They could sell us trees from sprouted acorns that had come from bottomland oaks, plus they could do custom growing for us. We could collect acorns and they would grow them in a separate area for us. The nursery also had a patented system for growing two-year-old trees that were six feet tall with thick, fibrous roots. These trees cost $7.25 each, but their potential for success in wetland areas was much higher.

Lisa Hoffmann, who had been working on the crew every summer since 2000, was a forestry student at Southern Illinois University in Carbondale. I told her everything I knew about trees, which wasn't all that much scientifically. But my plan seemed pretty simple: Plant trees with the right genotype in a suitable location where the ground was high above the water table and where there was less chance of them getting flooded out. These young trees would survive and start producing the acorns and nuts to sustain more wildlife.

In the late fall of 2002, Lisa and I took a small plane ride along the river to find oak trees. The leaves had fallen off most trees, but they still clung to the oaks, so we could identify them. And even though Lisa turned green from airsickness, we marked their location on maps. Then we recruited Boy Scouts and other groups and took them out in boats to collect the acorns. We found some monster acorns. They were so big you could have made them into Christmas ornaments. We collected bags and bags of acorns and took them down to the nursery. The nursery would sprout our acorns and grow them for two years while we found places to plant them.

I didn't want to wait a year. The nursery already had sprouted acorns from lowland oaks that would be ready to transplant in 2003. I wanted to start with 3,000 trees that were already growing at the nursery and transplant them on Mississippi River islands.

The tree-planting project was going to be a major shift into new territory for Living Lands & Waters, and so were the education workshops we were planning. I had to keep fund-raising and planning for the next cleanup season, but also I worked with Lisa and Tammy Becker as they developed the new programs.

Tammy split her time between working at her mother's house in Highland, Illinois, and the Living Lands & Waters office in East Moline. In addition to planning the education workshops, Tammy found herself getting drawn into helping our new office manager, Laura Lopez, with grant requests, fund-raising packets, and general correspondence. I also hired Judy Patchin as a bookkeeper to keep track of the ever-growing complexity of our finances.

I planned to raise enough money to pay for the workshops so the participants could attend for free. We also were working with Bryan Hopkins to get continuing education credits for the teachers who wanted them. We needed to make the workshops as attractive as possible to ensure good participation.

Since we had limitations on the number of people per workshop, I planned to stress quality over quantity. I wanted our workshops to present a broad-based and balanced view of the river. Thousands of environmental programs already existed and I didn't want to duplicate them. I wanted to present all perspectives—fisheries biologists, commercial fishermen, barge captains, foresters, and conservationists, to name a few.

The workshops would be a forum where everyone who worked on the river could have a turn speaking to the participants. My idea was to let people talk about how they see the river and how it affects them.

Fisheries biologists could discuss how they study fish populations, how they develop fishing regulations, non-native species and threatened or endangered species, how they electroshock fish and how they measure water quality. Commercial fishermen could talk about fish markets and how they fluctuate; what kinds of fish they catch and their seasons; what tactics they use for catching fish, and what kind of nets; and what problems they have with weather, river levels, heavy currents, and debris. Barge captains could talk about how they navigate on the river, how they lock-through the dams; what kind of boats they use and how far they travel, what kind of cargoes they carry, and how the crews are organized; and what challenges the river presents to them. Foresters could talk about doing tree surveys and planting seedlings, the monoculture of silver maples and the problem of invasive species, and the management of bottomland forests. Bird biologists could talk about migration flyways, habitats, and species. All of them could describe the best thing and the worst thing about their job.

I also wanted to provide participants with as much "river time" as possible. We would use the classroom on the barge for some presentations, but I wanted to get people out in boats and walking on the islands and in the woods. We would take the teachers on a tour of a line boat—from the pilothouse to the engine room. Commercial fishermen could demonstrate their techniques, showing the nets in action and holding up the freshly caught fish for everyone to see. Foresters could give guided tours through the woods, and archaeologists could take them to prehistoric sites. These firsthand perspectives would both educate and excite the participants. I wanted our workshops to be fast-paced and fun, with a lot of subjects and characters.

Tammy took a few trips in January to meet with Bryan at his office in Jefferson City, Missouri. He was compiling a book filled with lesson plans and river-related information which we would hand out to the workshop participants. He also was going to manage the registration through his office. Tammy was doing everything else—recruiting teachers to attend the workshops, identifying the experts to make presentations, finding the locations in various Mississippi River towns, and obtaining the necessary permissions.

The coming year's schedule was taking shape. I planned to start the cleanup season on the Ohio River in the middle of February and work upriver as far as we could through April. Then we would hitch a ride to St. Louis to start our May education workshops. We would do five workshops moving north from St. Louis to Hannibal. Then at the end of May, we would hitch a long ride up to Minneapolis, where I had hired Anne Hunt to organize another multicity campaign of community cleanups called the Big River Cleanup. In June, we would partner with the Audubon Society to conduct the Big River Cleanup, then work with them as we leap-frogged downriver cleaning up areas that we had never cleaned before. I wanted to keep up our momentum over the summer with cleanups all the way down to St. Louis. In the fall, we would go up the Missouri River as usual, then return to the Mississippi to conduct several educational workshops and start planting trees. At the end of November, we planned to go back to Paducah, Kentucky, to overwinter our barges at Marquette Transportation's headquarters.

In the middle of February, as planned, we reactivated the project on the Ohio River with a crew of six people. This marked the first time we started the season with an entire crew of veterans from the previous year.

I was able to negotiate a long-term lease through the state of Iowa to get another surplus deck barge from the Army Corps of Engineers. It was the identical barge that they had let us use in 2000. So we had four barges and a towboat, plus our four plate boats. We were all pretty excited about our fleet.

The Ohio River was filled with its usual plethora of garbage, and we slowly made our way as far as Tell City, Indiana. We also had our usual share of accidents. One night, the whole crew left the barge to take our boats to a cleanup in another city. I got a call that one of our plate boats had sunk. When I returned, I discovered that the boat sank because a hit-and-run barge had collided with us. The impact knocked the starboard rails off the house barge, and that barge came within six inches of smashing through my office. We never knew who hit us.

We turned back at Tell City and went around west and north to St. Louis. On May 7, Bryan Hopkins led our first workshop and started a general pattern that we have continued. We gathered everyone in the classroom for an introduction to barge safety and the Living Lands & Waters project. Then each presenter talked for 20 minutes to an hour, and the participants did some hands-on lessons about watersheds and water quality. For presenters, we used our contacts with the Corps of Engineers, the Fish and Wildlife Service, state conservation agencies, local colleges, barge companies, and commercial fisherman.

During the sessions, the crew prepared a noon meal and everyone ate lunch out on an island. In the afternoon, the workshop participants went for a walk to learn about wildlife, forests, and wetlands. A fisheries biologist discussed invasive species in the river such as Asian carp and Zebra mussels. A commercial fisherman set nets and showed the fish that he caught. We cooked samples so people could have a taste test. At the end, we asked participants to fill out evaluation forms. Everyone went home with an inch-thick booklet from the Missouri Department of Natural Resources and numerous handouts from the other presenters.

As we worked our way upriver conducting workshops in different towns, we found out that May was not a good time for attracting teachers since the schools were shutting down for the summer. We still had decent turnouts, but we were trying to draw interest in small towns and rural areas with low populations. Also, because it was our first run, we didn't have a base of teachers to draw upon. There was no word-of-mouth yet between friends and colleagues. All during this process, Tammy tried different marketing strategies and communication techniques. Still, the evaluations were very positive and many people said it was by far the best workshop they had ever attended. We knew those participants would help build the program.

In an interesting coincidence, I also received an honor in the field of education. In the middle of May, I was called up to the Quad Cities to accept an honorary degree from St. Ambrose University. I received a doctorate in public service at its commencement ceremony. I was proud to become a doctor, and my mother joked that I had skipped over the difficult part of writing and defending a thesis. Both my parents had worked hard to get their master's degrees. As a side benefit, I found that the conversations in bars with girls lasted a lot longer when you told them you were a doctor instead of a professional garbageman.

We did a limited amount of cleaning up as we moved upstream, but our main focus was the education workshops. I don't believe that the crew was too stoked on the workshops. They had to sit around during presentations and couldn't just go out and pick up trash.

Our last workshop was in Hannibal, Missouri, on May 15, and then Captain Mike drove our fleet upstream to start the Big River Cleanup.

We were expecting 800 people to help us with a concentrated campaign of cleanups starting in Hastings, Minnesota, and moving up to Minneapolis.

I was amazed at how the Mississippi River changed once we passed Dubuque, Iowa. I couldn't believe how tall the bluffs were. Some of them looked like low mountains similar to the Ozarks, with cliffs rising 600 feet. The nature of the river changed as well. The water pooled in wide lakes just above the dams, and the stream became narrower and threaded with backwater channels as we approached the next dam. The water was clearer, too. The U.S. Fish and Wildlife Service managed about 200 miles of the riverfront in Iowa and Wisconsin from La Crosse to Prairie du Chien, and there was very little development—just a cabin here and there.

Big River Cleanup, entailing 11 separate cleanups, was well-received in the Twin Cities region. These cities had been restoring their riverfronts since the 1990s, and the Mississippi was becoming a topic of civic pride. Anne Hunt had been organizing for months, and there was a lot of buzz about the cleanups.

The garbage barge concept was still new and fresh, and it had a strong visual appeal. I wanted to involve hundreds of people over nine days to really make a difference they could see. We had numerous corporate sponsors, including Cargill, Lafarge, and Flint Hills Resources. Cargill and Lafarge each made a three-year commitment of funds, which really helped me with planning for the future. We also had partnerships with environmental organizations, government agencies, and civic groups.

Cargill offered its employees "service-project days" and paid them to work for a good cause. The employees could choose from a number of projects, and more than a hundred of them chose the river cleanup. They just shut down the office that day because everybody went to work with us on the river. I was gratified to get such an upwelling of support, from the company president on down the line.

Flint Hills was a new sponsor that Anne had found to help pay for the Big River Cleanup. It also offered a service day, and again more than a hundred employees volunteered to come to a cleanup. They had a ball. A side benefit came out of the day as well. I happened to mention that I was considering a big cleanup in Washington, D.C., and one of their workers, Fran Sheperson, told me that their parent company, Koch Industries, had its foundation office there. She called the next day with the foundation's information, and it became my first contact in D.C., since I didn't yet know anyone there.

The first cleanup took place June 14 in Hastings, near the confluence of the St. Croix and Mississippi rivers. We provided most of the infrastructure for the 11 cleanups, although other boats came out when we expected an especially large group of volunteers. After concentrating on workshops in May, we worked relentlessly, picking up garbage with back-to-back cleanups. We kept moving from one cleanup to the next like clockwork.

In the morning, we helped volunteers pile the garbage on the shore, and then in the afternoon our small crew would pick up the combined trash from the hundreds of volunteers. We hauled it by the boatload, unloaded everything on the barges, and in nine days we completely filled up two barges. We rose at 5:30 in the morning and worked until 11:00 every night, and we were all bone-weary.

In the midst of all this activity, I also had to field interviews with the media. It was an added stress because I always had to be upbeat and on point. I had learned that lesson the year before when I had been joking around on camera and didn't realize the reporter was broadcasting live. I looked like a complete jackass and vowed not to repeat that mistake.

On the fifth day of cleanups, we arranged to transport 150 people down a narrow gravel road to the Spring Lake boat ramp. This area was remote, and we had found a really good spot to target with a large group.

The National Park Service had recently acquired a chain of islands about two miles upstream from the boat ramp, and we could ferry volunteers there with a 15-minute boat ride. Our main targets were four cabins on the island that looked like they'd been built and then abandoned by squatters. The backyards were filled with trash—shingles, carpets, tarps, appliances, barrels, barbecue grills, and nearly a barge load's worth of Styrofoam blocks that had been used for dock floats. We identified three sites and planned to emphasize teamwork to tackle them. We split up the big group and formed human chains to take out the junk. When people worked hard together side by side, they motivated each other. The group spirit at a cleanup could surpass any at a sporting event or music concert.

On that clear, windy day, people were laughing and joking around as they waited in small groups to board the boats. The volunteers were pumped up, and that got us pumped, too. Some of them had participated in cleanups before and understood how much fun it was to work hard together. They would help build piles of garbage that were mountainous by the end of the day—so much stuff that it would take one person years to accumulate it. The group could collect it in a few hours, and everybody would feel like champions. How often do people have a chance to work hard together and then, at the end of the day, see the results of their group efforts? People were hungry for that kind of experience, and the cleanups helped fulfill that need.

I recruited some extra boats through my contacts at previous cleanups. One of the operators was Chris Jackson, whom I had met in Burlington, Iowa. He was an avid duck hunter and an excellent welder. He also had been driving boats since he was a kid and was an excellent operator.

We quickly seated dozens of volunteers in 14 boats at the ramp, and the little fleet left together like a naval armada. Near the shore, the river was shallow and filled with stumps for the first 500 feet. The boat drivers went slowly until they reached the deep water in the channel and then started speeding upstream. I was in the lead boat, and I dropped off the first group of people and helped orient them at the trash sites. The group started to take the junk to the shore, and I told them I'd be back in about a half-hour with the next group.

As I drove back to the boat ramp, I saw Margo Abts coming upstream in one of our boats, urgently waving her hand over her head. I slowed down and she came alongside. "There's been a serious accident back at the boat ramp," she told me. She didn't have much more information, and I jetted back wondering what had happened. I felt sick with worry. There had never been an accident at a cleanup and I just hoped nobody was hurt.

When I arrived, everybody was in shock. I found out two people already had been airlifted to the hospital. They had been injured right at the start as the fleet was leaving the boat ramp. The accident, rescue, and evacuation had all occurred in the 45-minute period while I was taking the first volunteers upstream to the cleanup site.

When all the boats had taken off together, they churned up waves. The backwashed waves crossed and combined, creating an effect like a white-water river. The boats in the back drove into the turbulence and were tossed by the waves. The chaotic water popped up in unpredictable peaks, and a wave tipped one of the local boats helping us that day. Everybody in the boat fell topsy-turvy into the river, except one man who held on to the side of the hull.

The throttle was stuck at three-quarters speed, and the empty boat started turning in tight circles over the people in the water. Two of them were hit by the propeller, and the boat was making another pass when the guy hanging onto the gunwale pulled the "kill" switch to stop the motor.

Chris Jackson, driving the rearmost boat, picked up the people in the water and pulled them to safety. When he saw the injuries, he called 911 and rushed back to the boat ramp. The hospital sent their medevac helicopter to pick up the injured people. It landed in a field on top of the river bluff and whisked them to the hospital.

I didn't know what to do. Most of the volunteers were still working out on the islands and didn't know anything about the accident. For that matter, several people from the boat accident still wanted to go out. The accident had cast a pall on the cleanup, but the volunteers out on the river were still working hard and doing a good job. I went back out to the island to help maintain the momentum of the volunteers. It was difficult to stay upbeat with my stomach tied in knots worrying about the injured people.

We sent flowers and cards as the volunteers recovered in the hospital. I checked on their progress every day through friends. They were discharged from the hospital fairly quickly, but it would take them months and a lot of further treatment to recover.

We all felt terrible about the boat accident—I felt physically ill—but we still were committed to six more cleanups in the Twin Cities area and to the hundreds of people who wanted to participate. The next cleanup was an employee event sponsored by ATA Airlines. On that hot Saturday, we spread out in the woods to pick up scattered trash. I was running back to the boats when I spotted two women comforting an older man seated on a log. He was pale and wobbly and started to slump over. I thought he was having a heart attack or a stroke. We tried to help him walk to the boat, but when he stood up, he just collapsed. We soaked a T-shirt with water and put it on his head, then helped him limp back to the shore, but the aluminum plate boat had become like a solar oven. I poured cold drinking water on his wrists to cool him off. I didn't know what was wrong but I knew he needed medical attention, so I called 911 while I was taking him back. Instead of the boat ramp, we met the ambulance at a barge dock because it had a street address. We later learned that he was suffering from heatstroke and recovered at the hospital emergency room.

I was heartsick. Two medical emergencies had occurred almost back-to-back after never having an injury in five years with thousands of volunteers and hundreds of cleanups. We still had two more cleanups on the schedule, so we just had to keep going.

We completed our 11th cleanup at the Ford dam in the Twin Cities. With the exception of the two unfortunate incidents, Big River Cleanup had been an overall success. We had worked with 35 organizations to bring more than a thousand volunteers to the cleanups. I just wish the accidents hadn't happened. As it turned out, however, our run of bad luck wasn't over.

We moved our barges to Redwing, Minnesota. A large assemblage of volunteers had gathered there with people from the Audubon Society, ARTCO barge lines, and several school groups. As usual, the volunteers were eager to get out on the river and make a tangible difference.

Instead of driving a boat like I usually did, I accepted the offer of a man called Captain Ron, who wanted me to go out with the volunteers in his excursion boat. So I rode in a 1940s-era vessel that seated a dozen people. It wasn't the best boat for a cleanup because it was slow and too deeply drafted to get close to shore. Still, I sat with a mother who brought her five foster children to the cleanup. She was very inspirational and I could tell that the kids liked her a lot. I spent most of the time talking to her and her kids.

Captain Ron drove us to the first cleanup site, but we found very little trash there. We finished quickly, reboarded the boat, and cruised to the second site. That site proved to be mediocre, too, and we were driving to the next site when the foster mother pulled out a bag of trail mix. She had plenty of food and offered some to everyone in the boat.

An older man asked if the mix contained peanuts, because he was allergic to them. We told him there was a good chance there were peanuts, but he reached into the bag anyway. Before we knew it, the man's face started to swell and his skin turned red. I knew his throat could close up and cut off his breathing. He could die right there in the boat. I urgently called on the cell phone to get one of our boats, and Yam came speeding back toward us.

I spoke to the man. "Sir, you're having an allergic reaction. You must have eaten the peanuts in there. We're going to get you back."

The man insisted that he was okay but his throat was starting to swell up so much that he could barely talk.

I said firmly, "No, sir, you are going to get in my boat right now."

Yam pulled up beside us, and we helped the man aboard and safely seated him. I took the tiller and just hammered down the throttle. In a half mile, I saw the Sheriff Department's boat, and we flagged it down. Fortunately, Anne had arranged for a patrol boat to be on hand. I explained the situation, and the sheriff's deputy took the man because the patrol boat was the faster boat between us.

Yam and I watched the patrol boat disappear upriver with its emergency lights flashing and a big rooster tail shooting out in its wake. I looked over at Yam and he raised his hands in disbelief. What was happening? It seemed like an emergency struck every time we went out.

When the man returned to the ramp, he walked to his car where he had allergy medicine, and that took care of his situation.

After this series of problems, I took a harder look at what we were doing. We'd had a marine safety expert conduct a survey at the start of the season. He inspected our barge and noted the number of fire extinguishers and their locations. He showed us where light switches needed to be and we labeled them. He made a report on what we had and what we needed—we had to fix this and cover that, install this and get rid of that. He told us to display some signs and to buy additional fire extinguishers. This marine safety survey was extensive and complete.

He had judged our operations safe, but we still made some slight changes that he suggested. Now, we reviewed our procedures and cross-checked our equipment. We determined that we were being cautious enough, and the accidents were the result of unusual circumstances. It was just a horrible coincidence that they all happened within two weeks.

We continued downriver with our plan to stop at 10 or 12 towns along the way. With most of these towns, it was the first time we'd been there. That had the expected up-and-down results.

No one showed up for the cleanup on July 12 in Wabasha, Minnesota, a small river town named after an Indian leader from the 1800s. It was also the town where the movie *Grumpy Old Men* was filmed. We parked our boats at the ramp, and the crew waited with shovels, work gloves, great jokes, and water for the volunteers; we just didn't have any volunteers.

Finally, a middle-aged married couple who had driven from Rochester, Minnesota, on a weekend trip, strolled down to look at the river. The whole crew started clapping, and I walked up to them with outstretched arms. I said, "All right, you made it! You're going to the cleanup. Perfect!"

We gathered around them and started shaking hands, patting them on the back, and thanking them for showing up. We didn't give them a chance to say no. We basically kidnapped them, but they had a really great time. They came back and hung out with us, and the husband rode the barge downriver for a ways. They still come to our cleanups when we're in the area.

That time, I was actually relieved that nobody showed up because there was hardly anything to clean up. Thousands of boaters used the upper reach of the Mississippi above Dubuque but they were very respectful of the river. We had a hard time finding even beer cans in the weeds.

Not surprisingly, the most volunteers showed up when we had good advance word in the towns. We tried to take the time to go and talk to people, explaining why we were cleaning up and piquing their interest. Over time, we learned that contacting organized groups was the key to getting the word out in the community. Flyers were almost a waste of time.

Some towns, though, had no boating or hunting clubs, nor any civic groups like the Rotary and Kiwanis; the Eagles or the Lions; the Optimists or the Knights of Columbus. In places like this, I discovered that people working at gas stations knew just about everything that went on in town, and they knew whom to contact. Armed with this knowledge, I would call the gas station in these towns and the owner would tell me what I needed to know.

When we had cleanups where hardly anybody showed up, the people who coordinated it felt bad. Sometimes they would get mad at their friends for not showing up. I told them, however, that we didn't care if there were two people or 200. A movement builds on momentum, so 10 people this year might be 20 next year. I don't do discouragement—it doesn't get you anywhere.

In July, Heidi Moran-Sallows came onboard in Winona, Minnesota, with paints and paint supplies for our towboat. She was a student at The School of The Art Institute of Chicago, and we hired her to paint our towboat's superstructure in a unique and colorful way. The towboat originally had a white superstructure and a black hull like the majority of towboats on the Mississippi River. We got a small grant to pay for a new paint job, and I wanted a more distinctive look. Heidi created a fantastic scene with a huge tree trunk, fish, and other wildlife rendered in swirling, bright colors. She worked until late August to finish the job before returning to art school.

In early August, we got down to Clinton, Iowa, and Chris Fenderson came onboard for a three-day tryout. He was a friend of Yam's we both knew from the skateboard park in Davenport. A big guy with a sarcastic sense of humor, he was working at a fabrication shop in Iowa City, Iowa, as a welder, and that was a skill we lacked on the project. Luckily for us, he was tired of the monotony of the shop and had just quit his job. He put all his stuff in storage and came onboard with two duffel bags.

After his tryout, he joined the crew. Chris had never operated boats, but he learned quickly. To his advantage, he knew how to ride a motorcycle, and the hand throttles on a bike were similar to the tiller arm on a boat. He also had experience as a driver with forklifts, skid-steers, and all kinds of trucks.

In the middle of August, we repeated the big community cleanup in the Quad Cities and had a hard time finding enough garbage to keep hundreds of people busy. We had been cleaning there for six years, and the Mississippi's shores looked great.

Paint is more than a protective coating on the MV River Cleanup. Artist Heidi Moran-Sallows puts the finishing touches on her masterful paint job.

A week after that, we did a cleanup on the Rock River in the Quad Cities. Nice houses line the river and, along with a large population of boaters, the residents asked us to clean "their" river.

When the cleanup was over, we hosted a river festival with bands at a tavern near the Rock River. My earlier dislike for staging these events was reinforced. Reportedly, two guys arrived inebriated after the last band stopped playing and started wrestling each other. They purposely knocked glass bottles off a table where they shattered on the ground. As they kept wrestling, they stepped in the broken glass. One of them was barefoot and got cut up. About a month later, he hired a lawyer and threatened to sue Living Lands & Waters. The frivolous lawsuit never went anywhere, but the experience further soured me on the whole festival idea.

After that, I decided to stop hosting river festivals for the general public. I thought a better idea was to have a Barge Party and invite all our true supporters. We could make it into a fund-raiser, but mainly we could celebrate our project's successes with the people who actually helped build it up. I didn't waste any time setting it up, and we had the first Barge Party that August, which 150 people attended at the Davenport Sailing Club just ten feet from the river's edge.

We worked our way downriver at the end of August, which was the start of our fall season. As our barge rounded the confluence at Grafton, Chris and I drove a plate boat ahead to scout out a place to park. When we turned to head up the Illinois River, we saw a replica 19th-century sailing ship parked on the shore. It was strange to see a tall-masted ship on the river, but this vessel turned out to be even more unusual—it was full of beautiful Canadian dancers doing yoga. Chris and I approached this unique vessel with dropped jaws.

The dancers were part of a troupe that used the ship as a stage for the productions they performed at waterfronts around the world. The ship's transmission had broken down near Grafton on their voyage from the Great Lakes. Because I had local contacts in the marine industry, I was able to aid them with their repairs. It was nice to be able to help someone else out since so many people had helped us over the years.

In the process, Chris and I befriended quite a few of the performers. Since we were neighbors on the river, we invited them over to the barge and then took them on a boat ride. The weather was perfect and everyone was enjoying the excursion until Bighead carp started flying out of the water. These non-native fish can grow up to 100 pounds, and the sound of a motorboat makes them jump out of the water like ballistic missiles. In a moment, they were jumping behind our boat, in front of our boat, over our boat, and then into our boat. At first it was funny, but then an eight-pounder flew up and smacked the girl sitting next to me square in the mouth. It hit her so hard that she almost rolled out of the boat. I grabbed her to keep her from falling overboard while Chris grabbed the fish and threw it back in the water.

The girl was bleeding profusely from her mouth, and I was afraid the flying fish had knocked out her front teeth. The rest of the girls started screaming. All this time, Bighead carp kept leaping out of the water all around and over us. It was total chaos. We drove straight back to shore, and I rushed her 12 miles to the emergency room. She didn't lose any teeth, but her wounded lip required seven stitches. She accepted the scaly slap in the face like a trouper and was laughing about it. She said that now she had a great story to tell.

Bighead carp are one of several Asian carp that were introduced to North American fish farms to keep down the algae in ponds. They accidently escaped into the Mississippi and spread quickly through most of its tributaries. I first saw a Bighead carp in 1999, and now there are literally millions of these fish multiplying in our rivers. Non-native, invasive species, such as Asian carp, Zebra mussels, and the round goby fish, to name a few, are one of the biggest problems that the river is facing today. They are competing with the native species and are causing havoc for people who use the river such as recreational boaters, commercial fisherman, or an occasional Canadian dancer.

On September 5, we had a small cleanup with employees of several of our sponsors. Then our next cleanup was near Grafton with the local Piasa

Palisades Group of the Sierra Club and the Army Corps of Engineers. This was another of many good cleanups with these partners.

At the end of September, we parked our tow near East St. Louis, put our boats on trailers, and drove 200 miles to Kansas City, Missouri, to help with the Missouri River Relief cleanup. The day before the cleanup, a Kansas City group hosted the "Week-of-Water" learning festival for 800 students at Berkley Riverfront Park on the Missouri River waterfront. The weather was crystal clear and warm for the festival, but it changed overnight to become cold and rainy for the cleanup on Saturday. Three separate launch sites were provided for the volunteers, and the Living Lands & Waters boats were operating from two barges tied up at Berkley Park. As volunteers lined up to go out on the river in the terrible weather, we stood on the small sand barge and helped them board the boats. With the conditions so uncomfortably dreary, I wanted to excite and energize the people. It was fun to be on the river, and it didn't matter that the weather was cold and rainy. We never cancelled a cleanup due to bad weather, unless there was lightning or gale-force winds. As each boat came alongside to pick up the volunteers, our crew led the cheering and clapping, "Give it up for your boat driver! Yeah, let's hear it for the Fish and Wildlife Service!"

After Kansas City, we returned to our barges on the Mississippi and brought them up to Saint Charles. Missouri, to help with another cleanup. In October, we headed back up the Mississippi River and moored in Burlington to do the last cleanups and education workshops for the year. Tammy conducted her first education workshops by herself without the help of Bryan Hopkins, who couldn't work very far beyond the borders of Missouri since he was employed by that state's Department of Natural Resources. The workshop was nearly full, with about 30 participants, and she was pretty nervous. At one point the barge ran aground, but, despite this mishap, Tammy just kept smiling and acting like everything was on track. The participants never knew there was any problem whatsoever.

Several of the people in Burlington who had helped us at cleanups in the past owned cabins on Big Island, just downstream from town. They were members of a boating and hunting association that owned most of the island. When we proposed planting a thousand trees on Big Island, the guys we had worked with thought it was a great idea. But when they presented the tree-planting proposal to their association board, they met stiff resistance. The other members didn't want strangers coming to the island, even if it meant Big Island would get thousands of dollars' worth of trees and a project that would improve the wildlife. After all, most of them were hunters. The proposal sparked a series of contentious meetings. After a while, I realized they thought we wanted to use hundreds of people as we did at cleanups. Once we assured them that we would scale down the project to a small, select group of people, they agreed to let us plant the trees. They just didn't want their privacy invaded, and I couldn't blame them.

In the end, the association was very supportive. They let us use ATVs and a tractor with a trailer to move the trees to the planting sites; they provided a portable tank to water the trees, and they mowed down the tall weeds at the planting sites. They also agreed to take care of the young trees for the first few years when they would be most vulnerable.

The transplants came in black plastic pots and stood up as tall as a person. We packed them tightly in the plate boats, and they looked like miniature forests sticking above the gunwales. I was pleased to see the boats loaded with trees instead of garbage, and I hoped the trees would live to reproduce and thrive for a long, long time.

We transplanted a thousand trees over two days in November when the trees had lost their leaves and were dormant. The weekend was raw and chilly, and a light rain steadily fell as we worked in the misty forest. We divided into pairs and switched off the tasks—one person worked the shovel and the other would hand-tamp the root balls into the ground. The black soil was moist, and it was easy to dig the holes. Nevertheless, we were sweating under our rain gear.

We didn't have much money to plant trees the first year, but overall we planted three thousand in three states—Illinois, Iowa, and Missouri—as we moved downriver.

Two of our plate boats and a recreational boat prepare to lock-through one of the 29 locks on the Upper Mississippi River.

When I first thought about planting trees, people told me to start small and do one little project. But I didn't want a minimal attempt. If we were going to do something, then I wanted to make an impact. I also wanted to spread the trees out so we wouldn't put all our eggs in one basket.

The tree-planting project enabled us to partner more with state agencies. We depended on them for their expertise and for getting landowners involved. We also brought in new people who were interested in trees and habitat restoration but hadn't been involved as much on the cleanups.

The project became more complicated because we had two aims at once. We were still cleaning up the river as a crew, but then some of us would go away to collect acorns or to pick up trees and plant them. That meant two schedules for the two different functions. We had to juggle people, trucks, boats, and tools. Sometimes we would split the crew between cleaning and planting. That was the first time I ever broke up into two crews, but I liked getting two things done at once.

Living Lands & Waters took a big leap in 2003 by branching out into education workshops and tree plantings. We had taken the initial steps and gained experience, and I wanted to expand them. The cleanup component grew, too, and got more complicated. I found myself juggling three huge projects, and each one was morphing into bigger and more complex programs.

I designated program managers for the first time. They ran their own shows, but I stayed involved as a laborer, planner, fund-raiser, and troubleshooter. They were exploring new territory for us and nobody knew what to do—we had to make it up as we went along.

I started telling people that we moved in these new directions because they rhymed—beautification, restoration, reforestation, and education. I joked that I had always wanted to be a rapper but had never worked that out.

From the beginning of the 2003 cleanup season, we were developing a more sophisticated system to maintain our equipment and to ensure safety. We began having regular crew meetings and making decisions as a group. People were staying longer on the project, and they brought their experience and insight to the table.

I was recognizing my limitations. I couldn't do everything all the time. I was becoming a bit worn out and overwhelmed after six years of wide-open, full-speed-ahead action. The strain I felt was more than physical—it was mental, too. I had to plan the logistics and develop the goals while forming strategies for the project's future. It took a lot of energy to develop and nurture relationships with sponsors, partners, supporters, volunteers, and the crew.

In addition to the on-the-ground aspects of the project, I had to stay apprised on organizational issues. I worked closely with the Living Lands & Waters board members and with the office staff. Our new office manager, Laura, handled the grant requests, fund-raising packets, and general correspondence. Judy, our bookkeeper, was working hard to stay current with our finances.

I wasn't starting to burn out, but it had been "go, go, go" and I knew that I needed to chill out once in a while. So I spread out the workload. Yam took over managing our safety program at the start of the season, and we subsequently held regular safety meetings and fire drills. We had a mandatory policy for life jackets at all times and became disciplined about wearing hard hats. Yam wrote a safety test, and everybody had to pass it. Anybody new on board the barge got the safety orientation and had to take the test right away.

Since we had a towboat and four barges, we modeled our operations and safety procedures after the marine industry. Captain Mike brought his vast experience with barges and renewed his coaching skills to train new crew members as competent deckhands.

Chris Fenderson was an excellent metal fabricator and a competent mechanic. I asked him to become our operations manager, and he accepted the daunting task of maintaining and repairing our machinery. He kept the maintenance schedules and worked with Captain Mike to keep the towboat and barge rigging in good order. If Chris wasn't qualified to work on a piece of equipment, we worked together to find the right person to do the job.

Despite the division of labor, everybody still had to remain flexible. We were traveling continuously and switching things up, so it was hard for any one person to oversee everything. If something needed to be done, people just did it. No one ever said, "That's not my job." I still had to be in charge, but I made a pleasant discovery: People felt empowered when I gave them responsibility.

As part of the project's evolution toward more of a corporate operation, we drafted employee policies and wrote an employee handbook, and everyone was supplied a uniform life jacket. Still, I didn't want to become too much like the military—there were no bunk inspections or regulation "lights out." We were simply using our collective experience to create sound policies.

At the end of November, we took our fleet of barges and boats to Paducah and tied up again at the Marquette fleet. As we cleaned the barges and stowed the gear, I was already planning for the next season. One major new step would be taking our operation to Washington, D.C. If we could help clean up the rivers at our nation's capital and use a garbage barge as the centerpiece of the cleanup, we would make a statement about all our rivers. We were poised for our next new leap.

My goal of cleaning up the rivers in Washington, D.C., took its first steps forward in 2004. When I flew there that winter, I met Alex Beeler from Koch Industries, who offered to show me around town and introduce me to people who might be able to help. He knew the town really well, both geographically and otherwise, and I literally would have been lost without him.

The first meeting I attended was held at the Department of the Interior in a huge room with a giant oak table surrounded by 20-plus chairs. Gail Norton, head of the department, was leading the meeting with officials from the Bureau of Land Management, the Fish and Wildlife Service, and other agencies, along with several congressmen and people from think tanks. The topics on the agenda were grazing, water rights, and fire management. I listened but didn't say anything. I didn't think it was my place. I thought, "What the hell am I doing here? Who am I to be at this meeting?"

Afterward, Secretary Norton invited us to go upstairs to her office. Six of us out of the 20 at the meeting went up, where she had a big tub of beer and some hors d'oeuvres. I was hoping to meet decision-makers in

D.C., but I hadn't expected to be drinking beer with them on a balcony overlooking the city. When I talked to her, I said, "I see you've got some really nice pictures of all these wonderful places in the United States, but you don't have anything of the Mississippi River. I think the river is like a national park."

That was the beginning. I had to fly back and forth several times to set up the cleanup. Early on, I figured I'd better do an initial scout for garbage. First, I had to find a guide, and that was a job in itself. I finally called a bass fishing association that hooked me up with a fisherman in Alexandria, Virginia. I asked him if he would take me out on the river to look for garbage and he just laughed.

I said, "Yeah, dude, I'll pay you a hundred and fifty dollars to just take me out and look for garbage."

He thought I was nuts, but said, "You want to see garbage. I'll show you garbage, man."

Along with Alex Beeler we boarded the fishing guide's boat on a bitterly cold day to go out on the Potomac River. The boat had a windshield but only for the driver, so Alex and I, bundled in our winter coats, hunched down to avoid the biting air. The trip paid dividends right away. I noticed unbelievable amounts of trash that had never been touched, just right on the bank.

The guide pointed to a small opening in the winter-gray trees on the Maryland shore, and we slowed down to turn into the hidden inlet. We puttered into a back bay called Oxen Cove, where we came upon an eye-popping accumulation of garbage that had been collecting there forever. I could not believe what I was seeing; I had never seen anything like it in my life.

The garbage circled the cove for a quarter-mile, and the trash was piled up two feet thick under the trees in some spots. It then tapered to a foot high on the shore and finally to six inches at the water's edge. It was like a treasure trove of trash, shiny and colorful with all the bright cans and plastic bottles. I guess in reality I should not have been shocked, considering the population density of the D.C. area and the fact that Americans go through 2.5 million plastic bottles every hour. And the tour was just beginning. The guide was laughing as we blasted along the shoreline and said, "You haven't seen anything yet."

We cruised to another cove, and this one was even worse. It was inaccessible from land, and the shores were teeming with trash. We motored into cove after cove where debris had just washed in and settled. We saw hundreds of tires and barrels everywhere, and enough garbage to fill a supertanker.

Alex continued to set up introductions, and I began a routine of flying to D.C. for meetings and then back to the Quad Cities to do more planning. On one trip, Alex suggested a dinner meeting with a prominent foundation that operated an educational center on the shores of the Potomac. One of its programs was an annual cleanup day, which had started in the early 1990s after the people at the center grew tired of looking at the garbage on their riverfront. This single effort had morphed into 150 cleanup sites in three states, similar to the river sweeps on the Ohio and Illinois rivers. Alex thought they would be a natural ally for our three-week cleanup in April.

This seemed like a perfect partnership to me, too, and I thought they would appreciate working with us because we would bring our heavy-duty, trash-hauling boats. What they were doing was awesome, but their cleanups were typically land-based. They didn't use boats to attack trash from the river like we did. I had seen on my scouting trip that the worst sites could only be reached by flat-bottom boats in the shallow water. Plus, by using a barge, we would collect a mountain of trash, and that silent spectacle would make the loudest statement of all about the neglect of our nation's rivers.

At a dinner meeting with the educational center's executive director and a board member, I was peppered with hostile questions. "Your effort is not sustainable," they challenged. "The trash will just come back."

I answered that the garbage didn't belong in the river and that whatever we picked up would not be there anymore. I asked, "If we didn't do it, then who would?" I also pointed out that we would be targeting areas that were inaccessible except by boat.

As the questions continued, I began to sense that they were concerned that we would be encroaching on their territory. I tried to point out all the extra elements we would add to their existing cleanups. We would be working for several weeks instead of just one day. We planned to concentrate on cleaning the river near their headquarters. There was a bay right across the way that was filled with barrels, tires, and litter. The experience for volunteers of going out on the river was an important feature, in addition to picking up the garbage. Most of the people we would take out in our boats had never been on the river.

Yet the antagonism remained, and I began to feel like walking out. I didn't understand what the problem was. Why couldn't we work together to clean the Potomac River and at the same time make a statement about all our rivers?

This cold shoulder would be repeated with other groups in D.C. I had seen territoriality on the Illinois and Ohio rivers, but I was amazed at the infighting here. From what I had seen, there was plenty of garbage for everyone. I kept stressing my main goal, which was to bring attention to all America's rivers, not just the ones running through the Beltway.

Judging from the amount of garbage, I would have expected people to welcome the cleanup with open arms, but that wasn't the case. I was extremely upset there wasn't exactly a warm welcome at first, but then I thought about it in simple terms and knew that there was a need for us to go and clean up.

After I thought about it, I could see the situation from their point of view, but the miles of garbage-laden shores just stuck in my mind. They might have regarded the cleanup effort as a one-time event that would not be sustainable through the years. Knowing how hard it is to build momentum for a cleanup project and how passionate people felt about their organizations, I could understand how they might be worried that we would steal their thunder.

I had stepped into a hornets' nest—the District of Columbia was the most political place in the world. It didn't matter what you did. A task as simple as picking up garbage was not simple—and there were people that made sure it wasn't.

But there was one person who definitely met us with wide-open arms and that was Robert Boone, founder of the Anacostia Watershed Society. Within a few minutes of meeting him, he said, "I think it's great that you guys are coming to help us out. As you can see, we can use all the help we can get."

We wanted to complement the local organizations, not compete with them. We had our own sponsors. We weren't taking any money away from these groups. As a matter of fact, the cleanup brought sponsors to the table. We had been working over the years on five big rivers with hundreds of groups and countless volunteers. Our goal was to include everybody and exclude nobody. I was committed to do everything I could to work with people.

While I was wading through the mire of political intrigue, I still had a ton of logistics to organize. The first priority was securing a barge. The whole deal hinged on having a disgustingly huge pile of garbage stacked on the barge. I envisioned the garbage barge floating on the river with the Capitol and Washington Monument in the background. I looked all over, but there were no barges within 150 miles.

Luckily, I had contacts at American Waterways Operators (AWO), the national organization of the marine barge industry. Even they had a hard time, but they eventually located a barge in Norfolk, Virginia. It was 180 miles away, but we could use it for free. I drove down to Norfolk on one of my trips back East to look at the barge. It was a behemoth, 150 feet long by 40 feet wide by 8 feet tall, and it would create the floating foundation for a very impressive mountain.

Next, I had to locate a towboat to push the barge up to Washington. I found out that the towboats drafted so deep that they typically don't go above the I-495 Woodrow Wilson Bridge in Alexandria, so I had to find a place below the bridge to park the barge. I contacted the construction company that was working on the bridge to find a spot in their fleet. All these logistical details were fragile and tentative.

Complicating the problem was the fact that I was in Illinois trying to make these arrangements by phone. I realized that I needed someone on the ground in D.C. to work out the mass of details. I considered sending Tammy Becker, but she would need a car and an apartment. It was too expensive, plus she was busy making arrangements for our education workshops when we returned to the Midwest.

I talked with Alex about the problem, and he said a public relations firm could help. Apparently, you couldn't do anything in D.C. without a PR firm. I said I couldn't afford to pay for one but asked if they could. Four PR agencies made presentations to me about what they would do, how they would do it, and what they could bring to the table. I had never dealt with a PR firm, and it felt weird to be picking one out of a lineup of competitors.

I picked Susan Davis International (SDI) because I liked the people and thought they could help me navigate the political minefield I had stumbled into. I told SDI that I already felt squeezed out and hadn't even arrived yet. They said they knew people all over town and could help smooth the way.

SDI would help set up all the logistics. We made a list of 52 different groups we wanted to work with on the project and eventually partnered with 36 of them on cleanups.

There were several groups we were really happy to work with—the Potomac Conservancy, the Earth Conservation Corps, and the Anacostia Watershed Society. The Anacostia River is a tributary of the Potomac, running around the east side of the city. I was particularly glad when Robert Boone joined our coalition because I had read about his accomplishments. He had done scores of river cleanups and was still really motivated after 20 years.

I gained a key ally when I called Doug Siglin, who ran the Anacostia River Initiative for the Chesapeake Bay Foundation. I started with my

Volunteers sort garbage for recycling during one of many cleanup sessions in the Capital River Relief campaign on the Potomac and Anacostia rivers.

usual intro. "Hey, I work on the Mississippi River. I'm helping to clean it up. My name is Chad."

He said, "Pregracke?"

I was surprised that he knew my name, and he said he knew about me through his mother, who lived in Davenport, Iowa. She had been sending him newspaper clips about my cleanup project on the Mississippi. He had actually called me a couple of years earlier to say that I should call him sometime, and look him up if I ever came back East.

I couldn't remember his call, but I said, "Dude, I'm coming out there and wanted to see if you'd like to partner with us."

Doug knew the political food chain because he had been a player in the Chesapeake watershed for a long time. He helped smooth over the bumps to make the cleanup work for all the partners. "What's your agenda? What do you want?" he'd ask. "Okay, we can try to fit that in here."

Doug worked well with SDI on the news conferences and helped determine who should get a place at the podium and how long they should speak. I didn't know anything about news conferences. I had never had one. But that was how things were done in D.C., and I understood that the media attention could carry the message. At the very least, I wanted to show the empty barge at the start and the full barge at the finish.

We had to set up two big news conferences, and that opened a whole can of worms. Where should it be? What if it rained? Should we have it inside a building or outside on the river? I just wanted to do the cleanups, and all these details drove me crazy. We decided to have the opening news conference April 1 on a big tour boat in Alexandria. We wanted to stage the final news conference around Earth Day, in a location with the Washington skyline in the background.

Several groups, including Doug's group, wanted their efforts to focus on cleaning up the Anacostia River, so I needed to find a place to park the barge up toward D.C. I checked several places, but nobody wanted to have a garbage barge. I also needed a place to unload the garbage, but that was difficult, too, because D.C. is not very industrial. There were no terminals on the riverfront and very little barge traffic on the river. I'd heard about a heliport on the Anacostia River near the confluence with the Potomac that had an old dock facility. If we could park there, we would be exactly where we needed to be for the news conference. We also could launch our volunteer cleanups on the Anacostia River out of the boat ramp at the Anacostia Park.

Doug and I went to meet Don Scimonelli, who ran the heliport, and he said, "Yeah. You can park right out there. That'll work; no problem. Can you just help me clean up around here?"

I thought, "Wow, is this guy serious?" With hardly a word, we had a nice place to park in a spot protected from the wind and waves. I wasn't used to this in D.C. He even said we could unload the garbage there. His neighboring businesses just happened to be set up to help us—a scrap-metal yard was located four blocks away, a transfer station for municipal garbage was just two blocks away, and the neighboring business had an end-loader we could use if we needed. After four months of planning and stressing, Doug and I had solved some giant problems in just ten minutes.

I had a similar reaction at Belle Haven Marina in Alexandria, Virginia. It was a really nice place that I thought would be ideal for picking up volunteers for the Potomac cleanups. I met the marina manager on my very first visit, told him what we were doing, and asked him if we could use his facility. He said, "Sure, no problem." Why wasn't everybody like that?

The politics among the other organizations continued to be relentless. We had to have a banner printed to recognize the coalition members and the cleanup sponsors, and that became yet another point of negotiation. We had decided to call the project Capital River Relief, but we still had to decide who would be listed on the banner. How big would the names and logos be? How big should the banner be?

I found out that I needed to get an official permit to pick up garbage. I nearly fell down when I heard that. You had to get a permit for everything in Washington—and not just one but three or four. We were working in two states and the District of Columbia. We had to get two permits from the National Park Service—one from the office in D.C. and one from the other side of the river.

I next had to work out the logistics of lodging and transportation for my crew. SDI helped find a hotel that would donate rooms, but there was no parking for our huge trucks. I determined how far we would travel every day and the routes to take. We had a crew of nine, and our biggest truck seated six people. We didn't have a van, so I talked to John Eckstein at Marquette and he loaned us one for a month. I still had to figure out how to shuttle the crew and our boats, but the van made it easier.

We needed a skid-steer to handle the garbage on the barge. I had to find out who rented them and arrange for delivery at the bridge project; I needed to coordinate this with the bridge company to move the barge into place when the skid-steer arrived, and I had to arrange for a crane to put the skid-steer on the barge and then get the barge moved back on the river. Making these arrangements was like choreographing an intricate outdoor performance. It required exact timing, pinpoint accuracy, and delicate negotiations. I was on the phone continuously.

In the midst of making all these arrangements, I also was working every day on the Ohio River. That part I could handle. Even more satisfying was a trip we took up to Wisconsin with our boats to help the U.S. Fish and Wildlife Service with a streambank-stabilization project. We cut and planted 12,000 willow stakes along the shores of the Mississippi River so their roots would prevent the bank from eroding. The USFWS had showed us a big stand of willows, and we were able to trim the existing willow trunks and branches into two-foot stakes. We boated bundles of these stakes to the work site and stuck them in the sand and mud where they could take root and grow. This proved difficult at times because the surface of the ground was still frozen then. Sometimes we worked as the snow fell. One nice perk, though, was that we saw the first line boat of the year after the ice broke up on the Upper Mississippi River.

Two weeks before the cleanup was scheduled to start in April, the barge in Norfolk still wasn't confirmed. While I was speaking at an engagement in Iowa, I called the barge company. I explained that the barge was a make-or-break deal—no barge, no cleanup.

McDonough Marine had offered it for free, but they were holding out for a paying customer. If they could hire it out for a year, they didn't want to let me borrow it for a month. I understood their position, but I really needed it. Everybody at SDI and Koch thought that I had the barge sewn up.

I finally landed the barge with less than a week to go, but I wasn't done yet. It took two steps to get the barge up to D.C.—one tugboat guided the barge out of Norfolk to a dock, and another tugboat from Moran Towing brought it 150 miles up the Potomac River. They charged us only the price of their diesel fuel.

The place to park it was still up in the air because the deepwater tugs would not go above the I-495 bridge. The Woodrow Wilson Bridge Project was the second largest infrastructure project in the country and had been going on for eight years. Edward Kraemer & Sons Construction Company had a fleet below the bridge with spud barges and cranes right in the middle of the river next to the channel. Belle Haven Marina was located just downstream. There couldn't have been a better place to park the barge until I moved it up to the heliport later in the month when we would be cleaning the Anacostia River.

I talked to a friendly guy with the bridge project, but he was with their PR firm and didn't deal with the construction side of things. I begged him for a parking place, and he said, "No, I don't think so. We don't know if we're going to have room."

At the end of my rope, I confessed my dilemma to Derek LaVallee at SDI. He promptly called my contact at the bridge project, and they must have talked PR guy to PR guy. They both wanted to make the arrangement work. The barge was already on its way upriver when we finally secured the parking spot.

It was time for us to get the show on the road. The crew cleared out of the house barge in Paducah and we convoyed to D.C. We didn't have enough trucks to pull all of our trailers, so we had to stack two boats on each one. We made quite a sight driving down the highway. I didn't have a plan for getting them unloaded, but I knew we'd figure something out when we arrived.

We got to D.C. a few days early to launch the boats and scout for trash. I found a marina with a portable crane to off-load the boats. We loaded the skid-steer on the barge and built a fence around the deck. We were finally ready for prime time.

A light rain fell on the day of the news conference. The tour boat offshore in Alexandria bustled with media people and dignitaries—several congressmen, the mayor, and John Paul Woodley, Jr., the Assistant Secretary of the Army (Civil Works). Everyone was dressed nicely, and we moved the podium inside to escape the dreary cold weather. I myself was dressed in orange foul-weather gear and wore a plain sweatshirt under my bib pants with wide black suspenders. I really stood out in the power-suit crowd.

My crew mingled with the SDI staff and 20 young people from the Earth Conservation Corps (ECC). We would be bringing them with us to collect garbage after the news conference ended.

Doug Siglin had told me about the ECC during my first visit to D.C. Most of them lived in the inner city, and they performed environmental service projects like planting trees and picking up trash. It was a great organization, and we were excited to take the kids out on the river.

I was extremely nervous. We were waiting for the bridge company to bring the barge, and I wasn't sure that it would show up. They offered to move it for free, but they would not commit to a schedule because bridge building was their first priority. Yet the empty barge at the start of the cleanup was the purpose of the whole event. I wanted to show the difference we had made when the barge was heaped up at the end of the project with a huge pile of tires, barrels, and bags of trash.

I tapped my foot and snatched glances toward the bridge. Finally the barge emerged from the misty rain. It looked small but grew bigger as it came up the gray river. The eight-foot sides gleamed with a silver sheen from the rain, and the flat deck was puddled with water in the low spots. The barge looked shipshape with the skid-steer parked on the wide deck and shovels stacked neatly next to the fence. The barge turned slowly and revealed the Capital River Relief banner with all the names and logos.

Just then our entire crew spotted one of our 16-foot passenger benches floating upside down in front of the barge. Nobody else noticed, but we were horrified. We had come there to clean up, and now our bench was littering the river like any other piece of trash. Chris Fenderson jumped in a plate boat and zipped out to grab it.

SDI had drafted talking points, and Derek went over them with me. I liked the gist of what was written; the ideas were exactly what I wanted to convey. But the text sounded fluff-ball and phony. I told him it was lame and I wasn't going to read it.

He said, "What do you mean?"

I said, "I mean, I'm not doing it. I know how to give speeches."

Now Derek became nervous, too. But I knew what I wanted to say, and I winged it. I made a good impression and followed up the speech with a series of interviews.

Once the news conference was over, it was time to get going. We planned to leave immediately with the ECC volunteers in our plate boats and start cleaning. Somehow, though, there was a miscommunication and they didn't know they were supposed to go out on the river to get garbage. They were all dressed in nice clothes and wearing nice tennis shoes. Still, they were willing to go when I told them we had plastic trash bags to wear as rain gear.

We were about to take off when I asked where the life jackets were. The crew looked back and forth at each other and then raised their arms and shrugged. Damn, I'd had a million things to remember for the news conference but forgot the life jackets. I sent two crew members by boat for two miles back to Belle Haven Marina, and we stalled—smiling and acting like everything was going according to plan.

When the life jackets arrived at last, we boarded the boats and took off on our first garbage run. The raindrops stung my face as I drove across the rippling water, but I was smiling through the discomfort—we were finally cleaning up the Potomac River. That part we had down cold.

Or so I thought. On the third day of the cleanup, I tied my boat on the rocks next to the boat ramp during the morning session and left it there because we didn't need it that afternoon. When I came back, I found the boat four feet up on the rocks. I had to ask a rugby team to pick up the boat and put it back in the water.

I didn't know anything about tides. I had never experienced them before, and neither had any of the crew. We were all Midwesterners. We had seen rivers rising and falling, but tides were different. They happened twice a day but not at the same time every day, and their levels varied.

We had to start living by the tides. They dictated where we could go and when we could go there. When I was making arrangements to move the garbage barge up to the heliport on the Anacostia River, I found out that we couldn't go under the bridges at high tide. Fortunately, Doug gave us the tide schedule and newspapers published tide charts that told us how to plan our river travel.

Nevertheless, it took a while to figure out the tides. We would scout out a trash site and plan to take volunteers there the next day, but when we got there, the site would be completely submerged. We did several clean-ups where we waded in the woods in two feet of water because there was nowhere else to take the volunteers. Or we would drive by, see the high water, and find another place to clean up.

We did cleanups twice a day, with a morning and an afternoon session, and we had 30 to 60 people per session. We did that for three days in a row and then took the fourth day off. But we rarely had a day for sight-seeing or even relaxing. We had to haul the garbage stockpiled on shore or fix equipment or prepare for the next three-day stint.

We had no lack of targets. The Potomac and Anacostia rivers were a garbage-rich environment. The trash was piled so high in places that you could fill up a garbage bag without moving—just jump out of the boat, sit down in one place, and sweep the garbage like leaves into the bag. We could clearly see where we had been. That was great, because people had a lot of fun at the cleanups and could instantly see results.

We changed our original plan to clean the Potomac and ended up doing more than half our cleanups on the Anacostia River. That change was in response to the fact that some of our key partners were focused on the Anacostia. One of the trashiest sites was along Anacostia Park's riverfront. We were appalled to see an entire mile jammed with garbage.

People wouldn't expect to see cans, bottles, and tires cluttering up Yellowstone or Yosemite, and yet they tolerated it here in Washington. I had always regarded the Mississippi River as a treasure that should be treated like a national park—that was a big reason why I started to clean it up. When I looked around D.C., I had to shudder. People came from all around the world to tour our nation's capital.

From time to time, naysayers predicted that the garbage would just come back, so what was the point? I answered that question with another question: If we don't clean it up, who will? I tried to keep things simple. We took people out on the water in our boats. We gave them the experience and exposed them to the problem. We let them be part of the solution. Most of the time people were disgusted by the garbage but gratified to clean it up. Wasn't that worth all the effort we could give?

Our aluminum-plate boats truly created a sensation. People had never seen commercial fishing boats from the Midwest. Back East you couldn't even rent boats like that. They were originally designed to haul tons of fish. We had to have the big flat-bottom boats to navigate the shallow water in the little coves and back bays.

We were excited to be in Washington, especially in April. We saw the cherry trees at the Tidal Basin changing from dark branches to brilliant pink blossoms to fresh green leaves. We saw the skyline every day from the river with the dome of the Capitol in the background and the Washington Monument thrusting more than 600 feet in the air. The sharp outline of the National Cathedral rose up from a distant hill. We took garbage-laden boats under the arches of stone bridges decorated with bronze statues. We drove the empty plate boats flying full-speed ahead on the water next to highways gridlocked with traffic.

We had never stayed in a big city before, and the experience was much different from living on islands or small towns on the Mississippi River. Everything was difficult for us—parking our big trucks, driving while towing trailers in traffic, finding places to park all our boat trailers, locating deep places to launch our boats, and making arrangements to moor them at night.

After a while we knew our way around really well, and it seemed like we became residents. We had a good commute: We would drive out to Belle Haven Marina in the morning when everybody else was driving into the city. In the afternoon, when the rush-hour traffic reversed direction, we drove into the city when most people were leaving.

That's not to say we didn't have problems. We were crowded together in our motel rooms, and the walls seemed to shrink the longer we stayed. I had to switch some roommate assignments to keep people from bickering, and I had to iron out several conflicts so that no one quit the project in D.C. If anybody had bailed out, it would have put a huge strain on the others. Everybody was worked to the bone, but Tammy became especially stressed out. She had the extra obligation to plan the upcoming education workshops, scheduled in less than a month. She was so hardworking that she stayed on her computer until 1:00 a.m. trying to hammer out all the details. She was miserably low at times, close to crying and ready to quit.

The food situation didn't help. We tried to prepare our own food to save money, and grocery chain Whole Foods Market donated wraps for our volunteer lunches and food credit cards for our crew. We often ate the wraps that were left over from the cleanups. I know I personally consumed a lifetime's worth of wraps that month.

The last cleanup and final news conference was set for the day before Earth Day. We had been operating in D.C. for 25 days and had worked with 36 different groups and more than 670 volunteers. The Capital River Relief effort had completely filled the giant barge with garbage. SDI contacted the local media and dignitaries, and I called Tim Wall at CNN. He said they would send a crew to cover it. We were expecting a big turnout of volunteers.

The news conference was held at Haines Point, at the confluence of the Anacostia and Potomac rivers. A host of dignitaries and celebrities were in attendance, along with the volunteers for the final cleanup, including the staff and volunteers from the Potomac Conservancy.

We had filled the garbage barge completely and parked it right off Haines Point. We couldn't have our sponsor logos displayed on park property where we set up the microphones, but there was no law against showing them on the barge offshore, and the cleanup banner was a big visual thank-you to our sponsors.

The logistical task was off-loading the barge. I found out who the Army Corps of Engineers hired to haul its river trash and called Goode Trash Removal. They brought 11 Dumpsters to the heliport, and the owner's son and three of his friends came out to work with us on a Saturday. They even gave us a break on the price. The garbage transfer station was only a few blocks away, but the recycling centers were far.

We didn't have a crane, so we had to unload everything by hand. The Georgetown Sailing Club came out to help us, but many of them were wearing sandals and deck shoes—not the best footwear for what we were doing. We shared our clunky rubber boots with them instead. We made like ants, walking in a line with armfuls of trash bags and barrels. But they loved it! With such manpower we filled each 40-cubic-yard dumpster by hand in 20 minutes or less.

We loaded the tires into our boats and then trailered them to the tire-recycling facility, located out in the country. We completely unloaded the barge in a day, and it was great to see the results of our labor. It made the perfect ending to our D.C. cleanup.

After that, we cleaned the barge thoroughly and removed the temporary fencing we had installed. I arranged for removing the skid-steer and returning the barge to Norfolk. We visited the people who helped us to thank them personally and to say, "See you next year."

We had to leave quickly to get back in time for the Missouri River Relief cleanup on Saturday, April 30. After an exhausting month we drove straight through to Alton, Illinois. I had arranged with Captain Mike to bring the barges up from Paducah, Kentucky, and they were waiting for us about a mile downstream at the fleeting service in Wood River, Illinois. We had to scout for trash where the Missouri meets the Mississippi. There was no time to recover or reflect on our experience in D.C.; it was just—boom—we're taking people out on the river again—just on a different river. We pulled up to the Alton boat ramp early Thursday morning, and Yam Louck, Chris, and I rolled out of the truck. We started hooting and giving each other high-fives. We were bleary but happy to be back in the Midwest. It already felt different.

That point was reinforced when we eyed our boats, stacked on each other. Chris and Yam looked questioningly at me. We had to have the top boat unloaded by a crane. Less than a minute later, a guy drove up in a white Ford Ranger and asked us how we were going to lift those boats off. When we said we didn't know, he offered to bring his boom truck down to the ramp. A half-hour later, he hoisted the boat into the river with his crane. I asked him how much we owed him and he wouldn't take any payment. I thought, "Man, it's good to be back in the Midwest."

After the cleanup at the confluence of the Missouri and Mississippi rivers, we started our education workshops in the first week of May in Alton. As with the year before, May was a terrible month because the teachers were busy with their end-of-the-year activities. Tammy tried to get the word out to teachers by contacting every school district within a hundred miles of the river. She tried direct mail, email, and telephone calls. The best marketing was by word-of-mouth from teachers who already had participated telling their colleagues.

We were learning to roll with unexpected changes that turned up at every workshop. We purposely didn't hand out agendas or schedules to teachers so we could be flexible. The weather provided the most challenges, since we had to adapt the program for rain and heat. We had equipment breakdowns and scheduling difficulties with presenters coming and going at different times. Yet even while Tammy was scrambling to solve a problem, the teachers were oblivious to her difficulties. She always kept smiling, and the participants thought everything was going according to plan.

We finished the last education workshop of the first part of the season in Burlington, and I gave the whole crew a week off around the Fourth of July. We had never really recovered from the cleanup campaign in Washington.

Everyone rejoined the barge in mid-July, and we hitched a ride all the way up to La Crosse, Wisconsin. After doing a workshop and cleanup, Captain Mike drove the barges to Lansing, Iowa, a small river town with frame houses, brick churches, and a main street fronting the river.

The mayflies had hatched, and they flew in thick clouds around the streetlights at night in such swarms that they dimmed the illumination. They were so numerous that their dead bodies covered the streets like snow and made the pavement slippery. In certain years, I was told, some towns used snowplows to clear the bridges of them. The mayflies became a housekeeping chore on the barge, and someone had to shovel mounds of dead bugs that accumulated like leaves around our navigation lights.

Back when I was shell-diving, we would feel these creatures underwater in the cocoon phase of their life cycle. They felt spongy and covered the bottom for miles like a foam carpet. Sometimes they would crawl under your wetsuit and bite with their little pincers. Yet the mayflies were a sign of a healthy river, and they provided a feast for the fish and birds.

We had a well-attended cleanup in Lansing. The mayor came aboard the barge and gave us the key to the city—a flat outline of an old-time key about two feet long that was made by a local smith. We proudly hung it above our dining table on the barge. Our entire visit was very enjoyable. The town let us stay in a huge old restored house on a hill. It was newly redone, and they gave us a radically reduced rate. We looked down at the barge parked in the shadows of a 150-foot bluff on the Mississippi shore. It was a nice change of pace for us to stay in a regular house for a few days.

As we were leaving Lansing, we picked up a news team from the *Chicago Tribune* who rode the barge to Prairie du Chien, Wisconsin, and stayed with us for our three-day visit there. It was also a special stay. We parked our tow at the city's riverfront park, where the steamboat *Julia Belle Swain* docked overnight on its round-trip from La Crosse. The downtown, two blocks from the river, was filled with Old West—style brick and wood-frame buildings. One night we even saw the aurora borealis, the northern lights.

I had long been fascinated by the town. Prairie du Chien was built on the site of an ancient Indian settlement near the confluence with the

*Another great day on the river. Over the years, we've enjoyed
the company of up to three dogs at one time living with us.*

Wisconsin River. The regional tribes came together here in the summers
for a celebration of feasting and trading. You can still see six-foot mid-
dens of mussel shells from the prehistoric clambakes. Prairie was also
the oldest European settlement in Wisconsin, dating back to the 1600s,
and I set up my hookah diving rig and spent a few hours searching the
bottom for antique beer bottles to add to my collection from my shell-
diving years. Back then, I had found some bottles that had been at the
bottom of the river for more than a century. When the current rolled
them in the sand, this created pretty patterns and swirls in the glass. My
brother once found an antique bottle labeled "Liquid Hair" at the bottom
of the Illinois River, which was worth $600.

I didn't find any bottles but I did make an interesting discovery. The
bottom was covered two feet deep with the shells of dead Zebra mussels,
an invasive species that had overtaken the river ten years prior, and
thousands of big Washboard mussels were living in this new substrate.

I thought it was very promising that the native mussels had survived the invasion of Zebes and were thriving once again.

We held an education workshop in Prairie and staged a cleanup the next day. Not many volunteers showed up, but that was good in a way because the river is fairly clean and the garbage is really spread out. The U.S. Fish and Wildlife Service and the Audubon Society brought boats to take the volunteers out on the river. An amusing note was added when the employees of a casino in Iowa came in their gaudy pontoon boat painted a robin's egg blue. They loaded their giant boat with garbage and brought it to the barge.

We put a few people in each boat, and the boats pulled up to a site, the volunteers jumped out, grabbed the garbage, piled it up on shore, and then drove to the next site. We leapfrogged like that for several hours and covered a lot of ground. For lunch we drove back to the barge, where we had fresh-delivered pizza for everyone. Some of the crew kept loading the accumulated garbage, and after lunch the volunteers helped off-load the garbage onto the barge. I didn't think there was much garbage, but I was impressed to see that we filled three heaping boatloads with 5,000 pounds of junk.

Later that afternoon Chris Fenderson took charge of dismantling a wrecked houseboat. The crew used chop saws and cutting torches on the metal frame of the hull, and we hauled the pieces back to the barge. The USFWS had asked us to remove this eyesore from the Iowa shore near their headquarters, and we were happy to do them a favor. Their offices were also located near Effigy Mounds National Monument, a place where Indians built mounds in the shapes of falcons, bears, and other creatures. You could stand on the 100-foot-tall bluffs and see the earthen figures down below.

The *Chicago Tribune* published our story as a feature article on the front page. A NATIONAL GEOGRAPHIC photographer named Annie Griffiths Belt happened to be visiting her parents in Wisconsin when the *Tribune* article came out. The photo of me and the garbage caught her eye, and she read the article. She was working on a book about America's last wild places, from which all the proceeds were slated to go to environmental organizations. She called and, after telling me about the book, said she wanted the first proceeds to go to Living Lands & Waters. It was a major donation and I was delighted by the unexpected generosity.

The *Chicago Tribune* reporter and photographer left the barge in Prairie du Chien, and we traveled south to Dubuque, where we did a workshop and cleanup. We forged on to the Quad Cities and parked at the Davenport Sailing Club for our annual Barge Party and fund-raiser. We rented a big tent, set up tables, and catered a dinner for 250 people. We gave tours of the barge, and I made a brief presentation about the project, introduced the crew, and thanked everyone for their support.

We stayed on to do a cleanup on the Rock River and prepare for a massive project called the X-Stream Cleanup at the end of August. This was an extension of our original efforts in the Quad Cities. I had first proposed the idea the previous year, when I attended a follow-up meeting after our Quad City cleanup. We had been working in Iowa with the Scott County Public Works Department and a group called Keep Scott County Beautiful, a local affiliate of Keep America Beautiful. We had reached the point where the local groups were organizing everything for the cleanup and we just showed up with our boats. Scott County was great to work with and even helped us get rid of the garbage.

In 1999, the *Quad City Times* had organized a kids' cleanup on an urban stream called Duck Creek while we were cleaning on the Mississippi, and the effort worked really well. The creek cleanup complemented what we were doing on the river, and it gave more people a chance to participate. That separate cleanup gave me an idea that had been building in my mind ever since, and I brought it up at the meeting.

"Next year we should create an opportunity for people to clean up their local creeks if they want," I said. "We could have sites on the Mississippi River like we always do, but also have a bunch of sites on the feeder streams."

Everyone thought that was a good idea, and we started to do some detailed planning over the next two meetings. The committee worked for the rest of the year to nail down the logistics and coordination. A multisite cleanup was much more difficult and complex to coordinate. It required recruiting site leaders; arranging food, water, equipment, and safety; and disposing of the garbage.

In 2004, we set up for the first X-Stream Cleanup by conducting smaller cleanups in Princeton, LeClaire, and Bettendorf, Iowa, and Port Byron, Hampton, and Rapid City, Illinois. The X-Stream cleanup featured a big cleanup on the Mississippi in Davenport and smaller cleanups at 28 satellite sites on feeder streams. The local media supported the effort with frequent free advertisements. The X-Stream Cleanup brought out 1,300 volunteers who picked up 80,000 pounds of trash in one day.

The X-Stream Cleanup became the next incarnation of our community cleanups. By expanding it into a massive one-day cleanup at a multitude of small sites, people could get together with their neighbors and grab the garbage before it had a chance to float into the Mississippi. In the future, the X-Stream Cleanup organization could be the centralized group that would buy supplies, arrange for garbage pickup, and make it easy for people to tackle cleanup sites in their own backyards. I liked the concept because it empowered people to do something positive right where they lived.

After the X-Stream Cleanup we took our barges to Plum Island in the Illinois River near Starved Rock State Park. We had a monthlong mission to accomplish on the island.

The Plum Island project had its origins back in June when I got a call from John McKee of the Illinois Audubon Society. The society had just purchased Plum Island, a 45-acre island located in the middle of the Illinois River next to the North Utica Lock-and-Dam and beneath the 100-foot bluffs at Starved Rock State Park. The park is only 90 miles from Chicago and attracts 1.3 million visitors each year. Its name stems from an ancient legend about warring tribes. One tribe drove an enemy tribe up on the rocky bluffs and laid siege until its enemies starved. It's a rare place on the Illinois River where glacial melt-water carved out deep canyons and where rare birds have rookeries. Bald eagles over-winter near the dam, where they can feed when the rest of the river is frozen solid.

Plum Island had been developed in the 1930s as a resort. A bridge had never been built and access was always difficult. A cable car had oper-ated to and from the park at one time, and five acres had been cleared for a grassy airstrip. Recently, a developer had subdivided the island and planned to build condominiums. He was delayed due to a lack of per-mits, and this created an opportunity for the Audubon Society to orga-nize a coalition to stop the development. After three years, a petition with 20,000 signatures, the coordination of countless groups, and dedicated persistence, the society finally purchased Plum Island. Now that it had title to the land, it intended to manage it as a nature preserve.

The first order of business was to remove all the man-made items that didn't belong in a preserve. The ruins of the cable cars still existed with a rusty metal sign that read, "Last car leaves at 8 p.m." Four cabins and a bathhouse stood abandoned in various stages of disrepair. Old machinery littered the woods—tractors, backhoes, mowers, and trailers. Junk piles, corroding barrels, and dilapidated sheds were scattered around three-quarters of the island. A wrecked houseboat was rusting on the beach. All this ugly debris was very visible from the overlooks at Starved Rock.

John McKee had heard about Living Lands & Waters and knew we had equipment on our barges that could access Plum Island. He wanted to see if we could help. When I drove over there, I noticed right away the developer's signs with lot numbers regularly spaced around the island. I felt good that this signage was just more trash to be removed rather than a sign of luxury condos to come.

I estimated it would take us 30 days to clear the island. I checked our cal-endar and found nothing set in stone for the month of September. We had tree plantings scheduled, but we could split up our crew and supplement our labor force with volunteers. I called back and said we could start in September and it would take a month. He said, "This September?"

I replied, "Yes, this September. We'll bring barges, skid-steers, and our tools. We'll load everything on the barge and remove it."

John was blown away at the short notice. He thought we wouldn't be able to start for at least a year or two. We talked about payment, and he thought that Audubon could raise the money. After all, they had raised more than a quarter of a million dollars to buy the island. In the end, Living Lands & Waters covered a substantial money gap, but it didn't matter. I was happy to help restore this unique ecological niche. Most of the activists who worked on the Plum Island project felt the same way. For example, Don Goerne ran a lawn-and-garden store a half-hour away from Starved Rock. He sold and repaired Toros and then managed the Audubon campaign for three years in his spare time. Ironically, we recovered a wide golf-course mower that he spotted in the weeds on Plum Island. Don got it running, and we drove it up the ramp onto the barge.

Although our barges were parked only 90 miles from Plum Island, we had to follow the rivers and take the long way around. In early September we embarked on a 400-mile cruise down the Mississippi and up the Illinois. The location had an additional advantage for me, since it was fall and time to start fund-raising and planning for next year. The Living Lands & Waters office was less than a two-hour drive away.

When we arrived at Plum Island, we parked the garbage barge next to a V-cut in the blast spoils. The Corps had dynamited the limestone bedrock to create a nine-foot navigation channel and had piled the rock in a 20-foot ridge along the edge of the island. They left a cut in the ridge to allow equipment access. We put our ramps out and used our skid-steers to move the debris onto the barge.

We had to dismantle a scattering of ugly buildings. We started at the top and moved downward, taking everything apart piece by piece. We had burn permits, but we couldn't burn the shingles and had to haul them to the barge. Ultimately, they went to a landfill. We burned wood that couldn't be salvaged, although I tried to recycle as much of the materials as possible. I found plenty of good wood, including true two-by-six boards in the shower house. I de-nailed them at night after work and saved them for a later use.

On the shallow side of the island rested a 40-foot houseboat that had been abandoned for five years. It sat directly across from Starved Rock State Park, and I felt bad that visitors had to look at this rusty derelict. I was amazed that something hadn't been done about this eyesore a long time before we got there. We dismantled it and hauled the pieces away in the plate boats. We had to be careful not to load the boats too much or they would get stuck in the shallow water. One interesting find was pieces of pottery on the beach from a prehistoric village just upstream from Plum Island.

The leaves changed while we were working, and vibrant red and yellow outlined the limestone towers while tall pine trees provided an accent of deep green. The park was crowded on the weekends at first, but fewer people came as the weather turned colder. Almost every newspaper in Illinois sent someone to report on the Plum Island cleanup. Whether they stayed with us for a few hours or a few days, the extensive coverage showed me how important this project was to the citizens of Illinois.

My estimate turned out to be right: It took us exactly 30 days to clear the island. We filled two barges, and one was full of scrap metal, including three tractors that we had to cut into pieces to drag up on the deck. Plum Island looked so much better when we finished. It was rewarding to restore an island that would be seen by more than a million people every year.

Audubon organized a final cleanup on the last day to remove the small litter and debris. The weather was crisp and cool as we took dozens of people to the island, including several classrooms of kids, and they swept the whole area clean, down to picking up nails. People were really eager, and it felt like a spring cleanup. Usually we were worn out by autumn, but the level of enthusiasm charged us up.

We ate lunch together at a covered shelter in Starved Rock Park and then took 115 people back to the island for the dedication ceremony.

Eric "Yam" Louck makes an attempt to
clean the towboat's engine room—a dark, poorly ventilated place.

The weather was clear and windy as we gathered at the head of the island for the speeches. Illinois lieutenant governor Pat Quinn flew in for the event. Several people gave speeches, and when my turn came, I said we were happy to do our part with the cleanup, but the praise really should go to the people who worked so long and so hard to save the Plum Island from development.

As the ceremony came to an end, the last speaker asked everyone to turn around and look at the eight-by-four-foot "For Sale" sign displayed on the shore. We had precut the posts with a chainsaw, and an Audubon volunteer pushed over the realtor's sign—revealing a new sign behind it that read, "Audubon Society Nature Preserve." Everyone cheered and clapped. It was one of the most gratifying projects I have ever worked on.

Our season was drawing to a close. We conducted an education workshop at Starved Rock, and simultaneously I sent a small team to plant trees at Big Island near Burlington, Iowa. We took our barges down to Alton, where Azcon off-loaded all the scrap metal with their electromagnetic crane on rails. We had collected so much scrap metal and the market price was so high that the proceeds paid an end-of-the-year bonus for the crew.

We moved back up to Grafton and off-loaded the last of the tires. We did a big tree planting at Pere Marquette State Park in Illinois and then took the barges all the way back to Paducah, where we packed up and parked them at Marquette headquarters for the winter. Since starting the cleanup project, we had never ended a season with such spirit and strength. When I looked back on 2004, it seemed like we had condensed two whole years into one.

The obstacles and hurdles in D.C. were exhausting and daunting, and the back-to-back cleanups in April were grueling, but we were gratified to meet all our goals. Despite a difficult beginning, we were ultimately well received by other groups. We established good partnerships and hopefully started long-term relationships. In the end, we had 670 volunteers, 36 groups, and one gigantic barge load of garbage. We were already looking forward to building on our success and returning next year.

The trip to the East Coast had made me appreciate the Midwest and the freedom of the rivers here. When we returned, we were also struck by the absence of garbage. In many places it was becoming hard to find trash, and it seemed like new litter was not appearing in the river as much as before. That's exactly what we had been working so long and so hard to see happen.

We had solid and seasoned crew members who had been aboard for years and were taking charge of their own areas of expertise.

On a sad note for me but probably a good note for them, I lost my two longest-serving crew members at the end of 2004. Lisa Hoffmann left the crew after working a total of five seasons—three years during the summer and two years full-time. She went to work managing a state-owned tree and plant nursery near Montrose, Iowa. Yam finished his "ten-day camping trip" with the project after extending it by 1,792 days. After five years, he left the barge and returned to his college studies. Lisa and Yam took their dog, Jonas, too, and the barge was now without its loyal mascot.

We continued to expand our education workshops into the second year, and now we had waiting lists due to the excellent word-of-mouth from teachers who attended our first series of workshops.

The river-bottom tree planting project also made progress. We expanded our range from Wisconsin to Kentucky. When we returned to our previous sites in Iowa, Illinois, and Missouri to plant more trees, we found that 90 percent of the transplants had survived the first year—an outstanding accomplishment.

One of the most rewarding projects we've ever done was clearing the debris off Plum Island. Usually the fall is a low point for morale, but when we arrived at Plum Island it felt like spring had returned. Our equipment and crew were the perfect combination for the job and we were happy to join the Audubon Society and the countless other groups who worked so hard to create a nature sanctuary there.

The Plum Island job made me realize that Living Lands & Waters had evolved into a unique river cleanup operation with the right equipment and experience for these special projects. Perhaps more important, we also had the organizational flexibility and financial freedom to identify a problem and react quickly to solve it.

In 2004, I felt like we had reached an optimal size—a manageable staff, sustainable finances, great equipment, and a diversified board of directors. Our three main activities—river cleanups, education workshops, and reforestation—were continuously improving. We were small but effective, and if we got much bigger I wouldn't be able to go out on the river and work outside in small boats. Instead of bigger, we were getting better, and we had a whole new year ahead of us to advance the cause.

We started 2005 in Paducah, Kentucky, in the middle of February. The crew consisted of Tammy Becker, Chris Fenderson, Woody Spring, and some new members: Dave Andrews, who quit his paramedic job to join; Geoff Manis, who started as an office intern while earning his degree at Western Illinois and then switched to the barge; and Julie Rowan, whom we met at our first tree-planting at Big Island, where her family had a cabin. She stopped out of Northern Iowa University to join the crew.

We jumped right into cleaning up on the Ohio and Tennessee rivers and oriented the new crew members to the routine on the barge. Even though we had cleaned some sites for the past four years, there definitely was still no lack of garbage. In three weeks we picked up more than 800 tires and 27 refrigerators in a 20-mile stretch. Soon after we started the season, we had our first education workshop on the Ohio River, and there was so much demand we had to schedule another one, and even then there was a waiting list.

Winona State University students came down from Minnesota for a "community service" spring break in the middle of March. They were able to stay at a hunting lodge that had pool tables, a big-screen TV, Ping-Pong, and a jukebox. They enjoyed the facilities at night and worked hard during the day. Anybody who takes the time to work like that over their spring break is special, but those kids had a good time, and we did, too.

We also were discussing with Winona State collaborating on a floating classroom for the river studies program it was developing. The university had envisioned becoming a river studies school, and I had just obtained a used boat that would be ideal for that purpose.

A routine meeting had led to our good fortune in getting that boat. Over the winter I had helped arrange a meeting between John Deere and the National Fish and Wildlife Foundation in hopes that the two organizations could establish a special fund to support environmental causes. The foundation had a program to take a donor company's money and match it to create a unique company fund. The foundation then would administer the fund in the company's name to support various organizations. This financial setup had the advantage of allowing a company like Deere to support a cause without the need to field thousands of requests for money.

During an introductory meeting with Jim Collins from John Deere and Don Waage from the National Fish and Wildlife Foundation to discuss establishing the fund, Jim asked me, "Chad, how would you like our houseboat?"

I'd seen the Deere boat before, but never very close. I gave a tentative yes but said I wasn't certain and would have to get back to him about it. I had to check with my board about such a significant addition to our fleet. He told me to hurry, because the slip lease at the marina was expiring.

Built in 1958, the John Deere corporate boat had two twin diesels, chrome, the works. The can of Pledge in the engine room gives the idea. It's probably the biggest houseboat I've ever seen on the Mississippi. It was like a yacht—62 feet long and 18 feet wide with a displacement of 48 tons. It had three levels—a lower story containing the bunkroom, kitchen, and pantry; a second story with a large living room; and the top story with the pilothouse and an open deck where you can see everything. I figured Winona State wouldn't mind having it.

At the end of March, we returned to Washington, D.C., for the Capital River Relief cleanups. Mike Havlis rejoined us in April to beef up the crew. We reactivated the coalition from the previous year, and our second time around was much easier. We knew the people and organizations, where to get supplies, where to park the barge, and how to compensate for the tides. We even had a nicer place to stay. The Radisson donated giant rooms, and they provided parking for our trucks. Like the year before, the opening news conference in D.C. featured the empty barge with banners in the background.

This year, we wanted to focus on getting more people from Capitol Hill and the White House. The entire contingent of White House interns came on a bus to help clean up, and numerous congressional staff members helped at cleanups, too. I wanted to show them the extent of the garbage problem and tell them that this is what a lot of rivers look like. On the boat ride back to the ramp after a cleanup, one of the staff members told me, "This has been a life-changing experience for me. I had no idea." I told the boatload of interns and staffers that they were all in a position to make serious change on a national level, which is one of the reasons we came to D.C. to do the cleanup campaign there.

At the closing news conference, we showed the barge overflowing with garbage. The reporters were fascinated in particular with the dozens of blue plastic barrels we collected. A reporter even wrote down the serial numbers to trace them back to their source, but we never heard the results of his investigation.

We returned to the Midwest at the end of April to help Missouri River Relief with their cleanup at the confluence of the Missouri and Mississippi rivers. I had again arranged for Captain Mike to bring the barges down from Paducah, and he noticed a vibration when he was running the towboat. We found out that the propeller shaft was bent, and we tied up for repairs at the fleeting service in Wood River, Illinois. We cleaned in the Alton area for a few weeks while we waited for the towboat to be fixed. While we were there, NBC News sent a team to cover the project, and they ran the segment July 4 on the *Nightly News with Brian Williams*.

At this point Kristen Ellis joined the crew. She had volunteered at a cleanup, and we were impressed with her. Kristen had graduated from the University of Missouri and spent a couple of years working as an assistant for wildlife researchers. She ran a few miles every chance she could, even after a hard day of working on the river. She was used to working outdoors and living under difficult conditions, and she started giving natural history presentations at our education workshops,

When the towboat was working properly again, we rode up to Starved Rock State Park and started our cleanup and education workshop season. Because we had learned that May was a bad time for the workshops, this year we waited until June, when schools were out and the teachers could attend more easily. We started moving down the Illinois River, tying up in towns where Tammy had scheduled workshops.

As part of a new initiative, we started to schedule smaller cleanups with the employees of our sponsors. We would go to a Cargill grain terminal and take a half-dozen people out on the river to clean up for a day. It was a great way to build lasting relationships. The employees returned to work and told their workmates stories about their time on the river and what they found.

The crew took a week off over the Fourth of July holiday. Afterward, we rejoined the barge and started heading up the Mississippi, staging our usual round of cleanups and education workshops along the way. We went to Burlington at the end of July, then Muscatine, and on to the Quad Cities. In August, we participated in the second X-Stream Cleanup and hosted more than 400 people at the Barge Party. At the end of August, we started working upriver and towing the Deere boat up to Winona State University in Minnesota for its river studies program. We even changed the name of the Deere boat to *River Studies*.

In the midst of our journey, Hurricane Katrina struck the Gulf Coast. Like the rest of America and the world, we watched on August 28 when Katrina made landfall just east of New Orleans. We didn't think too much about it at first because hurricanes were always hitting the Gulf Coast and Florida at that time of the year.

We were 1,500 miles away, preparing for a community cleanup in Sabula, Iowa. Seven months into our ten-month season, we were steadily working our way upstream.

When the New Orleans levees broke the next day, we remained unaware of the devastation. But later in the week, we were shocked by the scale of the flooding—the media were calling it the largest natural disaster in America's history. I called the Living Lands & Waters board members to suggest an emergency meeting. We had never canceled part of a season before, but I felt that it was necessary in this case. The board unanimously approved. I then called a meeting to discuss the situation with the crew.

Caution was in order because we were hearing reports of disease, looting, and gunfire. People were still stranded on roofs, and corpses were floating in the water. I was proposing that we go somewhere that was dangerous, and I couldn't expect everyone on the crew to go along.

"I'll take whoever wants to go, but nobody's obligated," I said. "There will be other things you can do if you decide to stay here."

It was an unnecessary gesture. The entire crew agreed that river cleanups paled in comparison to the work needed in the wake of Katrina. That very night we started to brainstorm what we'd need to bring. I had some experience with the flood of '93 on the Mississippi River and figured the immediate need for emergency items would be met by the Red Cross and FEMA. By the time we made it down there, they would need construction materials: plywood, drywall, roofing shingles, and nails to rebuild damaged buildings. Geoff started taking notes.

Everyone was eager to help, but at the same time an element of fear filled the room. What were we getting into?

We finished the Sabula cleanup the next day and called Captain Mike to let him know we were returning to the Quad Cities to unload the barge of garbage and to start gearing up for New Orleans. Our goal was to completely load up our barges with building supplies. The crew started making lists of lumber yards and supply stores they could ask for donations. We drew a circle within a two-hour drive of the Quad Cities.

Our first priority was to be as self-reliant as possible. We intended to take all the food, fuel, tools, and supplies we needed with us on the barge and arrive in New Orleans ready to go to work. We wanted to add people with useful skills to the team. The barge would be a floating "supply depot" as well as living quarters for an augmented crew anticipated to be 15 people. Immediately, past crew members and acquaintances started calling to offer to join us. They just knew we would be going to New Orleans to help.

We anticipated undertaking a variety of tasks—removing debris, rebuilding roofs, gutting houses, cutting downed trees, and so on. In order to do these jobs, the project would need a safe and secure spot to park the barges and trucks overnight, and a place to unload and store the supplies and building materials. Security became a bigger concern as reports of looting and shooting increased. We all wondered if we should hire a security guard to travel to work sites.

An increase in crew to 15 people meant we would have to raise the funds to pay for additional food, increased payroll, and workers' compensation insurance. I was worried about our people's health because of all the unknown variables and hazards, and I wanted everybody working with us to be fully covered. Fund-raising became tough because everyone we contacted said they'd already given to the Red Cross and Salvation Army.

Fortunately, I had a short list of people who said I should call them for special needs—and the hurricane relief effort certainly qualified as a special need. I asked the Roy J. Carver Charitable Trust and the Riverway Foundation for help, and they gave large amounts. I also contacted Jeff Foote of Coca-Cola, and their donation was also considerable. Riverstone donated about half of the building materials we brought down with us. Both Marquette Transportation and ARTCO provided "hitchhikes" for our barges to and from New Orleans. These towboat rides alone were worth about $10,000 each.

Within 12 days, the team had loaded more than a thousand sheets of drywall, four hundred sheets of plywood, four pallets of two-by-four lumber, and two semitrailer containers full of shingles, paint, and roofing materials from countless businesses and individuals. The list of supplies continued to grow as we sought advice from rescue agencies on the ground in New Orleans. I did go against their advice when I brought a dozen fans to dry out houses. I'd found these fans very useful after river floods, but they were useless in New Orleans because the power grid was knocked out and the houses had no electricity.

In order to be self-reliant we planned to take 2,500 gallons of water, 500 gallons of diesel fuel, and 500 gallons of gasoline. For equipment, we had the five work trucks owned by Living Lands & Waters, including a box truck with a load capacity of 12,000 pounds. The ground fleet would leave with five full-size trucks, a 20-foot camper, and two flatbed trailers loaded with Caterpillar skid-steers mounted with grapple buckets. The barge already had a skid-steer with forks aboard. The team also would bring nine chainsaws and plenty of power tools and hand tools.

Given the scale of the devastation and the confused response by relief agencies, we wanted to bypass bureaucratic red tape as much as possible. We wanted to target our efforts to help families with specific needs, but we also needed a way to identify people in need. We didn't know anything about hurricane relief efforts, so I tried to think who I knew down there, and suddenly it came to me—sponsors!

Many of our biggest sponsors are barge companies and grain corporations with facilities in the New Orleans area. Cargill operated a large terminal in Westwego, Louisiana, and my first call was to Rick Calhoun, who was in charge of shipping at Cargill.

Rick's first response was, "No way, don't go down, it's so bad there's nothing you can do right now to help." They were still pulling out bodies. Rick was in charge of a team at Cargill whose task was to tour the disaster area to assess the damage and help bring their employees back from the evacuation. Rick included me in their conference calls, so I could stay up to date on the situation and get guidance on what to bring down there and what to expect when we arrived.

Tammy, our education coordinator, had earned a bachelor's degree in social work and was reawakened to her training while preparing for the trip. She and I worked with Living Lands & Waters's New Orleans sponsors to compile lists of people who needed help and prioritized the overall list based on their needs. This was very difficult to do from a distance. We identified low-income families and those with inadequate insurance coverage, plus families with elderly or disabled members. These were put at the top of the list. We helped ease the burden on the sponsors by making calls to individual families most in need of assistance. Realizing that some families would require more, we wondered how to be fair with these inequalities and how to prevent any ill feelings. It was not an easy balancing act.

While we were preoccupied with this, the rest of the crew was very busy. First, they unloaded the garbage from our barges, then they helped solicit building materials. Teams of crew members then picked up the donated materials and started loading the barges. The unloading and loading of the barges was all accomplished in a week and a half.

I had never outfitted and organized such a large expedition, but I had faith from our years of living on the river that everything would work out for the best. I had labored under challenging conditions with the crew members currently living on the barge—Chris Fenderson (operations and safety coordinator), Tammy Becker (outreach coordinator), Woodson Spring (debris removal leader), Geoff Manis (carpentry), and Kristen Ellis (just plain bad-ass)—and they gave me confidence as we faced the unknown in New Orleans.

The former crew members who called wanting to join the effort included old hands like Dave Maasberg, Eric "Yam" Louck, and Mike Havlis, who brought their valuable experience in construction. Others who joined the trek south included my brother, Brent, and two retired men from Burlington, Iowa: Bill Pilger, a plumber, and Steve Rowan, a longtime Living Lands & Waters volunteer and Julie Rowan's father. Beth Irving, who in 2004 had worked with publicizing Capital River Relief events in Washington, D.C., dropped her public relations job in New York to come aboard. Ben Grafton, who was crew member Geoff Manis's cousin, signed on with his wealth of training in construction. Josh Crampton, a longtime volunteer, also had an extensive construction background and signed on to help. Finally, two entirely new people joined the trip to New Orleans, Jenn Branstetter, a longtime friend of Kristen's, and Shanti Kennedy, a friend of Brent's. More people kept calling as they heard about the mission.

We soon had a group of 19 people to form Living Lands & Waters's initial Katrina relief crew. They brought to the effort a wide range of skills, including a tree-service expert, a carpenter, a roofer, and a plumber. Over the next few months we would rotate in several more volunteers. In all, 29 people came to New Orleans at one time or another to help with Katrina relief.

Another concern we had to address was health. We were hearing numerous reports about mosquitoes, malaria, and what diseases we might pick up from the water. Tammy researched the medical issues on the Internet. She found out which inoculations were needed while my uncle, who is a doctor, gave advice on health issues. Two team members thought to rig the entire living quarters on the barge with mosquito netting, but it looked like a wedding gown and ended up being completely useless. As days stretched into weeks, I grew restless—I wanted to get going right away.

On September 16, the barges left for New Orleans and would take two weeks to make the trip. The crew of 19 piled into a convoy of seven work trucks and departed on September 27. On Interstate 55 near Memphis a tire flew off one of the trailers and rolled in nearly a straight line, crossing the median into northbound traffic. That near-disaster set us back a day. One odd sight I noticed when we were about three hours from New Orleans was the convoys of military vehicles and power-company trucks heading in the opposite direction. I couldn't believe they were leaving the area when it was so devastated. Our crew arrived in Westwego, Louisiana, on September 29—a month to the day after Katrina's arrival there.

Our base while working in New Orleans would be the Cargill grain terminal in Westwego, five miles upriver from New Orleans in an area spared from the floods. At night, the crew thought this weirdly lit, huge industrial complex looked like the Death Star from *Star Wars*.

Mel Menke and Jeff Koob of Cargill were waiting for us at 11:00 p.m. when we first arrived at the plant. They wanted to brief the crew about safety issues and rules. The Cargill response coordinators had been assessing employee needs and reconnecting families that had been displaced by the storm for a month prior to our arrival.

They told me to be up at 8:00 a.m. sharp the next day to meet the secretary of agriculture, who was coming to a meeting about Katrina's effects on America's grain exports. At 7:45, two helicopters landed at the Cargill facility, and the agriculture secretary and a group of congressmen disembarked from the choppers and were led into a meeting room at the Cargill plant. They were joined by Brig. Gen. Robert Crear of the Army Corps of Engineers, whom I recognized from an earlier river conference upstream. I reminded him that we had spoken before and pointed out that we were neighbors now—our barges would be tied up directly across the river from his towboat. He invited us over for dinner, and I hesitated before I answered. "General, I have 18 people with me." He just said, "No problem, we can handle it."

A week later, we motored over to the MV *Mississippi*—the Army Corps of Engineers's towboat. At 241 feet long and 48 feet wide, the *Mississippi* is the largest towboat in the world. General Crear had established his headquarters on board for handling the Corps's Katrina recovery efforts—dubbed "Operation Restore Hope." We enjoyed a hearty steak dinner with our army hosts, and then the general took us on a tour of the boat. After the tour, he gave us a briefing about the Corps's disaster response in the central control room, with maps and computers detailing the ongoing relief efforts. General Crear asked each worker to stand up and explain what their job was and what they were doing. I introduced our crew members and told what each of them did on the project. The general cracked up when I got to Geoff and said that his job was to bring women to the barge.

As we were setting up at the Cargill facility, the barges were making their way steadily downriver to join us. While we waited, we moved temporarily into FEMA trailers that were destined for Cargill families in the near future. I feared that our crew's morale would lag if they sat idle too long. We immediately started hauling the FEMA trailers that Cargill had arranged for employees who needed them, because we had the trucks to do it.

Damage at the Cargill facility itself gave us something to do right off the bat. Due to the hurricane, trees were down, and the company needed a trailer park to house some of its displaced workers.

At that time, only half the Cargill employees were back on the job at the grain terminal. The remaining employees were either displaced or still missing altogether a month after the storm. This slowdown in workforce resulted in a 50 to 60 percent reduction in capacity of terminal operations. Since the Cargill plant at Westwego is one of the largest grain terminals in the world, this severe reduction resulted in a backlog of grain all the way up the Mississippi River to Illinois, Iowa, and the upper Midwest. Hurricane Katrina had plugged up America's overflowing grain basket, and the bottleneck was right here in Westwego. If we could help in any way to get this facility running at full capacity, then we would indirectly be helping the farmers back home.

Some of the crew members cut and cleared the downed trees with chainsaws and trucks. Others used the skid-steers and a rented Ditch Witch to set up the site for 14 FEMA trailers on the Cargill grounds. Steve Rowan and plumber Bill Pilger and were the perfect people for installing the water and sewer lines needed for the FEMA village. This job took five days.

Tammy and I lived in the ancient 20-foot camper we hauled down from East Moline, where it had been parked since 1998. Back then I had shared it with two other team members at the end of the season when our houseboat started sinking. After the trailer park had been set up, the FEMA trailers looked like mansions compared to our beat-up old trailer.

While the crew was occupied, I joined the response coordinators who were going to check out some of the houses slated for gutting. This was my first excursion into the neighborhoods that had been flooded. The first thing I noticed when entering the storm-ravaged area was the wind damage—dead branches, downed trees, broken windows, and peeled roofs. Most billboards had sustained damage, and every McDonald's "Golden Arches" sign had been pummeled severely; many of them were destroyed. The high-level view from bridges crossing the Mississippi River revealed hundreds of roofs covered by blue tarps. The "Blue Roof" program was administered by FEMA and implemented by the Army Corps of Engineers to cover and protect structures with wind-blown holes in their roofs.

Although I was riding in the cab and not driving, I could see right away that we could easily get lost in the devastated neighborhoods. The city's maps did not conform to the new reality on the ground. High winds had blown over street signs and twisted others on their posts so they pointed in the wrong direction. Many signs were blown completely away. Streets were closed due to downed trees and power lines or city crews clearing debris. Drawbridges had been permanently raised, and some areas were closed off by military police. With no electricity, there were no stoplights or streetlights. There was no one to ask for directions.

Driving into a devastated neighborhood felt like entering a *Twilight Zone* episode, a dead-zone where a radiation bomb had destroyed all living things while keeping the city's buildings and roads intact. We drove through miles and miles of flood-ravaged buildings with high-water lines marking the walls like mammoth bathtub rings. The dirty flood-waters had coated the structures and vehicles with a drab grey-brown lacquer of dried silt. A thick layer of cracked mud caked sidewalks, car hoods, and truck beds.

In the worst storm-damaged neighborhoods, grimy cars and trucks had floated into piles between the buildings or were leaning against houses and trees. Other vehicles had been driven onto highway medians prior to the storm because that was the highest ground, but they had been flooded in place. They were parked in ghostly lines as though zombies had opened a "used car" lot. Chain-link fences had acted like fishing nets in the high water—everything buoyant had floated around until it was caught in the fences or deposited in the rubbish piled next to them when the water receded. Scattered trash and debris covered the ground, and the lighter stuff blew in the wind like autumn leaves.

The subdivisions were spooky and deathly still—no dogs barking, no lawnmowers roaring, no children playing. We saw no birds (except for crows) and no animals—not even squirrels. All the lawns were brown, destroyed by the briny water that killed all plant life below the flood line, including the shrubs and many of the trees. It was eerily silent except for the faint, forlorn whistling of the wind and damaged siding banging in a steady rhythm.

Eventually, we found the first house we were looking for. Search-and-rescue teams had marked this house and every other house in the area. They spray-painted a large X on the building, with the date of inspection above it, and numbers on the sides and bottom indicating who had checked it and what they had found (usually a "o" for nothing). It was sobering and creepy, however, to see a number indicating that a body or, worse, bodies had been found there.

Walking up to the house, I noticed for the first time how bad the dust was. The flood-deposited mud had dried in the sun, and now the wind blew it around. When I pried open the door to go inside, the thick coating of dust puffed all around, powdering our eyes and throats. At first I couldn't breathe without putting my shirt over my mouth. I was scared of the dust because I had heard reports about how toxic the atmosphere was after the hurricane. Mel and Jeff had both been in New Orleans for a month, though, and they laughed at me. "You're the Mississippi garbage man and you've got your shirt over your mouth?"

We slipped through the narrow entrance and stepped into a darkened living room with a soggy carpet squishing under our boots. The floodwaters had jumbled the furniture and household goods haphazardly—everything in the house was upside down or sideways and stacked in strange ways. A coffee table was resting on the kitchen counter. Even more ominous, every surface in the house was covered with a dark, furry substance—black mold.

I sidestepped around the jumbled mess in the house and approached the kitchen, where I got my first whiff of a post-Katrina refrigerator. I gagged and tried not to throw up. Even with the refrigerator door tightly shut, the aroma was asphyxiating. The food inside had been reduced to a rotten mass of molten slime that was going through yet another cycle of decomposition.

In this first brief encounter inside a flooded house, our noses and lungs had undergone a triple assault—first by the windblown dust kicked up from the polluted mud; then by the mold particles hanging in the confined air of a house that had been flooded and closed off for weeks; and finally by the overpowering reek of decaying food in one of the 150,000 appliances duct-taped shut and lining the streets of New Orleans. Welcome to the Big Easy.

On the way back to the Cargill terminal, we stopped to eat at a McDonald's in the relatively unscathed West Bank area. We'd been driving through miles and miles of devastated houses, then stopped and waited in line for swirly ice cream. I thought, "I can't believe that just ten miles away can be like that and right here is like any McDonald's, anywhere. Was I just down there? Did I see that? This is surreal."

Two days later, the barges arrived at the Cargill plant. Our house barge was the perfect base for us—it was on the river for easy access and provided

The contents of a flooded house spill from the kitchen door as Katrina relief worker Jeff Barrow throws another item on the pile.

ample space to set out supplies and materials. Cargill had a crane to unload us, and there was electricity and water. Cargill let us use their showers, telephones, and meeting rooms. The crew moved into their living quarters on the barge. They started to unload the construction materials and set up storage and staging areas on shore. After a month of preparation, planning, and travel, the Hurricane Katrina relief project was about to begin in full swing.

The scene in New Orleans was unlike anything I'd ever experienced or anticipated or imagined. We had originally hoped to help a hundred families, sending crews to three job sites per day. We realized from the start that Living Lands & Waters would be able to make only a limited impact, so we decided to focus on a targeted effort in order to have a big impact on the people we came in contact with.

I stayed with the original plan to divide the crew into teams and send them to three separate sites each day. This quickly became a planning nightmare: the crews sometimes got lost looking for job sites in the chaos that New Orleans had become after the storm. The closed roads and neighborhoods made street maps a hit-or-miss affair. It's hard enough to get your bearings in New Orleans, where streets in the centuries-old layout of the city accommodate bends in the river, but with the street signs blown down or twisted, it was nearly impossible to find the people we were supposed to help.

To reach the work sites, our trucks convoyed through "streets of garbage"—the contents of gutted houses piled high on both sides of residential streets for blocks. It became mundane to drive through these canyons of household debris with windblown litter in every direction. At every house, everything inside had been thrown out. It was a strange experience for an organization dedicated to cleaning up garbage to be immersed in a litter-strewn landscape that stretched far out of sight.

Kristen developed an uncanny ability to find her way around and became the designated navigator for the work crews. We quickly named her the KPS—Kristen Positioning System. One day she was driving the big extended-cab pickup truck at the head of a Living Lands & Waters convoy when she approached yet another unmarked street. She put the truck in park and jumped out to rummage through a debris pile on the corner. After a brief search, she smiled and raised a street sign hidden in the pile—it was the street we were trying to find. Everyone came to believe in the KPS, and she took her responsibility as guide seriously.

The empty neighborhoods were silent except for the distant "beep-beep-beep" of heavy machinery operating in reverse gear. Closed parts of town and business areas slowly reopened as the infrastructure was restored, but the schools remained closed for months. As a result, we never saw any children around. Twelve weeks after the hurricane hit, I heard on the radio that the first public school was opening and only 200 kids were going to school.

Our work consisted of gutting houses and clearing debris. We also delivered building materials to people throughout the New Orleans area so they could begin the rebuilding themselves. Most of the damage had resulted from flooding—the water had ranged from knee-high to over a person's head in depth, and it had remained in the houses for two to three weeks. By the time we arrived, the houses had been closed up for a month, and the interiors had become a perfect habitat for growing mold—not just black molds of that first house but a diversity of specimens ranging in textures and colors. The mold covered every surface without discrimination and looked remarkably like lichens and mosses one might find in a moist wilderness area.

Because of the mold and the toxic waters that had soaked everything below the high-water mark, we dressed in white Tyvek protective suits and wore rubber or latex gloves despite the heat and humidity of southern Louisiana. Everyone wore a respirator and changed the filters regularly. We spent $1,600 on respirators alone.

"Before going to New Orleans, I was really nervous about the mold," Beth told me. "After a while I got used to working in it, and then I was nervous because I wasn't nervous anymore."

High winds had blown down trees and ripped up roofs, but the bulk of the relief work involved hauling flooded household effects to the curb for removal by city authorities. We looked forward to tree clearing or roofing jobs as a healthy break from working in the mold.

The New Orleans area had become pockmarked with temporary landfills of household debris piled in open spaces and on highway medians. For the time being, just to store it, the city work crews made mountains of garbage in the city parks. Mounds and mounds of couches, other furniture, kitchen goods, carpets—all the contents of the houses—filled the park landscape for blocks and blocks.

In the Gentilly neighborhood, north of the French Quarter next to Lake Pontchartrain, heaps of debris covered 50 acres in rows towering up to 100 feet high. These man-made mountain ranges grew as 2,500 truckloads a day hauled debris from the neighborhoods and added volume continuously to the huge piles. An equally large accumulation of trees and branches waited to be chipped into mulch. Battalions of duct-taped refrigerators and freezers stood at attention awaiting freon removal and a one-way trip to the scrap-metal yard.

When the crew entered a house unopened since the flooding, they felt like they were going into a ransacked nightmare world of moldy piles and jumbled slopes. Everything buoyant in the house had floated in the rising waters, moved around in the house, and then had sunk back to the floor in chaotic patterns. Dressers came to rest on top of beds, and chairs stacked up like a game of pick up sticks. The ceiling tiles and insulation fell under their wetted weight, and the moldy material blanketed everything like a sooty-pink snowstorm.

The crew started by picking the yucky stuff off the top and moved steadily down through the mysterious mess, carrying everything to the curb and piling it there. Kitchen cabinets contained vile remnants of floodwater in the stacked dishes, bowls, and cups. The contents of refrigerators produced rotten food that had decayed a second and third time—rot had grown on rot. Frozen chicken was transformed into a yellowish, green-grey substance with the consistency of gravy. The stench was unbearable. It made us gag—or worse on occasion—whenever we encountered this unique fragrance.

Terry Becker is a middle-aged man who retired from the barge industry and still helps with Living Lands & Waters. He flew to New Orleans, and we immediately took him to a house that we were gutting. He is a stocky man and a hard worker, so he dove right into the work. After half an hour, Terry kneeled by the curb and puked in the dead bushes. He had smelled his first Katrina refrigerator and it turned his stomach. He said, "I don't know if I can do this." But he went back in the house and got to work. He stayed with us four days and gutted houses like a madman—he just avoided the refrigerators.

We were amazed at the amount of stuff packed into a typical American's house. One kitchen cabinet from a small duplex yielded 23 frying pans among the dozens of pots, pans, griddles, choppers, blenders, and mixers.

When all the furniture, furnishings, clothing, kitchenware, TVs, appliances, and other items had been hauled outside, the crews rolled up the carpets and began to rip out the spongy drywall. A crew of six people could completely gut a single-story two-bedroom house in six to eight hours. The exhausting work was dreary and sad, particularly because we knew that the soggy, moldy parade of goods going to the curb made up all of a family's worldly possessions—from graduation photos and wedding gowns to toys and DVD collections. We tried to save some of the irreplaceable items, but many were too far gone to salvage. The work became even more difficult when the homeowners were present.

A flooded house is an especially bitter emotional pill for survivors to swallow, because all their possessions are destroyed but still on site and intact. Unlike a burned house, in which the possessions have been reduced to ashes, a flooded house retains the decaying remains of a person's worldly realm. It has to be heartrending to watch white-suited strangers, anonymous in their respirator masks, carrying all of your former world to a pile in the front yard.

The destruction brought out powerful emotions among the homeowners. They often fought about what should be thrown out and what should be saved. One time, two middle-aged brothers got into a fistfight while their elderly father battered them with his cane. A flooded house created strong emotions in us, too. I would see people break down in tears, or go off to the side to be alone for a while.

On the opposite side, I think it's human nature to try to find humor in such an ugly, demoralizing situation. So crew members would also crack themselves up on job sites to boost morale—dressing in a Santa suit discovered in a closet or donning a Mexican sombrero found hanging on a mold-infested wall.

One day, an especially steep and well-formed "Mount Trashmore" awakened my snowboarding instincts. I grabbed an ironing board, climbed to the top, and rode down the slope of compressed debris. A wipeout, I reflected afterward, would have been gnarly. Chris videotaped this exploit and narrated it like a big-surf contest. Later, he mock-interviewed me on tape about the adventure.

At one site, six workers in white Tyvek suits arranged themselves like bowling pins in a V, and I rolled a basketball into them. When the ball struck the first "pin," she fell and knocked the others down in succession except for the corner pin—Chris again—who wobbled back and forth but remained upright to deny me a strike.

We found that larger work groups performed better than smaller ones in terms of both efficiency and morale, so we began to combine the three teams into two groups and sometimes into one big group. A battery-powered boom box cranked out rock-and-roll, and the music transformed a brutal and bitter job into a kind of dance. We marched in and out of the house like ants at a picnic—carrying stuff to the curb and returning empty-handed for another load. The Living Lands & Waters skid-steer scooped up large, heavy items and piles of household effects and loaded them onto the growing hill of debris. The crew got used to the strangeness of our world and became desensitized to a certain degree.

I was unaccustomed to managing the kind of work involved with the Katrina relief efforts, especially comforting distraught residents. Scheduling house-gutting crews and tree-clearing or roof-repair jobs was especially difficult, since it was easy to misjudge the time it would take to accomplish the tasks.

When we first started, we appeared on jobs within an hour of when we promised. But sometimes we'd go to a place and the job took an extra couple of hours. The next people would be waiting at their house, and if they'd taken off work and we were two hours late, they could be upset. And then we'd have to go back if we didn't finish. This could become a vicious cycle as the jobs stacked up, and the chaos of planning overwhelmed me in a short period of time.

Yet many people welcomed us warmly no matter what time we arrived. In some neighborhoods, we were the first relief workers on the scene. At first, the National Guard troops stopped us because they wondered if we were looters. When we told them why we were there, the soldiers were both relieved and happy. Their joy might have been enhanced because we had as many as nine women on the crew.

The Katrina relief effort became an all-consuming special mission, but the ongoing needs of the Living Lands & Waters organization continued to gnaw at the back of my mind. Autumn was the time we wrapped up the year's season and started to raise funds for the next year. My major sponsors would be planning their upcoming budgets, and I knew I should be there to plead my case to them.

I thought about home only during stray moments. I was overwhelmed with our massive job at hand. I had to direct the crews to two or three jobs a day, with ever shifting numbers of personnel—12 to 18 people at different times—to make sure they stayed busy. My mind was constantly filled with: We have to get here, estimate the time, finish this job on time, meet these new people on time. I was getting stressed out badly.

Luckily, our team thrived on novelty and adventure. They were used to traveling continuously while living on the river cleanup barge. They were skilled at working with new people in new places, and had become accustomed to handling difficult and unexpected challenges with a never-give-up attitude.

On a river cleanup, things broke down and we had to roll with it. Keep charging on and switching your plans up—we were used to that. What was helpful in New Orleans was being able to stay on task despite what was being thrown at us.

Early on in the Katrina relief effort, I had called Michael Caminita, who worked for Illinois Tool Works (ITW), a giant manufacturing company in the Midwest that makes Miller welders, among other things, and is one of our sponsors. ITW gave me two names, and our crews gutted both houses. Mike told me that the authorities were opening his neighborhood for the first time since the hurricane struck, and he was going to inspect his house that afternoon. Mike's grandfather had built the house from scratch in the

1940s, and Mike was the third generation of Caminitas to live there. He gave me the address, and I said a crew would be there in the morning to help him gut it.

The next morning, we reached the site at 8:00 a.m. with eight workers. Mike wasn't there, so I called him at 8:15. He didn't answer. I called again a half-hour later, and still no answer. At 9:00, he finally answered and said he was stuck in traffic. He told me to go ahead and said that everything goes. By the time he arrived, we'd been working for an hour or so. We had made a huge pile that contained almost all his household effects. He couldn't believe how much we had accomplished and how much better his house looked without all the soggy furnishings.

We were about to leave when he said to me, "The reason I was late today is because I was so saddened after seeing it like it was yesterday that I was never coming back. Yet now, seeing it like it is down to the bare studs after gutting everything, you guys have given me hope." He repeated this last statement several times, and I realized that in New Orleans, restoring hope was more important than restoring homes.

Word spread fast about the Living Lands & Waters relief teams. We worked for Mike's neighbor, his elderly aunt, and more of his friends. As soon as we helped one homeowner, the word spread quickly and family, friends, and acquaintances would ask for help, too. Every one of them told a compelling story, and this snowballing stream of people needing help threatened to strain our resources. I'm not one to say no to somebody. To turn people down was just so sad.

When making arrangements with people over the phone, a certain amount of misunderstanding could occur. The hit-or-miss cell phone coverage in post-Katrina New Orleans added considerably to the confusion. At the Cargill terminal, the cell phones would cut out without warning. I also soon learned that insurance companies were "totaling" the contents of houses in flooded neighborhoods, so the crew became adept at completely gutting houses. This tendency sometimes created problems.

People would say, "Everything goes out of the house," and we'd ask them three times, "Everything down here goes—everything?" And they'd say, "Yes, everything, take everything." And so we'd take everything out, including fixtures like toilets and sinks, and they'd call the next day and complain, "You took our sinks out."

Even as our crews worked hard trying to clear the damaged homes, plenty of others on the scene were taking advantage of the people in the Big Easy. Price gouging and inflated billing seemed to be universal. The stoplights at nearly every street intersection in flood-stricken areas were not operational, but sprouted temporary signs advertising a blizzard of disaster-related services: Trees Cut, Sheetrock Removal, Interior Gutting, Foundation & Structural Inspections, Mold Disaster Unit, Tree Clearing, New Orleans Title & Insurance, Bankruptcy Help, Photo Restoration, In & Out House Gutting, We Buy Wet Cars, Multi-Task Disaster Clean Up, We Buy Houses with Cash, Need Movers, Class A Lawsuit for Broken Levees, and so on.

Many people were overcharging for their services. We were working for free and contractors were making a lot of money. Even so, there still weren't enough contractors to do the work. People waited weeks and months to get work done, even with the phenomenal prices.

The lawlessness of the recovery period affected us, too. The Katrina relief project suffered considerable loss due to a series of robberies. A thief stole a small generator from the back of one of our trucks, and many petty robberies occurred as well, such as missing pallets of water and Coca-Cola. The most dramatic heist occurred early on a November morning when river pirates boarded the barge in the dark and absconded with a large generator worth $3,500. We had used it to provide electric power to the barge when our solar panels ran out of juice.

How could someone steal a generator that large? A towboat came in around 4:30 in the morning when the crew was asleep. Two deckhands dragged up the 400-pound generator and stowed it on their towboat. We told Cargill about it and they checked with security, but they didn't have any cameras focused on our barge. Only one boat had come in unexpectedly and then took off, so they called the guy who ran that fleet and learned the same boat had made an unauthorized stop—they knew because they checked that boat's GPS. So the thieves probably just ditched the generator and went on their way. Cargill bought us a new one, even though they weren't responsible at all for the loss.

The emotional and mental fatigue was compounded by the unending challenges of even simple everyday tasks. Our truck tires seemed to attract nails like magnets. We had to fix flat tires often, sometimes every other day. Luckily, we had anticipated this and brought plenty of extra tires with us. In addition, shortages of services and supplies in New Orleans meant that even a trip to the grocery store became a marathon as we waited in line to get in and again to get out.

When we returned home to our barge quarters or the ancient trailer in the FEMA village, we were greeted by the aroma of grain in the air from the massive quantities at the terminal. Kristen said she felt like she'd awakened in a tortilla factory each morning when her alarm went off at 7:00. Grain spillage attracted prodigious numbers of grain-loving animals and birds—large flocks of pigeons swooped through the air during the day, while at night we saw a gigantic beaver and several nutria lurking in the weeds on shore. Seabirds hunted the schools of grain-eating fish that gathered in the waters around the oceangoing grain ships docked at the terminal. The conveyor belts worked 24 hours a day unloading the grain from river barges and storing it in a system of 24 concrete elevators ten stories tall. When a merchant ship tied up empty to the dock, the hull below the waterline would show plainly about 10 feet clear, and, within three days, the ship groaned under the tons of grain and settled to its topmost Plimsoll or load line. When one ship left, another would tie up at the dock and begin the process all over.

New Orleans reopened in stages. We visited Bourbon Street in the French Quarter when it opened for business. Not surprisingly, the crowd consisted primarily of male relief workers from out-of-state. In most bars, sales were cash only—no credit cards. Every street corner was barricaded, and uniformed soldiers stood watch with automatic weapons slung over their shoulders. Small convoys patrolled the area.

The crew went to the Quarter a few times to relax from our grueling labors. On two occasions, Jeff Foote from the Coca-Cola company treated us to dinner at the Redfish Grill, a fine restaurant and landmark. New Orleans mayor Ray Nagin ate there on the second night, and we had our pictures taken with him.

On the Saturday before Halloween, everyone dressed in costume—some went to a used-clothing store and others transformed items on the barge. Jenn and Kristen found two old-style dresses and became 1980s prom queens. Tammy wore a hard hat and a tool belt and went as a construction worker. I became a mobile garbage can by cutting armholes and a hole for my head in a trashcan and wore the lid as a hat.

We discovered that Tyvek makes a surprisingly versatile Halloween costume. Brent dressed up as a bunny rabbit with a little cotton tail and long ears. Geoff dressed in a white Tyvek suit to become a black-belted samurai with "Mojo Dojo" written in Oriental-style letters across his back. Jeff became "Harry Mold" and painted varieties of mold on his Tyvek suit. Three crew members dressed as Team Zissou from *The Life Aquatic with Steve Zissou* by transforming their Tyvek clothing into jumpsuits and donning red berets; unfortunately, they were mistaken on the street for FEMA employees and were heckled.

We were joined by hundreds of others dressed as the usual witches, ghouls, and pirates. A few adopted a Katrina theme. One woman personified Bureaucratic Red Tape by wrapping her torso in red plastic "caution" tape that was pinned with a dozen official-looking documents. She wore a black cape with "FEMA" printed on the back. A man dressed in dirty gray coveralls to portray a flooded house, with muddy high-water lines and a spray-painted "X" indicating he'd been inspected by search-and-rescue personnel. Most people thought his costume was more tasteless than funny.

At the beginning of November, the city opened up the Ninth Ward, where some of the worst job sites tackled by our crews were located. These houses were built in new subdivisions constructed on the edge of swampland, and they had sustained catastrophic damage. Cars and trucks had floated into massive piles next to the buildings. Tires had floated onto rooftops, and all the landscaping had been killed by the high waters. Dried silt covered every surface, and the house-gutting became extremely difficult due to the thick mud covering the floors.

In some houses, we found that water had risen above the doors and ceilings. We'd find four inches of mud on top of the carpet and two inches under it. The carpet was so heavy that we had to roll it up, attach a chain, and drag it out the front door with the skid-steer.

When it lay thickly on the floor, the black mud sucked at the workers' boots, but when it had been mostly scooped out, the floors became slippery. These mud-filled houses also contained wildlife that had washed or swum in from the surrounding wetlands. Tammy Becker picked up a dead fish in a chair and then, later in the same house, reached up and found another fish on top of a six-foot china cabinet. One time a crew member reluctantly used a shovel to decapitate a water moccasin that was coiled in a fireplace.

We continued working into the first week of December, when I was told that the project had outspent its budget, so I decided it was time to pack up and go home. I called around to get a ride for our barges back to Paducah.

Royce Wilken from ADM called me back and said, "I've got good news —we got you a ride; but the bad news is that it leaves in two hours." Luckily the team members weren't out working in the neighborhoods but were all on the barge maintaining equipment and cleaning. I called everyone into the kitchen and said, "Here's the deal, we've got two hours to get everything ready to go. Let's get all our stuff packed and off the barge."

Our barges left that day and we left the next morning.

When we returned to the Quad Cities, the entire New Orleans experience seemed like a dream. But our records showed that we had been there and accomplished a lot. In nine weeks we had distributed more than $50,000 in construction materials, set up a FEMA village for 14 families, delivered 12 FEMA trailers to individual sites, gutted 70 houses, patched 3 roofs, and cleared 15 trees.

In the end, everyone who participated was honored to have taken part in the restoration effort in New Orleans. Mike Caminita called us at Christmas to thank us again. He told me that the many people we had helped would also be blessing us. We were all happy to have done our part in the rebuilding, not only of homes but of lives.

The New Orleans experience had been a different set of challenges for us, and now that we were back in the Quad Cities, I had to play catch-up with fund-raising and planning for the next year. We had big plans to expand all of our programs. I wanted to develop a floating classroom for students as well as teachers and was looking into starting our own tree nursery using composted hog manure. In addition to maintaining our momentum doing cleanups on the Upper Mississippi, Potomac, Illinois, Ohio, and Missouri rivers, I wanted to expand our reach to the lower stretch of the Mississippi, from St. Louis to Memphis, and up the Ohio to Louisville. There was so much to do, and I was already behind. I had no choice but to push ahead full throttle. It had been another epic year.

EPILOGUE
Coming to a River Near You

As the river cleanup project has expanded, our mission has expanded, too. We're now also looking toward the goals of planting a million trees and starting a floating classroom, but our overall goal has stayed the same—a cleaner river.

In planting trees, I want to increase our efficiency and produce them for less money per tree. Our long-term goal includes starting a tree nursery in which we will grow a million seedlings from acorns and nuts. We'll focus on hardwoods to create more food for wildlife. I'm hoping to use composted hog manure as potting soil and to provide trees for free to farmers, cleanup volunteers, sponsors, and anyone else who's willing to plant them.

Currently we are in the process of building a floating classroom on a barge with its own staff and towboat. The classroom barge will travel on the big rivers of the Midwest independent of the cleanup operation. We'll draw on the more than 1,200 educators who have participated in our workshops and give them the opportunity to bring their classes out onto the river. The barge's superstructure will be built from the remains of Tuxedo's, the strip club we took down in 1998. But instead of walls, we'll have insulated garage doors that can be raised in good weather to create an open-air classroom. We want to start having thousands of students of all ages come to the river classroom.

One thing I like about the work we do is seeing immediate results, but with the education programs, I look at it differently. I realize that some results might not surface for many years or that I may never know the true outcome. My dad's 32-year teaching career is a perfect example. After retiring, he received dozens of letters from former students saying how he inspired them to go off in one direction or another in their lives. Hopefully we will inspire a few students to work in the future for the good of the river, and if not that, then at least we will have educated a lot of kids.

With these projects, I'm excited about the future. I'm charging ahead with so much to do, but that's how I've always done it—it's like, "All right that's done.... Next?"

One of my biggest downfalls is not taking the time to reflect on our accomplishments—I'm always too busy looking ahead. One reason is simply because there's so much work that needs to be done for the river.

At one point I was spending so much time at meetings, managing, budgeting, planning, fund-raising, and so on that I was becoming disconnected from the river. I really needed to start balancing my time better. That's where the board of directors and the office staff really helped with the management and business side of the organization, which allowed me to spend more time where I want to be—on the river.

Living Lands & Waters would not be where it is today without the hard work of all the board members, past and present, and of all of our crews. It's pertinent to the success of any not-for-profit organization to have an active board with diverse qualifications, such as banking, finance, insurance, law, marketing, and, in our case, marine operations. And fortunately, we have these bases covered, and I can't thank the directors enough for their efforts.

Writing this book has been one of the best things personally, because, before this, I'd never really looked back at what happened and how the project got to where it is. But even this book doesn't tell the day-in and day-out story of what it actually took to make things happen.

For ten years, I've been traveling almost nonstop, primarily through the river valleys of the Midwest—some of the most scenic areas in the country. I've been on a mission to clean up the rivers. It was a simple concept then and it's a simple concept now, but doing it has been far from simple or easy. I realize that we're not solving all the problems or necessarily saving America's rivers—we're simply doing our part, just as I hope you're doing yours.

We are working on huge rivers with huge problems and, in the grand scheme of things, garbage is probably the least of them. Some of the bigger issues such as siltation, runoff, and invasive species are not as easily solved. But if we can bring thousands of people to the shore, put them in boats, expose them to the river, and have them become part of the solution to the garbage problem, then they'll come back feeling like they have a stake in the river. It's hard to care about something you don't have a stake in. A lot of the people who come to our cleanups have never been on the river before, and they're not just going for a boat ride, they are working hard. If you can get people to come together for the river, then you're not only one step but two steps toward helping to address the bigger problems.

If we, the people, don't do it, then who will?

Looking back, the river cleanup project reminds me of a band on tour, but instead of a bus we've used a barge. We didn't travel the roads, we traveled the rivers. It's been a tour on a mission, and when we come to a town or city, our performance is a cleanup instead of a concert. We are always outsiders wherever we go, but welcomed outsiders. We're there to perform a service for the river and the community, and for that reason it's been easier to get a real feel for the town and to connect with the people. I can't begin to tell you how many great people have helped us along the way.

I've reached the conclusion that if this *was* a band, then I must not be a very good bandleader, because roughly 70 crew members have come and gone, and every one of them has worked hard to help our progression. If this was a band, then I've done every job from manager to lead singer to backup singer to booking agent to bus driver to roadie. As with every band, we even have groupies—long live the groupies! Sometimes I've been the only dude left in the band, but as always, the show must go on.

Over the years, some crew members have burned out with our nonstop go, go, go, and I didn't always take into account that cleaning the river wasn't everybody's lifelong mission. We've had many great times together as crew members, but we've also endured rough times with long hours, sweat, tears, blisters, and some truly hairy situations. Still, this didn't come without a strong sense of accomplishment and plenty of praise from people along the way. River cleanup could possibly be one of the most rewarding jobs in the world—for a few reasons: first and foremost, you get to live and work out on the river; second, you get to see the results of your work; and third, there's not a day that someone doesn't thank you for your hard work.

Plus, you occasionally get to find a message in a bottle. I could possibly have the world's largest collection of messages-in-bottles. They range from love letters to original songs written on sheet music to original art to something as simple as a name, address, and "response please." I considered answering those messages with a letter asking the senders to quit littering.

What is the strangest thing found by the river cleanup crew? Well, it could be the horse's head in a cooler or the prosthetic leg or our collection of stolen safes (usually found near boat ramps). The dumbest find was probably the money bag filled with many money bags (no money) and the bank-surveillance videotape that the brilliant robbers wrapped in plastic to make it waterproof. They threw it off a bridge, and we found the bag and video 300 feet downriver on an island.

It's funny that a project that started off with just me—one guy working alone—has grown to include tens of thousands of people. This has all been out of necessity. This is what it takes: teamwork. From the hardworking crews living in houseboats or house barges, enthusiastic volunteers at cleanups, like-minded friends in allied organizations, and generous sponsors who have given so much to make it happen, all of them have rallied to a cause that is so simple at its core but so universal in spirit.

Our fleet of open boats, garbage barges, the house barge, and the towboat parked at Prairie du Chien, Wisconsin, in July 2004.

I guess one of my sponsors said it best, "I'm not sure where the project is heading, exactly, but we're in it for the long haul, and it's going to be a hell of a ride."

Because of the number of volunteers who have helped, we were able to clean up far more than the crew and I could have done in our entire lives. One thing I've learned about volunteers is that it is much better to focus on the quality of the experience than the quantity of people at a cleanup. The one-on-one bond is really important, and I never forget the power of what one person can do if exposed to a problem and therefore motivated to do something. I think many organizers get hung up on numbers. That's a good selling point for fund-raising, but if you are making true connections on the individual level, then the numbers are not as important.

It's really taken tens of thousands of people who have helped push the movement forward—30,000-plus volunteers, hundreds of sponsors, and dozens of board and crew members who have helped put their sweat equity into building it up.

My motto has always been, Work *with* people, not *against* them. Some groups fight effectively through lawsuits and protests, and there's a need for that in certain cases; but that's not my way.

My goal all along has been to include everybody, not to exclude anybody. We've worked with all parties regardless of who they are or their political platform (now that I know what one is), because that's the only way that the clean-water movement is going to move forward. There are three things that have worked well for us and that we try to promote. First, pushing for a cleaner river. Second, promoting hard work, because it takes hard work to clean rivers—a discarded barrel doesn't just jump in your boat. Most people work hard and they respect hard workers. And third, promoting the people who make it happen—the other organizations, all the volunteers, and the sponsors who pay for it.

I have also tried to make sure that we complement other groups and don't compete with them—we work with more than a hundred groups every year. A lot of people tell me that I should promote our organization to keep it sustainable, and I think that's partially true. But the mission of cleaning rivers is more important than the sustainability of one organization.

We want to be able to complement what other organizations are doing, so that's one of the reasons we don't put Living Lands & Waters stickers all over our Living Lands & Waters boats and Living Lands & Waters trucks and Living Lands & Waters life jackets (get my point?). We want to work with organizations, give them a boost, and then we roll, and they're the ones who are sustaining the movement in their communities.

After this book, I guess I do hope you'll remember our organizational name (it's Living Lands & Waters), write it down, tell your friends, and go to our website at livinglandsandwaters.org—but seriously folks, more important than that, send cash fast!

When I first started out, I didn't have a master plan to start an organization—I didn't really know what an organization entailed. From the beginning, I've used what I've had at the time, while keeping my eye on what we've needed. That goes for equipment, people, knowledge, and so on.

In addition, we've worked with other organizations and been able to watch them grow into strong partnerships. We've helped get plate boats for both Missouri River Relief and the Earth Conservation Corps, two allied organizations. Since our first cleanup with Missouri River Relief in 2001, it has had more than 5,000 volunteers who've picked up more than 300 tons of garbage, plus it brings its equipment to help us at our clean-ups. In Washington, D.C., the Earth Conservation Corps is now actively cleaning up the Anacostia River, and its members have come to help us on the Mississippi.

Even when partnerships might have started out a little rough, they usually smoothed out over time. For example, we've now worked with Friends of the Illinois River on cleanups, and they've brought more than 8,000 volunteers to the river. They even helped raise money for us to go to New Orleans after Katrina.

In my experience, people don't just *give* to causes, they *invest* in causes. They are also investing in the people who are moving those causes forward. And people identify with an organization that has a charismatic person associated with it, for example, Robert F. Kennedy Jr. with the Waterkeepers. Although I can't compare myself to someone like him, my association with Living Lands & Waters has filled a similar function to a large extent.

The garbage got into the river one piece at a time, and that's the only way it's going to get out of the river. Each piece represents neglect, but it can also represent hope (after it's picked up). As far as the garbage prob-lem goes on the Mississippi, the cleanups are working. We've seen results time and again. People aren't trashing the river like they once were.

What matters is how many people care about our rivers, streams, lakes, oceans, or just plain clean water. I'm still amazed by it—I had abso-lutely no idea going into the project just how many people care about our rivers. With our equipment, we've created an opportunity for people to get out there and do something positive. I have learned so much about boats, barges, sinkings, logistics, planning, organizations, crew dynamics, and much more. But probably the biggest thing I've learned is that no matter where I go, people care about clean water.

This concern is found not only on an individual basis but on a social and political level, too. There is a big movement for cities and towns to reconnect to rivers. In just the short time I've been working on the cleanup project, it's been fantastic to see that so many places are turning to the river as their front door and the centerpiece of their communities. And the same thing is happening all around the country and the world.

Living Lands & Waters has accomplished a lot, and that's great, but there is so much more to be done—every waterway in the country needs help, from the tiniest trout stream on down to the sea. And not just waters, but forests and deserts and mountains and beaches, you name it. And not just the natural world, either. Pick a cause that's dear to you and work hard for it.

We all make a difference, even if we don't intend to, and it's either negative or positive. My question to you is, how big a difference do you want to make? I can't say how big a difference I've made or will continue to make, but I know this—I will plant a lot of trees and leave a cleaner river.

I've never thought of myself as an environmentalist. I've considered myself a regular person who saw a problem and wanted to do something about it. I truly don't have an ending here because even though we've been doing this for ten years, I feel like we're just getting started. But I can tell you one thing: We're probably coming to a river near you.

APPENDIX I
Start Your Own Crusade: 13 Tips

1. Get involved with your cause, and not just by joining but by becoming active. Serve on a committee, help with fund-raising, coordinate an event, do whatever you can—but do *something*.

2. Work with what you have at the time.

3. If you start with nothing but an idea, then there's nothing to lose. What have you really lost by making a phone call if someone says no?

4. Don't expect anything from anybody—you'll just set yourself up for disappointment and despair.

5. Set high goals but realize that the bigger the goal, the more persistence, dedication, focus, and sacrifice it will take to achieve it. Big goals are accomplished only by taking small steps, and it starts with a single, small action.

6. Work as hard as you can every day and know that you can only do so much. As long as you've worked as hard as you can, then that's all you can do.

7. Plant trees. Lots of trees.

8. Your greatest weakness could be your biggest asset. It depends on how you look at it.

9. It's who you know, yes, but it's also who you don't know *yet*.

10. Pick your battles and try to stay focused, because there are so many different problems that you could easily become distracted.

11. Don't expect the government to take care of something. *We* are the government.

12. If you're just starting out and someone tells you to have your people call their people, say, "Okay, my mom will call tomorrow."

13. Don't forget to water your trees.

APPENDIX II
Trash Statistics, 1997–2005

15,991–tires
9,832–balls
3,970–steel drums
2,092–five-gallon buckets
27,172–bags of trash
141–washing machines
97–barbecue grills
46–boats
1–1970s Ford Econoline van
63–bicycles
46–250-gallon drums
18–tractors
9–car engines
29–lawn mowers
8–motorcycles
45–dishwashers
19–bathtubs
65–duck decoys
6–football fields of one-inch-
    thick foam
397–tons of metal
3–school bus tops
1–piano
123–buoys
1–unleaded gas pump
681–antifreeze bottles

90–sinks
11,803–feet of barge rope
237–gas tanks/cans
1–mannequin hand
7–Porta Potties
345–coolers
70–freezers
430–milk crates
119–life jackets
66–trash cans
663–chairs
19–couches
1 –1950s International
    Harvester truck
1–car
6,338–feet of barge cable
29–mattresses
1–septic tank
815 –propane tanks
545–refrigerators
169–water heaters
148–TVs
143–stoves
72–toilets
35–air conditioners
30–messages-in-bottles

ACKNOWLEDGMENTS

From Chad:

It would be impossible to individually thank everybody who has helped beautify and restore our rivers. That list would take up several entire books in itself. There are thousands of volunteers and supporters who have contributed to the cause. You know who you are and what you've done, and my sincere thanks to every one of you. To the dedication, sacrifice, and sweat equity of the crew members, you have made this whole deal happen. I feel indebted to each of you. My deep gratitude to the LL&W office staff. Your services are invaluable. And to the LL&W board of directors, past and present, I am in awe of your hard work and the time you have devoted. Your expertise and advice has made this organization what it is today.

I'd like thank the marine industry as a whole for all the equipment, guidance, and free rides. I want to recognize the media for pushing this movement so far forward. I've been honored to meet many outstanding reporters and to hear their phenomenal stories. I am extremely grateful to the sponsors who have supported us and continue to keep us afloat.

To Jeff Barrow, co-author, thanks for all the great cleanups and for the long hours on the phone and in person everywhere from trucks to barges to bars to open boats and open fires, reaching from the East Coast to the Gulf Coast, to get the book written. I couldn't have chosen a better partner to work on this book. It's been great.

I'd like to thank Lisa Thomas and the entire team at the National Geographic Society, including Dana Chivvis, Melissa Farris, Cameron Zotter, John Paine, and Walton Rawls.

Most notably, I want to thank my mom and dad for having me, and my older brother, Brent, for all the beatings I took as a kid. In particular, my mom, KeeKee, helped grow this project from the very beginning and my dad, Gary, worked hard for us from fixing equipment to driving trailers to building our shop. Dad, when it comes to work, you are the most persistent person I've ever met, and I'm grateful for the example you set for me.

In writing this book, we had to streamline the narrative to the highlights along the way. Originally, we detailed nearly every episode and identified almost everybody who took part in the project. If you're not named in the manuscript then you're probably like Cathy Pfaff, who was ruthlessly removed by one of our editors.

From Jeff Barrow:

With so many to acknowledge, I've limited my thanks specifically to those who helped with this book. Yet, there are hundreds of colleagues in journalism and companions on the river who have taught me along the journey, and I hope you will accept my deep gratitude and praise.

First, I want to acknowledge my father, John C. Barrow, who encouraged me to become a writer, and my mother, Marilyn C. Barrow, who for years urged me to write a book. Now that I've completed this one, she wants me to write more.

Second, I want to thank Chad Pregracke, who agreed to work with me as a first-time author to help him tell his story. When I initially mentioned the book idea, he winced as though I'd punched him in the lower back. I think he realized what an arduous task it would be. In addition to his work on the river, Chad has inspired me with his upbeat attitude, his attention to accuracy, and his ability to concentrate on the sometimes grueling, book-writing process. Plus, he's funny and cracks me up. I'm looking forward to the next ten years as he continues his quest, and I hope we'll build on the friendship we've forged in cleaning rivers and writing this book.

I'm much obliged to Basin Ross Herbertson, Tim Nigh, John Brady, Lesa Beamer, Warren Taylor, Holly Neill, Scott Swafford, and Valerie

Ritter for reading early manuscripts and providing valuable insights and criticism. I also want to recognize Steve Schnarr for his enthusiasm.

I'm grateful to Dave "the River Slave" Marner for sharing his photos and to Dory Colbert for taking my portrait on such short notice and under difficult conditions. You're a pro!

Merci beaucoups to Elisabeth James, our attorney at the Sandra Dijstra Literary Agency, who was *formidable* with her experience, wisdom and grace.

Many people gave their valuable time to tell their parts of Chad's story and, in particular, I want to thank Brent Pregracke, KeeKee and Gary Pregracke, Rodney Shaw, Heidi Buracker, Tony Polito, Rachael Carlin, Lisa Hoffmann, Eric Louck, Bryan Hopkins, Tammy Becker, Mike Havlis, Dave Maasberg, Alain and Cathy Pfaff, Tom Harper, Gerry Brown, Terry Becker, Mel Menke, Mark Carr, Chris Fenderson, Kristen Ellis, Jenn Branstetter, Beth Irving, and Captain Mike Hanlin.

I owe a big thanks to the dynamic duo in the LL&W office, Madeline Luloff and Anne Powers, who always treated my requests for documents, reports, photos, and computer time with friendliness, efficiency, and good humor. Along with Tammy Becker, they were the crucial e-links between Chad and me as we worked on the manuscript.

I was blessed with the opportunity to work in inspirational settings on the shores of two mighty rivers. My thanks to John Brady, who arranged for me to use Club Medfly on the Missouri River, and to KeeKee and Gary Pregracke, who generously allowed me the use of their house and the attached studio apartment on the Mississippi River.

This book wouldn't be an accurate and complete story without transcriptionists, and I'm deeply grateful to Alexis Malone, Liz Klug, Shannon Diaz, Courtney Waters, Shanon Reineke, Tammy Becker, and Carol Kadlik.

Finally, I want to give high praise and thanks to Lisa Thomas, our editor at National Geographic, and the team in the NGS Book Division who worked on this project. Needless to say they were as professional, efficient, and gracious as one would expect from such an eminent institution, but beyond that, they were patient, kind, and fun.

INDEX